Advances in Personality Psychology

Volume Two

Edited by
Andrzej Eliasz, Sarah E. Hampson
and Boele De Raad

Psychology Press
Taylor & Francis Group

HOVE AND NEW YORK

First published 2005
by Psychology Press
27 Church Road, Hove, East Sussex BN3 2FA

5910722920

Simultaneously published in the USA and Canada
by Psychology Press, 711 Third Avenue, New York, NY 10017

Psychology Press is an imprint of the Taylor & Francis Group

© 2005 Psychology Press

Typeset in Times by RefineCatch Limited, Bungay, Suffolk

Cover design by anú design

British Library Cataloguing in Publication Data
A catalogue record for this book is available from the British Library

Library of Congress Cataloging-in-Publication Data
A catalog record for this book is available from
the Library of Congress.

ISBN 1-84169-546-7

Contents

Figures

Tables

Contributors

Phillip L. Ackerman is Professor of Psychology at Georgia Institute of Technology, USA.

Nathan Brody is Professor of Psychology at Wesleyan University, USA.

Austin Timothy Church is Professor of Psychology at Washington State University, USA.

Michael W. Eysenck is Professor of Psychology at Royal Holloway University of London, UK.

P. J. Hettema is Professor of Psychology at Tilburg University, the Netherlands.

Marcia S. Katigbak is Research Associate at Washington State University, USA.

Edward Nęcka is Professor of Psychology at Warsaw School of Social Psychology, Poland.

Boele De Raad is Professor of Psychology at University of Groningen, the Netherlands.

Jan Strelau is Professor of Psychology at Warsaw School of Social Psychology, Poland.

Błażej Szymura is an Assistant Professor of Psychology at Jagiellonian University, Poland.

Bogdan Zawadzki is an Associate Professor of Psychology at Warsaw University, Poland.

Series preface

The aim of *Advances in Personality Psychology* is to be a scholarly source for new theoretical developments, emerging research paradigms, and promising applications of personality psychology. This aim is accomplished by bringing together original reviews and critical evaluations of important new developments in personality psychology. It provides a forum for a variety of contributions: integrative reviews of current developments, overviews of research programmes and international collaborative projects, methodological advances, collaborative papers emerging from conference symposia, and updates on new developments in the application of personality psychology to fields such as psycho-diagnostics, clinical, industrial/organizational and educational psychology. This series is intended to be a valuable resource for researchers, teachers, and students of personality psychology.

Advances in Personality Psychology is an occasional series. The first volume was published in 2000, and subsequent volumes depend on the availability of manuscripts reaching the required standard. The series editors appoint volume editors in consultation with the executive committee of the European Association of Personality Psychology and the publisher. Publication in this series is principally by invitation. All submissions are peer reviewed.

Sarah E. Hampson, Guildford, UK and
Peter Borkenau, Halle, Germany
Series editors

Preface to volume 2

The second volume of the Advances in Personality Psychology series contains mostly chapters that constitute developed versions of selected lectures and papers presented during the Tenth European Conference on Personality Psychology that took place in Krakow in 2000. Editors of this second volume have chosen those presentations representing three major issues in personality psychology discussed during the conference: (a) personality, affect, and arousal; (b) personality and intelligence; (c) personality structure.

The volume begins with findings on the impact of cognitive biases on experiencing anxiety as well as on energetic aspects of information processing and influence of temperament on reactions triggered by traumatic events. In Chapter 1 Michael W. Eysenck deals with one of the Big Five dimensions – anxiety/neuroticism. However, Eysenck, contrary to the dominant descriptive approach, presents the underlying role of cognitive biases in experienced anxiety. He identifies two classes of cognitive biases: the first typical of persons with high anxiety, and the other with the opposite biases specific for so-called repressors who are defensive. The repressors tend to score low on trait anxiety, however their defensiveness makes them different from truly low-anxiety persons. These two sorts of cognitive biases account for significant differentiation among three types of anxiety measures: self-reports, behaviour, and physiological functioning. Highly anxious individuals tend to report higher anxiety than is measured behaviourally and physiologically. In contrast, repressors' anxiety levels estimated from self-reports are lower than those assessed by behaviour observation or physiological functioning. These high discrepancies among anxiety estimates in the repressors make the study of this group of particular theoretical importance. The author explores the cognitive and emotional mechanisms of anxiety within the framework of his four-factor theory. According to this theory, four sources of information have an impact on the experience of anxiety, namely: (a) the environment; (b) physiological states of the body; (c) one's own behaviour, and (d) negative thoughts concerning threatening future events.

Chapter 2, written by Jan Strelau and Bogdan Zawadzki, refers to the relations between two features of temperament with mental health, post-traumatic stress disorder (PTSD) and somatic diseases. All three presented studies were conducted within the Regulative Theory of Temperament (RTT) developed by Strelau. The theory offers a functional approach to temperamental characteristics, and these functions provide the basis for formulating hypothesis concerning emotional reactivity and activity. Research is referred to which examines the role of temperament as a moderator of relations between stressors and mental health, temperament as a predictor of PTSD in response to flood trauma, and temperament as a risk factor of somatic diseases (lung cancer and coronary infarct).

Emotional reactivity is viewed as a temperamental risk factor (TRF) for emotional and somatic disturbances. With high levels of emotional reactivity, a tendency to be depressed when facing stressful life situations is observed, which may lead to somatic diseases. The role of activity as a temperament dimension is more complex in reaction to difficult life situations, i.e. on the one hand, it helps to cope effectively with life stress, while on the other it may cause overstimulation and eventually lead to emotional and somatic disturbances.

In Chapter 3, Joop Hettema presents a biological model useful for conducting research on energetic aspects of information processing. This chapter introduces specific terminology derived from the proposed model, which identifies biological systems as the basis for social information processing. The model incorporates three different energetic systems (after Pribram and McGuiness): arousal (regulating input processes), activation (preparation of actions through maintaining tonic readiness to continue ongoing behaviour), and effort (co-ordination of the arousal and activation systems, which mostly consists in uncoupling output processes from input processes). Within each system, information processing operates on different dimensions starting from controlled/volitional processes to the automatic/emotional ones. Hettema's research indicates that persons occupy different positions within the dimensions and these particular positions are highly cross-situationally consistent. Moreover, Hettema points out a strong relation between arousal, activation and effort dimensions with data processing on the level of goals and beliefs, which correspond to primary and secondary control, respectively. Primary control lasts as long as the individual dealing with external environment requirements is able to preserve a sense of well-being. When current events disturb one's behaviour and the individual is no longer able to keep a sense of well-being, this implies a loss of control over the environment. As a result, secondary control is activated. This involves cognitive processing by the individual, particularly activation of beliefs and expectations. They serve as a basis for choosing environments, ways of behaving, and interpretation of ongoing events. Complex relations between emotional and volitional information processing form person-specific patterns.

They give rise to individual differences in goals and beliefs about the world. The main conclusion drawn from the research presented is that individual differences in data processing are better viewed as types than as traits. They are not definable in terms of particular, isolated dimensions because they are subject to more complex relations. These differences are person-specific coherent patterns of goals and beliefs determining individual ways of behaving in a social environment. The author stresses that no cross-situational consistency was ascertained, but it was confirmed – in congruence with Cervone and Shoda – that there was coherence in the field of information processing.

In Chapter 4, Błażej Szymura and Edward Nęcka present data concerning the association of attention processes with extraversion, neurotism and psychotism. Studies conducted by the two authors concern the functioning of individuals who show different levels of these personality traits in specific situations requiring strong selective attention, divided attention, or prolonged concentration. They have found that a high level of neuroticism corresponds to decreased accuracy in fulfilling tasks that require selective attention. Differences between extraverts and introverts are found only when participants are asked to do particularly complicated tasks that require divided attention. In these circumstances, extraverts cope with the tasks very well while introverts tend to get easily overstimulated.

Nęcka and Szymura had previously studied the so-called Stroop Effect and obtained similar findings demonstrating that the Stroop Effect also reflects the process of selective attention. Studies conducted by the authors revealed that psychotic persons could not concentrate on significant information when they needed to divide attention among several actions. The authors interpret the findings in terms of the hypothetical biological mechanisms of the personality traits included in the study. However, they find it difficult to interpret the attention processes typical of the psychotic persons within the biological mechanisms identified for of psychotism. In conclusion, the authors provide the reader with practical tips on how to cope with attention processes deficits characteristic for individuals representing various personality traits.

In Chapter 5, Phillip L. Ackerman questions the validity of individual differences in different domains in isolation and proposes instead research on so-called 'trait complexes', which are combinations that include personality, interests and ability traits. Historically, these domains have been studied separately. However, when Ackerman and colleagues conducted a meta-analysis of personality–intelligence relations and related these results to data on the relations between personality traits and interests, they found evidence for at least four trait complexes (i.e. groups of traits from these three domains with common variance): 'Social,' 'Clerical/Conventional,' 'Science/Math' and 'Intellectual/Cultural.'

Ackerman presents construct and criterion-related validity data for trait complexes in the form of associations between trait complexes and related domains of knowledge such as the physical sciences, humanities, and business. For example, the 'Science/Math' trait complex was associated in particular with domain knowledge in the area of physical science, whereas the

'Intellectual/Cultural' trait complex was most strongly associated with domain knowledge in the humanities. Ackerman argues that domain knowledge, unlike intelligence, is a result of a long-term intellectual involvement in a particular field of activity, and reflects the impact of personality and interests. Consequently, trait complexes should prove useful for vocational counselling and occupational selection.

Chapter 6, written by Nathan Brody, discusses the similarities and differences between personality traits and intelligence. The author draws attention to the differences between the methodology of personality trait research and the methodology of general intelligence research, as well as noting the similarities and differences in the genetic roots of personality traits and intelligence. A major difference between the study of personality traits and intelligence is that intelligence is measured behaviourally whereas personality traits are not. Intelligence is measured by level of performance, which is a behavioural measure. In contrast, personality is typically measured by self-reports or reports by others. Brody argues that it would be difficult to measure personality behaviourally. For example, in contrast to performance measures of intelligence, a measure of personality based on a particular behaviour observed in a particular situation may not generalize to other situations. Brody concludes that whereas we can measure intelligence with performance tests that generate what may be regarded as the true score on the underlying latent construct, we can only infer personality and, compared to indicators of intelligence, these inferences are less reliable indicators of the true scores on latent personality traits. He discusses how these differences in measurement affect what we know about intelligence versus personality over the lifespan.

Brody reviews a number of studies from behaviour genetics regarding the heritability of intelligence and personality. He concludes that the evidence from behavioural genetics indicates that there are more similarities than differences between personality and intelligence. Brody questions the common belief that the heritability of intelligence is greater that the heritability of personality characteristics. Using extraversion, neurotism, and depression as examples, he shows that the research concerning the genetic background of traits based on complex indices of traits (i.e. based on multi-occasion multi-method measurement) demonstrates heritability rates similar to those observed for intelligence (approximately 0.7). If the usual personality self-ratings or single trait ratings are employed the heritability ratios range from 0.4 to 0.5.

In Chapter 7, Timothy Church and Marcia S. Katigbak present their studies on personality structure in the Philippines. They employed imported measures of the five-factor model as well as indigenous lexical and inventory approaches. The findings indicate that the Big Five personality model is an adequate personality model of the language of personality description in the Philippines. The data are in accordance with other studies, which reflect a certain level of universality of the Big Five model. However, the indigenous approaches to personality structure indicate that it is possible to identify additional personality dimensions, which are different from the Big Five and therefore demonstrate some culturally specific dimensions.

In the last chapter of the volume, Boele De Raad presents analyses of relations between personality traits and situations. The author proposes that personality traits refer to behaviour in situations. It this way, the definition of a particular trait implies a direct reference to the situation. Starting from this principle, De Raad undertook the task of elaborating a taxonomy of situations for the personality traits covered by the Big Five model. He applied three distinct methods for pairing trait descriptors with their relevant situations. All of them yielded similar solutions enabling the selection of four to six categories of situations. These results make finding of a taxonomy of Big Five relevant situations likely. The author underlines the importance of further studies in different samples as a desirable continuation of the research. De Raad also shows that the behavioural expression of dimensions of the Big Five with temperamental characteristics, i.e. Extraversion and Emotional Stability, may be more dependent on specific sets of situations, which distinguishes them from the other Big Five dimensions. De Raad concludes that research on situations may help us to develop better tools for personality assessment that incorporate situational information.

The papers collected in the volume have undergone a reviewing process. We want to thank the reviewers who significantly contributed in the preparation of the volume by providing us with their thoughtful comments on earlier drafts of the chapters. Let us mention them here: Michael Ashton, Elizabeth Austin, Dick Barelds, Guus L. van Heck, John A. Johnson, Tatiana Klonowicz, Rainer Riemann, Frank M. Spinath, Magdalena Marszał-Wiśniewska.

Andrzej Eliasz, Sarah E. Hampson, Boele De Raad

Chapter 1

Cognitive approaches to trait anxiety

Michael W. Eysenck

There is increasing evidence that individual differences in the personality dimension of trait anxiety can be understood in part within a cognitive framework. More specifically, individuals high in trait anxiety possess various cognitive biases (e.g. attentional bias; interpretive bias) which lead them to exaggerate the threateningness of external and internal stimuli. These cognitive biases have recently been shown to have causal effects on individuals' level of experienced anxiety. The original cognitive approach to trait anxiety was limited, because no distinction was drawn between two types of individuals scoring low on trait anxiety: (a) the truly low-anxious, who are non-defensive; (b) repressors, who are defensive. There is accumulating evidence that repressors possess opposite attentional and interpretive biases leading them to minimize the threateningness of external and internal stimuli. In contrast, the truly low-anxious do not possess cognitive biases or opposite cognitive biases. The repressor group is of particular theoretical significance, because repressors show large discrepancies across the three major domains in which anxiety is assessed: self-report; behavioural; and physiological. These discrepancies depend on repressors' opposite cognitive biases. It will be important in future research to integrate the cognitive approach to trait anxiety with a biological approach emphasizing the role of genetic factors in producing individual differences in trait anxiety.

INTRODUCTION

For many years, there was a considerable amount of controversy concerning the issue of the number and nature of major personality factors. However, in more recent years, there has been a growing consensus that there are five main personality factors, often referred to as the 'Big Five'. The research of Goldberg (e.g. 1981) was influential in establishing five major factors, but the most influential theorists to emphasize the Big Five have probably been McCrae and Costa (e.g. 1985). According to their approach, the five factors are neuroticism, extraversion, agreeableness, conscientiousness and openness to experience.

This chapter is concerned with one of the Big Five personality factors, which has been variously described as neuroticism or trait anxiety. Neuroticism and trait anxiety overlap substantially with each other, as a result of which measures of the two dimensions typically correlate about +0.7 with each other (Eysenck and Eysenck, 1985). The key difference between them is that trait anxiety correlates negatively with extraversion, whereas neuroticism typically does not (Eysenck and Eysenck, 1985). More generally, there is convincing evidence that most measures of trait anxiety and neuroticism (as well as measures of depression) correlate highly with a personality dimension sometimes labelled negative affectivity (Watson and Clark, 1984).

The approach adopted by most advocates of the Big Five factor approach to personality has focused on description rather than explanation. In general, there has been more progress in terms of identifying the structure of human personality than there has in terms of understanding the underlying mechanisms associated with individual differences along each of the dimensions identified. However, some progress has been made in recent years, with various researchers conducting twin studies in order to assess the role of heredity. For example, Loehlin et al. (1998) found that individual differences in all five personality factors were determined to a moderate extent by genetic factors.

Historically, the main attempts to explain individual differences in trait anxiety or neuroticism were provided by H. J. Eysenck (1967) and by Gray (1982), both of whom emphasized the role of genetic influences in determining individual differences in personality. For example, according to Eysenck (1982, p. 28), 'genetic factors contribute something like two-thirds of the variance in major personality dimensions'. Genetic factors exert their influence by affecting the responsiveness of various parts of the physiological system. More specifically, H. J. Eysenck (1967) argued that those high in neuroticism have greater activity than those low in neuroticism in the visceral brain, which consists of several parts of the brain (hippocampus, amygdala, cingulum, septum and hypothalamus). In similar fashion, Gray (1982) argued that anxiety depends on the workings of a septo-hippocampal system.

The biological approach adopted by H. J. Eysenck (1967) and by Gray (1982) has received inconsistent support from psychological research. So far as the hypothesis that two-thirds of individual differences in neuroticism or trait anxiety are attributable to heredity is concerned, one of the most thorough studies (with many twins brought up apart) was the one reported by Pedersen et al. (1988). They assessed neuroticism in 95 monozygotic twin pairs brought up apart, 150 monozygotic twin pairs brought up together, 220 pairs of dizygotic twins brought up apart, and 204 pairs of dizygotic twins brought up together. They found that monozyotic twins brought up together had a correlation of +0.41, against +0.24 for dizygotic twins brought up together. For twins brought up apart, the correlations were +0.25 for monozygotic twins and +0.28 for dizygotic twins. These figures suggest that about 31 per cent of individual differences in neuroticism depend on genetic influences. However, the mean age of Pedersen et al.'s sample (58.6 years) was higher than in most other studies, and a recent review has suggested that about 40 to 50 per cent of individual differences in neuroticism depend on genetic influences (Bouchard and Loehlin, 2001).

The findings from twin studies indicate that genetic influences account for half (or a little less than half) of individual differences in neuroticism or trait anxiety. Thus, it is clearly important to consider environmental factors in order to achieve a good understanding of neuroticism or trait anxiety. What about the second hypothesis of the biological approach, namely, that individual differences in trait anxiety or neuroticism depend on individual differences in the responsiveness of the visceral brain or septo-hippocampal system? The evidence is almost uniformly negative. Fahrenberg (1992, pp. 212–213) carried out a review of all of the available evidence, and came to the following pessimistic conclusion: 'Over many decades research has failed to substantiate the physiological correlates that are assumed for emotionality and trait anxiety. There is virtually no distinct finding that has been reliably replicated across studies and laboratories.'

The evidence from empirical research demonstrating the limitations of the biological approach produced a situation in which there was no overall theory of trait anxiety and neuroticism which appeared adequate. However, the situation has changed to some extent in recent years. One of the main themes of this chapter is to argue that many of the limitations of the biological approach stem from its failure to consider seriously the role played by the cognitive system. It is increasingly recognized by personality researchers that an understanding of cognitive processes and structures can serve to enrich theories of personality (McCann and Endler, 2000).

As will be seen, there is compelling evidence that there are systematic differences in cognitive functioning between individuals high and low in trait anxiety. More speculatively, these individual differences in cognitive functioning can be regarded as providing a partial explanation for the limitations of the biological approach. The remainder of this chapter is devoted to a consideration of cognitive approaches to trait anxiety, with the ultimate goal being to combine such approaches with the earlier biological approach.

RECENT RESEARCH

During the 1980s and 1990s, several theorists argued that a cognitive approach can play an important part in providing an understanding of individual differences in trait anxiety or neuroticism. Examples of such theories include those of Williams *et al.* (1988, 1997), Wells and Matthews (1994) and Eysenck (1992). There are many important differences among these theories, but they do share some major assumptions. Of particular importance, it was assumed in all of these theories that individuals high in trait anxiety or neuroticism possess a range of cognitive biases which lead them to exaggerate the threateningness of many stimuli. It was also assumed that individuals low in trait anxiety or neuroticism lack such cognitive biases. We turn now to a consideration of some of the evidence relating to these assumptions.

Cognitive biases

Several reviews of the literature on trait anxiety and cognitive biases have been published (e.g. Eysenck, 1992; Williams *et al.*, 1997), and so only a brief description of some of the main findings will be attempted here. In essence, the main focus has been on three cognitive biases. First, there is *attentional bias*, which is defined as a tendency to pay attention to threat-related rather than to neutral stimuli. There is convincing evidence that individuals high in trait anxiety have an attentional bias, and this bias tends to be stronger when the situation is stressful. For example, MacLeod and Mathews (1988) found that high-anxious students had an attentional bias for examination-related words shortly before an important examination, but did not do so several weeks beforehand. There was no evidence for an attentional bias among individuals scoring low on trait anxiety.

Second, there is *interpretive bias*, which can be defined as the tendency to interpret ambiguous stimuli and situations in a threatening fashion. There is convincing evidence that high-anxious individuals have an interpretive bias whereas low-anxious individuals do not. For example, Eysenck, MacLeod and Mathews (1987) and Byrne and Eysenck (1993) studied the interpretations given to auditorily presented homophones (e.g. PANE, PAIN) possessing a threat-related and a neutral interpretation and spelling. In both studies, it was found that individuals high in trait anxiety interpreted more of the homophones in a threatening way than did individuals lower in trait anxiety.

Third, there is *memory bias*, in which memory performance is better for negative or threatening information than for positive or neutral information. This memory bias has been found in tests of explicit memory depending on conscious recollection (explicit memory bias) and tests of implicit memory in which conscious recollection is not involved (implicit memory bias). Williams *et al.* (1997, pp. 285–288) discussed studies on explicit and implicit memory biases in anxious and depressed individuals, and came to the following conclusion:

> Out of nine studies using indirect [implicit] tests of memory in anxious subjects or patients, seven have found significant bias towards negative material ... no study has yet found word congruent bias in implicit memory in depression ... all published studies appear to find explicit memory biases in depression, yet only a third of the studies on trait anxiety or GAD [generalized anxiety disorder] find explicit memory biases.

There are various reasons why these memory biases are discussed much less than attentional and interpretive biases in the remainder of this chapter. First, it is not altogether clear why there are differing effects of anxiety on explicit and implicit memory bias, or why there are systematic differences between anxious and depressed individuals. Second, the findings seem less consistent than was suggested by Williams *et al.* (1997). For example, Richards *et al.* (1999) carried out three experiments to study implicit memory bias in high-anxious individuals. They failed to replicate previous findings, concluding: 'None of the experiments offered any support for the prediction of a threat-related implicit memory bias in high-trait anxiety' (Richards *et al.*, 1999, p. 67). Third, there is a lack of persuasive theoretical reasons for assuming that memory biases (whether explicit or implicit) play a major role in accounting for individual differences in trait anxiety. As we will see, the situation is very different so far as attentional and interpretive biases are concerned.

Pre-attentive vs. attentional processes

An issue of theoretical importance is whether the attentional and interpretive biases exhibited by individuals high in trait anxiety involve pre-attentive processes. Most of this research has focused on attentional processes, and the majority of the relevant studies have uncovered evidence that pre-attentive processes are important. For example, Mogg, Kentish and Bradley (1993) carried out a study using the emotional Stroop task, in which attentional bias is revealed by slower colour naming in the presence of threat-related words than of neutral words. The words were presented either subliminally or supraliminally. The high-anxious participants showed a selective bias when the threat-related words were presented subliminally, but they failed to do so when the words were presented supraliminally.

Van den Hout *et al.* (1995) also used the emotional Stroop task under subliminal and supraliminal conditions. They found that the high-anxious participants showed a significant selective bias effect when the threat-related words were presented subliminally, and the same was also the case when the words were presented supraliminally.

The available evidence suggests that interpretive biases probably do not involve only automatic or pre-attentive processes. There have been several studies (e.g. Calvo, Eysenck and Castillo, 1997; Calvo and Castillo, 1998; Calvo and Eysenck, 2000) in which the time course of the development of an interpretive bias for ambiguous material has been assessed. The consistent finding has been that it takes of the order of several hundred milliseconds for an interpretive bias to develop. The finding that interpretive bias does not develop rapidly makes it unlikely that the bias depends primarily on automatic or pre-attentive processes.

Causality

One of the major problems with most of the research on cognitive biases is that the evidence obtained is essentially correlational in nature, and thus precludes assignment of causality. More specifically, it has been found repeatedly that individuals who report high levels of anxiety typically have various cognitive biases, but it is not clear whether the cognitive biases play a part in producing the anxiety, whether anxiety produces cognitive biases, or whether the causality is bidirectional. However, some recent research (discussed below) has shed light on this important issue.

Mathews and Mackintosh (2000) carried out a study in which a number of different procedures were used in order to produce an interpretive bias in the participants. In essence, the situation was set up so that ambiguous material would predominantly be interpreted in a negative fashion. The key findings revolved around the discovery that state anxiety was increased when the procedures used necessitated the generation of personally relevant meanings, but this did not happen when personally relevant meanings were not constructed. According to Mathews and Mackintosh (2000, p. 602): 'These findings provide evidence consistent with a causal link between the deployment of interpretative bias and anxiety.'

There is also evidence that inducing an attentional bias can increase experienced anxiety. For example, MacLeod *et al.* (2002) compared individuals who received training designed to produce an attentional bias with other individuals who did not receive such training. They found that the individuals with an induced attentional bias had a more negative mood state than the individuals in the control when both groups were given a stressful anagram task.

If inducing an attentional bias can increase individuals' level of experienced anxiety, then inducing an opposite attentional bias (i.e. avoidance of processing threat-related stimuli) should lead to a reduced level of anxiety. This prediction was supported in a number of experiments reported by Mathews and MacLeod (2002) in which the participants consisted of individuals with initially high levels of trait anxiety. In one of their experiments, one group of participants high in trait anxiety received a total of 7500 training trials designed to induce an opposite attentional bias, in which they were trained to selectively avoid attending to threat. A second group of participants high in trait anxiety also received 7500 training trials. However, no attempt was made during these training trials to change their pre-existing attentional bias. The group receiving training to produce an opposite attentional bias showed a highly significant reduction in trait anxiety when tested after training. In contrast, the control group showed only a small and non-significant change. This is the most direct evidence available to date that cognitive biases can change levels of trait anxiety as well as having more transient effects on state anxiety.

Evaluation

The research discussed in this section of the chapter has revealed clearly that there are important differences between individuals high and low in trait anxiety or neuroticism in terms of their cognitive functioning. More specifically, those high in trait anxiety typically have attentional and interpretive biases which are not found in those low in trait anxiety, and there is some evidence that the same is the case with respect to implicit memory bias. In addition, there is recent evidence indicating that some of these cognitive biases (i.e. attentional and interpretive bias) have causal effects on the level of experienced anxiety. This is important, in part because it suggests the potential value of a cognitive approach to the personality dimension of trait anxiety. However, as discussed below, the main theoretical and empirical approaches that have dominated this area until comparatively recently are limited in a number of ways.

One of the major limitations of the theoretical approaches of Williams et al. (1988, 1997), Wells and Matthews (1994), and Eysenck (1992) is that they are based on the assumption that individuals scoring low on trait anxiety form a homogeneous group. However, there is compelling evidence that there are clear subgroups among those scoring low on trait anxiety. For example, some individuals with low scores on trait anxiety have low levels of physiological reactivity in stressful situations, whereas others have very high levels of reactivity. This pattern has been found in several studies (see Weinberger, 1990, for a review).

Another important limitation of previous theoretical approaches is that the focus was almost exclusively on the functioning of the cognitive system. This is a limited approach, because it is clear that there are various response systems involved in anxiety. For example, Lang (e.g. 1985) identified separate behavioural, physiological and verbal response systems. Most early theories assumed (explicitly or implicitly) that there would be high levels of concordance or agreement among these response systems. In fact, the typical finding is that there is a lack of concordance. For example, Craske and Craig (1984) studied pianists who were performing in public. Their key finding was that measures of anxiety from different response systems typically failed to correlate significantly with each other. The widespread lack of concordance which has been observed seems important theoretically, and can only be understood if one adopts an approach broader than the purely cognitive.

FOUR-FACTOR THEORY

Eysenck (1997) put forward a four-factor theory of trait anxiety which incorporated some of the theoretical ideas and empirical research discussed in the previous section. However, the theory is intended to be much more comprehensive in scope than previous theoretical models, and some of the assumptions on which it is based differ from those of other theories in the area. The four-factor theory of trait anxiety is based on the assumption that the following question is of fundamental importance to an understanding of trait anxiety: What are the major sources of information which jointly determine an individual's level of experienced anxiety? In other words, it is assumed that we need to have a theory of anxiety as an emotional state as a prerequisite for developing an adequate theory of trait anxiety as a personality dimension.

The theory is called the four-factor theory because it is assumed within the theory that there are four main sources of information which influence experienced anxiety. Before discussing these four sources of information, it is important to note that the impact of each informational source on anxiety depends on the amount of attention it receives and on how it is interpreted rather than on the 'objective' characteristics of the information source per se.

What are the four sources of information? First, and most important, there is the external environment. As Lazarus (1991) has emphasized, the experience of most emotional states is heavily dependent on the cognitive appraisal of the immediate situation. Second, there is attention to, and interpretation of, one's own physiological activity. The importance of this source of information in producing the experience of anxiety is revealed most clearly in patients suffering from panic disorder. Such patients are far more likely than normal controls to experience extreme anxiety and a panic attack under biological challenge (e.g. lactate infusion), even though the physiological responses of both groups are typically rather similar (e.g. Gaffney *et al.*, 1988; Schmidt *et al.*, 2002; Yeragani and Pohl, 1989).

The third source of information is one's own behaviour. At an anecdotal level, it is often reported by public speakers that they experience much more anxiety when they become self-conscious and start attending to their own behaviour. More direct evidence was reported by Derakshan and Eysenck (2001a). In their study, the participant remained silent while a confederate of the experimenters either spoke about his own behaviour in the situation, or he spoke about the behaviour of the participant. The key finding was that the participants' level of experienced anxiety was substantially higher when their behaviour was the focus of discussion than when it was not.

The fourth source of information consists of negative cognitions about possible threatening future events (e.g. worries). Borkovec and Inz (1990) considered the effects of worrying on emotional state. Generalized anxiety disorder patients and normal controls relaxed for some time and then engaged in worrying. Both groups exhibited large increases in rated anxiousness and unpleasantness between the relaxation and worry time periods. Similar findings were reported subsequently by East and Watts (1994) in a study on normal individuals who rated themselves as chronic worriers and by Wells (2002) in research on patients with generalized anxiety disorder.

Repressors vs. low-anxious

It is assumed within most theories of trait anxiety (including those of H. J. Eysenck and Gray) that low scorers on trait anxiety form a homogeneous group. However, this assumption is not incorporated into the four-factor theory. According to that theory, individuals scoring low on trait anxiety should be divided into two groups on the basis of their level of defensiveness. Individuals who are low in trait anxiety but high in defensiveness are categorized as repressors or as having the repressive coping style, whereas individuals who are low in trait anxiety and low in defensiveness are categorized as low-anxious. These categories were first popularized by Weinberger, Schwartz and Davidson (1979), who used the Marlowe-Crowne Social Desirability Scale as a measure of defensiveness. They found substantial differences between repressors and low-anxious individuals when placed in a moderately stressful situation. For example, they found that repressors' physiological and behavioural responses indicated much higher levels of anxiety than did those of low-anxious individuals.

The differences between repressors and the low-anxious reported by Weinberger *et al.* (1979) have been repeated several times (see Eysenck, 1997). The most thorough study to compare repressors and low-anxious individuals with respect to physiological, behavioural, and self-report measures associated with anxiety was reported by Derakshan and Eysenck (2001b). They obtained all three types of measure in a moderately stressful situation in which the participants were videotaped. All of the data were then converted to standard scores for purposes of comparison. As had been found in previous research, repressors had relatively high physiological anxiety but low self-reported state anxiety. In contrast, the low-anxious participants had relatively low levels of physiological anxiety and/or self-reported state anxiety. The pattern was similar when behavioural anxiety (based on ratings of the videotape evidence by independent judges) was considered. Repressors had relatively high levels of behavioural anxiety, whereas the low-anxious had a low level of behavioural anxiety.

What is of most theoretical interest from the evidence discussed in this section so far is the fact that the repressors showed large discrepancies between their self-reported anxiety on the one hand and their physiological and behavioural anxiety on the other hand. One possible explanation of these discrepancies is simply that repressors deliberately distort their self-reports to claim low levels of experienced anxiety even though they actually experience high levels. If that were the case, then the discrepancies would be illusory rather than genuine. This issue has been addressed in several studies. For example, Derakshan and Eysenck (1999) assessed levels of trait anxiety on the Spielberger State-Trait Anxiety Inventory on two occasions separated by approximately two months: (a) standard conditions; (b) bogus pipeline conditions. In the second condition, the participants were wired up to an impressive-looking piece of equipment (known as the 'bogus pipeline') which they were led to believe could detect lying. The bogus pipeline has proved effective in numerous studies in social psychology in increasing honesty. For example, it has been found that participants admit to much more prejudice under bogus pipeline than under standard conditions (see Jones and Sigall, 1971, for a review). The trait-anxiety scores of repressors were slightly higher under bogus pipeline than under standard conditions, but the difference was not statistically significant. This finding suggests that repressors do not deliberately distort their scores when completing measures of trait anxiety under standard conditions.

Derakshan and Eysenck (1998) argued that it is extremely difficult to decide whether repressors' self-reported levels of state and trait anxiety are genuine or subject to distortion. Accordingly, they devised an indirect approach to the issue, using a paradigm which did not involve obtaining self-report data. In their study, the participants had to perform a verbal reasoning task which was combined with a high or low memory load. It is known that the adverse effects of the high memory load on performance of the verbal reasoning task are much greater for individuals high in trait anxiety than for those low in trait anxiety. It is generally accepted that the main reason for this pattern of findings is that individuals high in trait anxiety engage in more task-irrelevant negative thoughts about themselves and about their inadequate level of performance. Such task-irrelevant thoughts interfere with task performance, and such interference effects are especially strong when there is a concurrent memory load. The key finding obtained by Derakshan and Eysenck (1998) was that the negative effects of high memory load on verbal reasoning performance in repressors were relatively modest, resembling the effects on low-anxious individuals much more than those on high-anxious individuals. These findings support the view that repressors genuinely experience low levels of anxiety when confronting complex tasks.

How can we account for the differences between repressors and the low-anxious? According to Eysenck's (1997) four-factor theory, the two groups differ in terms of important aspects of cognitive functioning. It is assumed that low-anxious individuals do not have cognitive biases relating to the processing of external and internal stimuli. The absence of cognitive biases helps to explain why low-anxious individuals show minimal discrepancies among measures of self-reported, behavioural and physiological anxiety (Derakshan and Eysenck, 2001b).

In contrast, it is assumed that repressors have opposite cognitive biases with respect to the processing of both external and internal stimuli. More specifically, repressors have opposite attentional and interpretive biases. This means that they tend systematically to avoid attending to threat-related stimuli, and they also tend to interpret ambiguous stimuli and situations in a non-threatening way. As a result, repressors tend to minimize the threateningness of their own physiological state and behaviour, and this helps to produce discrepancies between self-report, physiological and behavioural measures of anxiety (Derakshan and Eysenck, 2001b). More specifically, repressors' opposite attentional and interpretive biases lead them to ignore and/or mis-interpret the evidence of their own physiological state, future cognitions and behaviour.

The relevant literature on opposite cognitive biases in repressors has been reviewed by Eysenck (1997, 2000), and so only a few studies will be men-tioned here. So far as opposite attentional bias with respect to external stimuli is concerned, Schill and Althoff (1968) presented their participants with a mixture of aggressive, sexual and neutral sentences masked by noise. There was some evidence for an opposite attentional bias, in that repressors' ability to perceive the sexual sentences was significantly worse than that of the low-anxious or high-anxious groups. In a study more directly on opposite atten-tional bias, Fox (1993) used the dot-probe paradigm with participants who were repressors, low-anxious, and high-anxious in order to assess attentional biases for social and physical threat words. For present purposes, the key finding was that the repressors showed an opposite attentional bias for the social threat stimuli, whereas the low-anxious individuals did not exhibit either an attentional bias or an opposite attentional bias.

There is relatively little direct evidence that repressors possess an opposite interpretive bias (see Eysenck, 2000). However, potentially important find-ings were reported by Calvo and Eysenck (2000), who assessed interpretive biases by measuring the speed of naming target words which confirmed or disconfirmed the consequence implied by previous ambiguous sentences. Various time intervals between sentence and target were used in order to plot the time course of activation of threat-related and neutral target words. The low-anxious participants showed no attentional or opposite attentional bias at any time interval. In contrast, the repressors had an interpretive bias when there was a short interval between sentence and target word, but this bias totally disappeared at a longer interval. It could be argued that this reversal (which was not found in the data of the low-anxious participants) reflects the operation of an opposite interpretive bias.

Biases for internal stimuli

The evidence discussed so far has indicated that individuals high in trait anxiety have attentional and interpretive biases for external stimuli, that repressors have opposite attentional and interpretive biases for external stim-uli, and that individuals low in trait anxiety do not have cognitive biases for external stimuli. All of these findings are consistent with the predictions of the four-factor theory. However, the theory also predicts that the same pat-tern of cognitive biases will be present when internal stimuli are considered. Accordingly, there will now be a brief consideration of some of the relevant findings.

Evidence that individuals high in trait or social anxiety have an interpretive bias for their own social behaviour has been obtained in a number of studies. For example, Clark and Arkowitz (1975) found that individuals high in social anxiety rated their overall level of social skill in two social situations as significantly lower than did independent judges. In contrast, those low in social anxiety showed no discrepancy between their own assessment of their level of social skill and the judges' ratings. Beidel, Turner and Dancu (1985) found that socially anxious individuals' level of self-reported anxiety was much higher than judges' ratings of their level of anxiety in two different stressful social situations. However, self-reported and rated anxiety were comparable across all situations for those low in social anxiety.

There are two limitations with the studies by Beidel *et al.* (1985) and Clark and Arkowitz (1975). First, the judges and the participants did not have access to the same information when making their judgements. As a consequence, discrepancies between self-report and rating data may reflect differential access to relevant information rather than interpretive bias. More specifically, the anxious participants may have indicated that their level of anxiety was higher than judges' ratings because they had privileged access to internal information about themselves (e.g. heart rate). Second, in neither study was there any attempt to distinguish between repressors and the low-anxious. Both of these limitations were addressed in a study by Derakshan and Eysenck (1997), to which we turn next.

Derakshan and Eysenck (1997) obtained video-recordings of university students as they gave a short public talk about psychology in front of their peers. Several days later they watched the video-recording of themselves, and rated their level of behavioural anxiety on several scales, having been specifically instructed to base their ratings of behavioural anxiety only on the evidence available in the video-recording. Independent judges rated the participants' level of behavioural anxiety from the same video-recordings using the same scales. The repressors showed an opposite interpretive bias for their own behaviour, in that their ratings of their own behavioural anxiety were significantly lower than the judges' ratings of their behavioural anxiety. In contrast, individuals high in trait anxiety showed an interpretive bias, since they rated their own behavioural anxiety as significantly greater than it appeared to the judges.

Evidence relating to opposite interpretive bias for future cognitions was reported by Eysenck and Derakshan (1997). The university students who were the participants in their study were asked to provide information about the negative expectations they had concerning their likely performance in important examinations due to be held a few weeks thereafter. They were also asked to provide the same information with respect to a typical student. One key finding was that repressors had an opposite interpretive bias, in that they had fewer negative expectations about themselves than about a typical student. This difference reflected an opposite interpretive bias rather than an accurate appraisal, because the actual examination performance of the repressors did not differ from that of other students. The other key finding was that individuals high in trait anxiety showed an interpretive bias, in that they had more negative expectations about themselves than they did about a typical student. This was a genuine interpretive bias, because the actual examination performance of the high-anxious students was comparable to that of the low-anxious and repressor groups.

It is relatively difficult to assess interpretive bias for one's own physiological state. The main reasons are that it is not possible to control an individual's internal state in more than a very approximate fashion, and it is also hard to assess accurately an individual's internal physiological state. Preliminary evidence was reported by Derakshan and Eysenck (1997) in a study described above. They measured heart rate while their student participants were giving a public talk, and found that there were no group differences between the groups of repressors, high-anxious, and defensive high-anxious individuals. However, there were substantial group differences in the interpretation of their increased heart rate during the talk when the participants were asked to indicate the extent to which they attributed it to the situation being stressful and threatening versus exciting and challenging. The high-anxious and defensive high-anxious groups attributed their elevated heart rate mainly to the situation being stressful and threatening. In contrast, the repressors argued that their elevated heart rate was mainly attributable to the situation being exciting and challenging. These findings may indicate that the high-anxious and defensive high-anxious groups had an interpretive bias for their own physiological state, whereas repressors exhibited an opposite interpretive bias for their internal state.

In sum, the evidence available so far suggests that individuals high in trait anxiety typically show cognitive biases for various internal stimuli. In contrast, repressors generally exhibit opposite cognitive biases for the same stimuli. These findings are consistent with the four-factor theory. As was argued above, repressors' opposite attentional and interpretive biases for internal stimuli may well account to some extent for their lack of concordance among anxiety measures, with self-reported anxiety being relatively lower than their levels of behavioural and physiological anxiety. In similar fashion, the attentional and interpretive biases for internal stimuli shown by individuals high in trait anxiety may explain the finding that their relative level of self-reported anxiety is characteristically higher than their relative levels of behavioural and physiological anxiety.

There are at least two reasons why further research is needed before coming to any definite conclusions. First, there has as yet only been a limited amount of research focusing specifically on cognitive biases for internal rather than for external stimuli, and it will be important to replicate the main findings. Second, it is much harder to carry out methodological sound studies on attentional and interpretive biases for internal stimuli than is the case for external stimuli. It is difficult to control internal stimuli; it is difficult to obtain an accurate assessment of internal stimuli (e.g. physiological state); and it is difficult to assess the extent to which any given individual is attending to specific internal stimuli. Ingenuity will be required to obviate these problems.

CONCLUSIONS

Research over the past 15 to 20 years has provided convincing evidence that individual differences in trait anxiety can be understood (at least in part) from a cognitive perspective. Individuals high in trait anxiety possess attentional and interpretive biases, and may in addition possess an implicit memory bias. The theoretical importance of the attentional and interpretive biases has increased with the provision of strong evidence that these biases can have causal effects on individuals' level of experienced anxiety. Before such evidence was produced, virtually all of the relevant findings were essentially correlational in nature, so that it was not possible to infer the direction of any causality.

Research carried out in recent years (much of it within the framework of the four-factor theory) has provided reasonable evidence that individuals high in trait anxiety and those with the repressive coping style possess different cognitive biases which are applied to a range of external and internal stimuli. More specifically, individuals high in trait anxiety possess attentional and interpretive biases and may well have an implicit memory bias as well, and repressors have opposite attentional and interpretive biases. In contrast, truly low-anxious individuals have consistently been found to lack both cognitive biases and opposite cognitive biases. The clear differences between the truly low-anxious and repressors with respect to cognitive biases support the view (e.g. Weinberger, 1990) that low scorers on trait anxiety fall into two discriminably different groups.

One of the key assumptions of four-factor theory is that at least some of the discrepancies among self-report, behavioural, and physiological measures of anxiety can be understood with reference to the cognitive biases possessed by high-anxious and repressor groups. More specifically, the attentional and interpretive biases of high-anxious individuals lead their self-reported anxiety in stressful situations to be relatively higher than anxiety as assessed behaviourally or physiologically. The opposite pattern is observed in individuals with the repressive coping style, because their opposite cognitive biases lead their self-reported anxiety to be relatively lower than anxiety inferred from behaviour or physiological state.

In spite of the fact that progress has been made, it will be important in future research to address various issues. Three of the most pressing issues will be discussed here. First, there have been relatively few systematic attempts to distinguish between effects of trait and of state anxiety on cognitive biases. In general, the evidence suggests that attentional and interpretive biases are strongest among individuals high in both trait and state anxiety. However, very little is known about the relative importance of low trait and state anxiety in determining the opposite attentional and interpretive biases of repressors.

Second, the evidence that individuals high in trait anxiety possess cognitive biases for all four sources of information is generally stronger and more convincing than the evidence that repressors possess opposite cognitive biases for the same sources of information. How can we explain this difference? The answer remains unclear. However, inspection of the findings suggests that repressors only reliably exhibit opposite cognitive biases when the stimuli they are processing possess clear personal significance. Thus, some of the clearest evidence for opposite cognitive biases in repressors has come from studies in which the critical stimuli were the repressors' own behaviour (Derakshan and Eysenck, 1997) or their beliefs about their own future failure (Eysenck and Derakshan, 1997).

Third, the four-factor theory provides a somewhat limited account of repressors. The existence of opposite cognitive biases in repressors can potentially explain why their relative level of self-reported anxiety is substantially less than their relative levels of behavioural anxiety and physiological activation. However, the theory fails to account for the fact that repressors have relatively high levels of behavioural anxiety and of physiological activation in stressful conditions. In that connection, the study by Calvo and Eysenck (2000) is potentially of importance. They found that repressors showed an initial interpretive bias when presented with an ambiguous sentence, but this bias disappeared thereafter. The implication of these findings is that repressors have a two-phase reaction to potentially threatening stimuli. The first phase involves a fast and relatively automatic alarm reaction which may resemble the automatic emotional reactions of phobic patients to phobic stimuli (e.g. Ohman and Soares, 1994). The second phase involves the use of various opposite cognitive biases which serve to prevent repressors from full conscious awareness of their previous alarm reaction. It is obvious that the four-factor theory is designed to explain the second phase of repressors' processing of threat-related stimuli rather than the first phase. Accordingly, it should be a goal of future research to explore in more detail what happens during the first phase.

REFERENCES

Beidel, D. C. Turner, S. M. and Dancu, C. V. (1985) 'Physiological, cognitive and behavioral aspects of social anxiety', *Behaviour Research and Therapy* 23: 109–117.

Borkovec, T. D. and Inz, J. (1990) 'The nature of worry in generalised anxiety disorder: A predominance of thought activity', *Behaviour Research and Therapy* 28: 153–158.

Bouchard, T. J. and Loehlin, J. C. (2001) 'Genes, evolution, and personality', *Behaviour Genetics* 31: 243–273.

Byrne, A. and Eysenck, M. W. (1993) 'Individual differences in positive and negative interpretive biases', *Personality and Individual Differences* 14: 849–851.

Calvo, M. G. and Castillo, M. D. (1998) 'Predictive inferences take time to develop', *Psychological Research* 61: 249–260.

Calvo, M. G. and Eysenck, M. W. (2000) 'Early vigilance and late avoidance of threat processing: Repressive coping vs. low/high anxiety', *Cognition and Emotion* 14: 763–787.

Calvo, M. G., Eysenck, M. W. and Castillo, M. D. (1997) 'Interpretation bias in test anxiety: The time course of predictive inferences', *Cognition and Emotion* 11: 43–63.

Clark, J. V. and Arkowitz, H. (1975) 'Social anxiety and self-evaluation of interpersonal performance', *Psychological Reports* 36: 211–221.

Craske, M. G. and Craig, K. D. (1984) 'Musical performance anxiety: The three-systems model and self-efficacy theory', *Behaviour Research and Therapy* 22: 267–280.

Derakshan, N. and Eysenck, M. W. (1997) 'Interpretive biases for one's own behavior and physiology in high trait anxious individuals and repressors', *Journal of Personality and Social Psychology* 73: 816–825.

Derakshan, N. and Eysenck, M. W. (1998) 'Working memory capacity in high trait-anxious and repressor groups', *Cognition and Emotion* 12: 697–713.

Derakshan, N. and Eysenck, M. W. (1999) 'Are repressors self-deceivers or other-deceivers?', *Cognition and Emotion* 13: 1–17.

Derakshan, N. and Eysenck, M. W. (2001a) 'Manipulation of focus of attention and its effects on anxiety in high-anxious individuals and repressors', *Anxiety, Stress, and Coping* 14: 173–191.

Derakshan, N. and Eysenck, M. W. (2001b) 'Effects of focus of attention on physiological, behavioral, and reported state anxiety in repressors, low-anxious, high-anxious, and defensive high-anxious individuals', *Anxiety, Stress, and Coping* 14: 285–299.

East, M. P. and Watts, F. N. (1994) 'Worry and the suppression of imagery', *Behaviour Research and Therapy* 32: 851–855.

Eysenck, H. J. (1967) *The Biological Basis of Personality*. Springfield, IL: C. C. Thomas.

Eysenck, H. J. (1982) *Personality, Genetics and Behavior*. New York: Praeger.

Eysenck, H. J. and Eysenck, M. W. (1985) *Personality and Individual Differences*. New York: Plenum.

Eysenck, M. W. (1992) *Anxiety: The Cognitive Perspective*. Hove, UK: Lawrence Erlbaum Associates Ltd.

Eysenck, M. W. (1997) *Anxiety and Cognition: A Unified Theory*. Hove, UK: Psychology Press.

Eysenck, M. W. (2000) 'A cognitive approach to trait anxiety', *European Journal of Personality* 14: 463–476.

Eysenck, M. W. and Derakshan, N. (1997) 'Cognitive biases for future negative events as a function of trait anxiety and social desirability', *Personality and Individual Differences* 22: 597–605.

Eysenck, M. W., MacLeod, C. and Mathews, A. (1987) 'Cognitive functioning in anxiety', *Psychological Research* 49: 189–195.

Fahrenberg, J. (1992) 'Psychophysiology of neuroticism and emotionality', in A. Gale and M. W. Eysenck (eds) *Individual Differences: Biological Perspectives*. Chichester, UK: Wiley.

Fox, E. (1993) 'Allocation of visual attention and anxiety', *Cognition and Emotion* 7: 207–215.

Gaffney, F. A., Fenton, B. J., Lane, L. D. and Lake, C. R. (1988) 'Hemodynamic, ventilatory, and biochemical responses of panic patients and normal controls with sodium lactate infusion and spontaneous panic attacks', *Archives of General Psychiatry* 45: 53–60.

Goldberg, L. R. (1981) 'Language and individual differences: The search for universals in personality lexicons', in L. Wheeler (ed.) *Review of Personality and Social Psychology*, Vol. 2. Beverly Hills, CA: Sage.

Gray, J. A. (1982) *The Neuropsychology of Anxiety*. Oxford: Clarendon.

Jones, E. E. and Sigall, H. (1971) 'The bogus pipeline: A new paradigm for measuring affect and attitude', *Psychological Bulletin* 76: 349–364.

Lang, P. J. (1985) 'The cognitive neurophysiology of emotion: Fear and anxiety', in A. H. Tima and J. Maser (eds) *Anxiety and the Anxiety Disorders*. Hillsdale, NJ: Lawrence Erlbaum Associates Inc.

Lazarus, R. S. (1991) *Emotion and Adaptation*. Oxford: Oxford University Press.

Loehlin, J. C., McCrae, R. R., Costa, P. T. and John, O. P. (1998) 'Heritabilities of common and measure-specific components of the Big Five personality factors', *Journal of Research in Personality* 32: 431–453.

McCann, D. and Endler, N. S. (2000) 'Editorial: Personality and cognition', *European Journal of Personality* 14: 371–375.

MacLeod, C. and Mathews, A. (1988) 'Anxiety and the allocation of attention to threat', *Quarterly Journal of Experimental Psychology* 38A: 659–670.

MacLeod, C., Rutherford, E., Campbell, L., Ebsworthy, G. and Holker, L. (2002) 'Selective attention and emotional vulnerability: Assessing the causal basis of their association through the experimental manipulation of attentional bias', *Journal of Abnormal Psychology* 111: 107–123.

McCrae, R. R. and Costa, P. T. (1985) 'Updating Norman's "adequate taxonomy": Intelligence and personality dimensions in natural language and in questionnaires', *Journal of Personality and Social Psychology* 49: 710–721.

Mathews, A. and Mackintosh, B. (2000) 'Induced emotional interpretation bias and anxiety', *Journal of Abnormal Psychology* 109: 602–615.

Mathews, A. and MacLeod, C. (2002) 'Induced processing biases have causal effects on anxiety', *Cognition and Emotion* 16: 331–354.

Mogg, K., Kentish, J. and Bradley, B. P. (1993) 'Effects of anxiety and awareness on colour-identification latencies for emotional words', *Behaviour Research and Therapy* 31: 559–567.

Ohman, A. and Soares, J. J. F. (1994) ' "Unconscious anxiety": Phobic responses to masked stimuli', *Journal of Abnormal Psychology* 103: 231–240.

Pedersen, N. L., Plomin, R., McClearn, G. E. and Friberg, L. (1988) 'Neuroticism, extraversion, and related traits in adult twins reared apart and reared together', *Journal of Personality and Social Psychology* 55: 950–957.

Richards, A., French, C. C., Adams, C., Eldridge, M. and Papadopolou, E. (1999)

'Implicit memory and anxiety: Perceptual identification of emotional stimuli', *European Journal of Cognitive Psychology* 11: 67–86.

Schill, T. and Althoff, M. (1968) 'Auditory perceptual thresholds for sensitizers, defensive and non-defensive repressors', *Percepetual and Motor Skills* 27: 935–938.

Schmidt, N. B., Forsyth, J. P., Santiago, H. T. and Trabowski, J. H. (2002) 'Classification of panic attack subtypes in patients and normal controls in response to biological challenge: Implications for assessment and treatment', *Journal of Anxiety Disorders* 16: 625–638.

Van den Hout, M., Tenney, N., Huygens, K., Merckelbach, H. and Kindt, M. (1995) 'Responding to subliminal threat cues is related to trait anxiety and emotional vulnerability: A successful replication of MacLeod and Hagan (1992)', *Behaviour Research and Therapy* 33: 451–454.

Watson, D. and Clark, L. A. (1984) 'Negative affectivity: The disposition to experience aversive emotional states', *Psychological Bulletin* 96: 465–490.

Weinberger, D. (1990) 'The construct validity of the repressive coping style', in J. L. Singer (ed.) *Repression and Dissociation: Implications for Personality Theory, Psychopathology, and Health*. Chicago: University of Chicago Press.

Weinberger, D. A., Schwartz, G. E. and Davidson, J. R. (1979) 'Low-anxious, high-anxious, and repressive coping styles: Psychometric patterns and behavioral and physiological responses to threat', *Journal of Abnormal Psychology* 88: 369–380.

Wells, A. (2002) 'Worry, metacognition, and GAD: Nature, consequences, and treatment', *Journal of Cognitive Psychotherapy* 16: 179–192.

Wells, A. and Matthews, G. (1994) *Attention and Emotion: A Clinical Perspective*. Hove, UK: Lawrence Erlbaum Associates Ltd.

Williams, J. M. G., Watts, F. N., MacLeod, C. and Mathews, A. (1988) *Cognitive Psychology and Emotional Disorders*. Chichester: Wiley.

Williams, J. M. G., Watts, F. N., MacLeod, C. and Mathews, A. (1997) *Cognitive Psychology and Emotional Disorders* (2nd edn.). Chichester: Wiley.

Yeragani, V. K., Balon, R. and Pohl, R. (1989) 'Lactate infusion in panic disorder patients and normal controls: Autonomic measures and subjective anxiety', *Acta Psychiatrica Scandinavica* 79: 32–40.

Chapter 2

The functional significance of temperament empirically tested

Data based on hypotheses derived from the regulative theory of temperament

Jan Strelau and Bogdan Zawadzki

This chapter presents the results of three studies aimed at examining the influence of two temperamental traits: emotional reactivity and activity in mental
health, post-traumatic stress disorder (PTSD) and somatic diseases (lung cancer and myocardial infarction). The data indicate that high emotional reactivity
may be considered a temperamental risk factor (TRF) of emotional disturbances and somatic diseases. The role of activity seems to be more complex
because it has two functions, which sometimes may be in contradiction. It leads
to more effective coping with life problems and regulates the arousal level by
supplying stimulation. As a result, high activity may be a TRF when it leads
to overarousal, but also low activity may have such a status when related to
non-effective coping with life stress.

INTRODUCTION

It was already the ancient Greek typology of temperament that developed,
as a result of observations, that inappropriate activity combined with the
amount and mixture of the four hormones constituting the physiological
basis of temperament, leads to different kinds of illnesses. Thus Hippocrates
and his follower, Galen, were the first to show that temperament plays an
important role in human functioning. The significance of temperament as a
factor that accelerates, or is conducive to, psychiatric disorders has been
strongly emphasized by constitutionally oriented researchers, such as Kretschmer (1944) or Sheldon and Stevens (1942). However, they entirely ignored
the contribution of environment to the origin of these disorders.

Pavlov (1927) was probably one of the first to show that temperamental traits,
when in interaction with an adverse environment, result in behaviour disorders. His experiments conducted on dogs demonstrated the functional
significance of temperamental traits, especially the strength of the central
nervous system (CNS), in the individual's adaptation to environmental
demands, such as strong stimulation, deprivation, and radical changes in the
surroundings.

Independently of age-specific activity and situations, many researchers
agree (e.g. Nebylitsyn 1972; Thomas and Chess, 1977; Kagan, 1983; Strelau,

1983; Chess and Thomas, 1989) that the functional significance of temperamental traits comes to the fore when individuals are confronted with difficult situations, extreme stressors or demands that exceed their capacities to cope.

Based on this point of view, different approaches have been developed, depending on whether these situations and demands refer to children or to adults. In research on children, specific concepts, such as 'difficult temperament' and 'goodness of fit' (see Thomas and Chess, 1977; Chess and Thomas, 1989), have been constructed, whereas in studies on adults concepts referring to different aspects of stress have gained widest popularity. This distinction, however, is not exclusive since both approaches can be found in studies on children and adults.

In several temperament theories the assumption that temperament plays an important role in moderating stress is incorporated as one of the most important postulates. For example, Kagan (1983, 1994) considered the two types of temperament distinguished by him – inhibited and uninhibited temperaments – as representing different vulnerability to experience stress under situations of unexpected or unpredictable events. According to Nebylitsyn (1972) and Strelau (1983) the functional significance of temperament is evident when individuals are confronted with extreme situations or demands.

In arousal-oriented theories of temperament, which refer to the concepts of optimal level of arousal or stimulation, temperamental characteristics are regarded as moderators in experiencing the state of stress under extreme levels of stimulation, as exemplified in the domain of extraversion (Eysenck, 1970; Eysenck and Eysenck, 1985), sensation seeking (Zuckerman, 1979, 1994) or harm avoidance (Cloninger, 1986; Cloninger, Svrakic and Przybeck, 1993).

The question arises as to why temperamental traits should be considered as important variables moderating stress phenomena. Temperamental traits have a moderator status, by which we mean, after Folkman and Lazarus (1988), that they constitute antecedent conditions that influence other conditions. The individual has a given temperament since birth and it is present before stressors and states of stress occur. If so, one may expect that temperamental traits modify all kinds of stress phenomena (Strelau, 1995).

Studies on temperament as related to stress take into account different aspects of stress. From the point of view of our studies the following three are of special importance:

- the impact of temperament in determining the intensity of stressors
- the role of temperament as a co-determinant of the state of stress
- the contribution of temperamental traits to the psychophysiological and/ or psychological costs of the state of stress.

As opposed to Lazurus and Folkman (1984) who underline the cognitive aspect of stress (perceived threat) and simply ignore arousal as an important component of this phenomenon, psychological stress is understood here in a different way. It is characterized by strong negative emotions, such as fear, anxiety, anger, hostility, or other emotional states evoking distress, accompanied by physiological and biochemical changes that evidently exceed the baseline level of arousal (see Strelau, 1995). Such an understanding of the state of stress, encountered among many researchers in the domain of stress (see Strelau, 1995), underlines the importance of both emotions and arousal as inseparable components of the state of stress. Both emotions and arousal are regarded as core concepts in temperament research, and thus constitute a good rationale for searching for links between the phenomena being studied here – temperament and stress.

Excessive stress, resulting from demands with which the individual is unable to cope, consists of extremely strong negative affects accompanied by unusually high elevation of the level of arousal. As consequence changes in the organism occur, which may result in variations in psychological functioning such as an increased level of anxiety and depression, or in physiological or biochemical disturbances expressed in psychosomatic diseases or other health problems.

Stress should be regarded as one of the many risk factors (external and internal) contributing to maladaptive functioning and disorders. When the state of stress interacts with other factors that decrease or dampen the consequences of stress, maladjustment or behavioural disturbances may not occur. Temperament determines individual arousability and constitutes the domain of personality that more than any other increases or decreases the probability of developing the state of stress, and as a consequence the psychological or psychophysiological costs of stress. This justifies the introduction of the concept of temperament risk factor (TRF), by which we mean any temperamental trait or configuration of traits that by itself and most probably in interaction with other factors acting excessively, persistently or recurrently, increases the risk of developing behaviour disorders or pathology, or that favours the shaping of a maladjusted personality (see Strelau, 1998).

Our own studies aimed at testifying the functional significance of temperamental traits are based on the Regulative Theory of Temperament (RTT; see Strelau, 1998). In short, RTT can be described by ten postulates. The following four served as a starting point for formulating our hypotheses:

1   Temperament reveals itself in formal characteristics of behaviour, which may be described in terms of energy and time.
2   Temperament characteristics are in their primary (inborn) form a product of biological evolution and there must exist some genetic bases as well as physiological mechanisms regulating the individual-specific level of arousal that co-determine individual differences in temperament.
3   Temperament plays a regulatory function consisting in modifying (moderating) the stimulative and temporal characteristics of situations and behaviour adequately to the individual's temperamental traits.

4   The role of temperament in regulating the relationships between persons and their environment becomes evident in difficult situations and maladaptive behaviour.

One of the common denominators of the studies presented in this chapter is that in all of them two temperamental traits were selected – emotional reactivity and activity – regarded according to RTT as moderators taking part in regulating the energetic aspects of situations and/or behaviours (Strelau, 1998). The structure of temperament as postulated by RTT comprises six traits that refer to the formal characteristics of behaviour and includes, in addition to the two mentioned above, briskness, perseveration (both refer to the temporal characteristics of behaviour), sensory sensitivity and endurance.

Many studies conducted in our laboratory have shown that emotional reactivity and activity are of special significance in moderating the stimulative value of stressors or consequences of stress resulting in behaviour disorders (see Strelau, 2001a; Zawadzki, 2001; Zawadzki and Strelau, 1997). To avoid misunderstandings, both temperament constructs are defined for the purpose of this chapter as follows (Strelau and Zawadzki, 1993, p. 327):

- *emotional reactivity* (ER): tendency to react intensively to emotion-eliciting stimuli, expressed in high emotional sensitivity and in low emotional endurance;
- *activity* (AC): tendency to undertake behaviour of high stimulative value or to supply by means of behaviour strong stimulation from the surroundings.

Considering these traits as dimensions, the definitions refer to one of the two poles characterizing high intensity of both emotional reactivity and activity. Our studies (Strelau and Zawadzki, 1995) have shown that emotional reactivity correlates positively (above 0.50) with neuroticism as measured by the EPQ-R (Eysenck, Eysenck and Barrett, 1985), and with distress and fearfulness assessed by means of the EAS-TS inventory (Buss and Plomin, 1984). In turn, activity shows correlations exceeding 0.50 with extraversion and the Sensation Seeking Scale (SSS-V; Zuckerman, 1979) total score.

The chapter presents three different studies concerning distinct aspects of the role that temperament plays in everyday life when individuals are confronted with difficult situations.

STUDY I: TEMPERAMENT AS A MODERATOR OF THE RELATIONSHIP – STRESSORS AND PSYCHOLOGICAL HEALTH

As postulated by Selye (1975, p. 21): 'Deprivation of stimuli and excessive stimulation are both accompanied by an increase in stress, sometimes to the point of distress.' All the events in one's life that can be interpreted in terms of intensity of stimulation and, as a consequence, in terms of arousal effects, as assumed by Rahe (1987), may be regarded as factors subject to moderation by different temperamental traits. Which of the specific temperament characteristics plays the role of moderator, by elevating or reducing the stimulative value of life events, depends on the kind of event.

Ursin (1980) pointed out that, under a high level of arousal, the tolerance to life events of high intensity is lowered. This is caused by the process of augmentation of acting stimuli. Under a low level of arousal there is a decrease in tolerance to life events of low stimulative value (e.g. deprivation, isolation), resulting from suppression processes in relation to acting stimuli.

Without going into the specificity of the different arousal-oriented temperamental traits, one may predict that temperamental traits that refer to low arousability (see Gray, 1964; Strelau, 2001b) as, for example, extraversion, high sensation seeking, or strong type of nervous system, when in interaction with life events characterized as demands of low stimulative value, such as deprivation or isolation, act as moderators that increase the state of stress, leading in extreme cases to excessive stress. In turn, temperamental traits characterized by high arousability interacting with highly stimulating life events as, for example, death, disaster, or traumatic stressors, act as moderators to increase the state of stress, again leading in extreme cases to excessive stress expressed in behaviour disorders. Introversion, low sensation seeking, or a weak type of nervous system are examples of such traits.

As argued by Strelau (1998) a life event that induces a state of stress of low intensity may be moderated by emotionality or other temperamental traits in such a way as to increase the state of stress, which has an impact on health status. The same state of stress, in terms of intensity, may result from low intensity life events interacting with high emotionality, as well as from high intensity life events interacting with low emotionality.

Taking into account these considerations we hypothesized that life events result in changes of psychological health measured by psychological distress and well-being. However, the relationship life events–psychological health will be, modified by emotional reactivity and activity. It was expected that emotional reactivity increases psychological distress whereas activity enhances well-being. Also interaction between life events, ER and AC, was expected to predict psychological health status.

Method

The model applied in this study explained mental health (psychological distress and well-being) in terms of stress induced by lack of equilibrium between the stimulative value of life events and personal characteristics reduced here to temperamental traits.

Subjects

All subjects were investigated by mail in this study. The inventories were sent to about 5500 people. The final sample was composed of 1327 subjects: 802 females and 525 males, ranging in age from 19 to 81 years ($M = 36.30$, $SD = 11.07$). Females were in the same age range as males ($M = 36.61$, $SD = 10.88$ and $M = 35.82$, $SD = 11.36$, respectively; $t = 1.27$ $n.s.$). The subjects were selected from a sample of 1515 persons who sent back inventories, but 188 persons with missing data were excluded from the analysis.

Measures

For measuring the subdimensions of mental health – psychological distress and psychological well-being – the Polish adaptation of the Mental Health Inventory (MHI; Veit and Ware, 1983) was used. As underlined by Veit and Ware (1983), psychological distress contains symptoms of anxiety, depression and loss of behavioural and emotional control and may be conceived as a negative pole of mental health. Psychological well-being is regarded as a positive pole of mental health and comprises general positive affect and emotional ties (Veit and Ware, 1983). The Polish version of the MHI is a translation of the original instrument and shows very similar psychometric properties to the American inventory (Cupas, 1997). Although a general mental health score could be calculated, for this study lower level scales were applied, measuring psychological distress and psychological well-being.

Life events were assessed by the Polish adaptation of the Recent Life Changes Questionnaire (RLCQ; Holmes and Rahe, 1967; Sobolewski, Strelau and Zawadzki, 1999). Items describing life changes were translated into Polish, but rates of the stimulative value of all life changes were reconstructed and they are specific for the Polish population. In this study the analysis of the impact of stimulative value of life events was based on the assessment of their stressfulness obtained from population rates. The subjective assessment of the level of experienced stress did not bring any different results than the objective indicator, so it was dropped from the analysis (the correlation between both indexes was equal to 0.81, $p < 0.05$).

Finally, temperamental dimensions were assessed by the Formal Characteristics of Behaviour–Temperament Inventory (FCB-TI), developed originally in Polish by Zawadzki and Strelau (1997; see also Strelau and Zawadzki,

1993, 1995). The inventory measures six temperamental traits: briskness, perseveration, sensory sensitivity, endurance, emotional reactivity, activity. For the purpose of this study only two scales were selected: Emotional Reactivity and Activity (each scale comprises 20 items).

Procedure

The statistical analysis was based on hierarchical regression analysis (Aiken and West, 1991; Pedhazur and Pedhazur-Schmelkin, 1991). As a preparation for this analysis, the scores of life events were square-rooted, because of the substantial deviation from the normal distribution. The impact of age and gender on all variables then was removed by linear regression – the data were stored in the form of standardized residuals. Then, all interactions were computed as products of independent variables.

Analysis of the data was based on hierarchical regression analysis, starting from the highest level interactions (the 'top-down' model). For psychological distress the effects of all of the interactions as well as an effect of activity were not significant. Thus, the final model retains two effects: life events and emotional reactivity. For psychological well-being, the same statistical procedure was applied, which showed that effects of interactions were also insignificant. So, the final model explaining psychological well-being contains only simple variables, including activity.

Results and discussion

Basic statistics of the applied scales (means, standard deviations, Cronbach's alphas, intercorrelations, and initial correlations with gender and age) are presented in Table 2.1.

As shown in Table 2.2, the data partly confirmed our hypotheses. The rate of stressors, as expected, is positively correlated with distress and negatively with well-being. This finding is fairly consistent with data from other studies (Rahe, 1987; Brown and Harris, 1989) and indicates that stress increases the probability of emotional disturbances.

The results show, as expected, that emotional reactivity, which is related to emotional arousal, may be considered as a risk factor of affective disorders. The role of temperamental activity is less clear. On the basis of our theoretical model, activity may be treated as a regulator of the level of arousal, but also as a trait which should have a direct impact on the individual's adaptation to the environment (active persons are more able to manage life problems; Zawadzki, 2001). For these reasons the role of activity may be more complex than emotional reactivity. It may have positive as well as negative impact on mental health, which is reflected by the zero-order correlations between activity and distress (negative one) and with well-being (positive one).

When the whole model with emotional reactivity and stressors is concerned,

Table 2.1 Matrix of correlations among all variables with basic statistics of scales

Scale	No of items	Alpha	M	SD	Gender	Age	LE	ER	AC	PD
LE	75	–	504.47 (20.87)	396.29 (8.30)	0.07* (0.07*)	-0.15* (-0.17*)				
ER	20	0.83	11.83	4.63	-0.35*	0.06*	0.03			
AC	20	0.83	7.81	4.59	0.13*	-0.35*	0.13*	-0.29*		
PD	24	0.92	59.62	18.26	-0.21*	0.05	0.23*	0.42*	-0.07*	
PWB	14	0.89	47.67	11.84	0.13*	-0.11*	-0.08*	-0.36*	0.27*	-0.70*

Notes

LE = life events (in parenthesis data for square-rooted scores), PD = psychological distress, PWB = psychological well-being, ER = emotional reactivity, AC = activity. Females were coded as 1 and males as 2. Correlations significant at $p < 0.05$ (two-tailed) are marked by an asterisk (correlations were calculated on the basis of standardized variables).

Table 2.2 Results of the hierarchical regression analysis for psychological distress and well-being (and life events)

Dependent model	Psychological distress					
	F	F_{change}	R	R^2	Predictor	Partial correlation
LE, ER, AC and all 2-way interactions + 3-way interaction	54.84[a]*	2.06	0.47	0.22	–	–
LE, ER and AC + all 2-way interactions	63.59[b]*	0.65	0.47	0.22	–	–
LE, ER and AC	126.63[c]*	–	0.47	0.22	LE ER AC	0.23* 0.41* 0.02
LE and ER + LE × ER interaction	127.03[c]*	1.43	0.47	0.22	–	–
LE and ER (final model)	189.76[d]*	–	0.47	0.22	LE ER	0.24* 0.42*

Dependent model	Psychological well-being					
	F	F_{change}	R	R^2	Predictor	Partial correlation
LE, ER, AC and all 2-way interactions + 3-way interaction	38.35[a]*	0.04	0.41	0.17	–	–
LE, ER and AC + all 2-way interactions	44.76[b]*	1.65	0.41	0.17	–	–
LE, ER and AC (final model)	87.75[c]*	–	0.41	0.17	LE ER AC	−0.11* −0.30* 0.20*

Dependent model	Life events					
	F	F_{change}	R	R^2	Predictor	Partial correlation
ER and AC (final model)	15.69[d]*	–	0.15	0.02	ER AC	0.07* 0.15*

Notes

a – df = 7/1319, b – df = 6/1320, c – df = 3/1323, d – df = 2/1324;* p < 0.05. R – correlation between dependent variable and linear combinations of predictors; R^2 – variance explained by the model; F – test F for the regression coefficient; F_{change} – test F of significance of increment of predicted values; for descriptions of the models and variables see text and Table 2.1.

activity has impact only on well-being, but not on distress. We hypothesized that the impact on well-being reflects the direct role of activity (positive one), whereas the relationship to distress comprises both mechanisms (regulation, which leads to overarousal and direct effect, which may weaken negative emotions) and both influences (positive and negative ones). It may be easily seen in the correlation between activity and stressors. Sobolewski, Strelau and Zawadzki (2001) showed that activity correlates with individual-dependent stressors such as challenges and negative events whereas this trait does not correlate with stressors that are not dependent on individuals. Activity also shares a substantial amount of genetic variance with stressors dependent on individuals and – in a model of causal relationships between activity and challenges – it was established that it influences life events identified as challenges. Based on data from this study, it may be postulated that active persons are not only able to manage life problems, but at the same time they tend to search for some life events and are prone to experience more stressors (even those which are not desired by an individual). This last mechanism may lead to a state of disregulation and overarousal. Activity for these reasons may be treated as a trait, which protects from affective problems, but at the same time is a risk factor, because – *via* stressors – it may increase the probability of emotional disturbances.

This explanation, however, is limited by the fact that none of the interactions were significant. It is very difficult to explain this finding, which is inconsistent with our theoretical model and hypotheses. It is possible that the model concerning life events linked to temperament should introduce rather person-environment correlations than interactions (see Wachs, 1992). The role of interactions may be clearly analysed only if the person's independent stressors are taken into account, as demonstrated in the second study. If all life events are concerned, the correlations between temperament and stressors should be taken into account as well as the effects of temperament on life events. This possible effect was demonstrated by additional data, presented in the last part of Table 2.2. Here life events were treated as variables dependent on temperamental traits. It was shown that not only activity predicts the amount of life events. Emotional reactivity – even if the zero-order correlation was near to zero – shows positive influence on stressors, additionally to activity (emotionally reactive persons reported more life events). In spite of the interpretation of this effect (see Kohn, Lafreniere and Gurevich, 1991), the total influence of emotional reactivity on mental health is clear: direct and indirect (*via* stressors) effects on distress and well-being are similar. Both increase distress and decrease well-being. In the case of activity, both effects may be opposite: activity increases well-being and decreases distress, but indirectly (*via* stressors) it decreases well-being and increases distress.

Finally, some interpretation is needed regarding the dependent variables. As shown in Table 2.1, both dimensions of mental health are strongly inter-related ($r = -0.70$), but they seem to depend only in part on identical mechanisms. Surprisingly, distress was more predictable than well-being (22 per cent and 17 per cent of variance, respectively). Although the data for well-being demonstrates the positive role of activity, it seems that the arousal-oriented model of stress explains more negative emotional states than positive ones. Well-being may depend more on other environmental factors, like social support or cognitive personal characteristics, such as sense of coherence (Antonovsky, 1979), not introduced into the study. Thus, what we need is a broader model, which should comprise other personal or environmental factors that influence the positive pole of mental health.

STUDY 2: TEMPERAMENT AS A PREDICTOR OF PTSD UNDER EXPERIENCED TRAUMA RESULTING FROM FLOOD

The study conducted on subjects who experienced flood was based on the following four assumptions: (a) all kinds of disaster or catastrophic events may be considered as examples of extreme stressors; (b) disasters may be treated as typical events not dependent on the individual; (c) the long-lasting state of stress caused by those stressors results, among others, in post-traumatic stress disorder (PTSD); (d) temperamental traits play a role of moderators in respect to the consequences of the state of extreme stress by increasing or decreasing the risk of PTSD.

There are not many studies in which temperament traits were related to post-traumatic stress disorder. Among the candidates that may be regarded as predictors of PTSD such traits as anxiety, introversion and neuroticism have been mentioned (Davidson, Kudler and Smith, 1987; McFarlane, 1989, 1992; Lee, Vailland, Torrey and Elder, 1995). Probably the most complex study regarding personality predictors of PTSD has been conducted by Lauterbach and Vrana (2001). In a sample of college students who reported a wide range of trauma borderline personality, antisocial personality, sensation seeking and the three Eysenckian superfactors have been considered as predictors of PTSD and retraumatization. The results of this study show that trauma intensity and personality variables are significant predictors of PTSD, explaining over 40 per cent of the variance.

Taking into account the literature review on disasters, as well as our own studies (see Strelau, 1995, 1998; Zawadzki and Strelau, 1997; Strelau et al., 2002) on temperament as related to stress phenomena, the following hypotheses have been formulated: PTSD is a function of the intensity of experienced trauma as measured by objective indicators. Emotional reactivity is positively related to PTSD whereas activity correlates negatively with symptoms of post-traumatic stress. Additionally, emotional reactivity and activity moderate the trauma–PTSD relationship.

Method

The model applied in the analysis required to assess trauma intensity, to ascribe temperamental traits a status of independent variables, and to consider the intensity of symptoms of the post-traumatic stress disorder as a dependent variable.

Subjects

The sample was composed of 279 subjects: 146 females and 133 males, ranging in age from 13 to 75 years ($M = 36.17$, $SD = 14.55$), who survived the Great Polish flood in 1997. Females were of the same age as males ($M = 35.66$, $SD = 13.72$ and $M = 36.73$, $SD = 15.44$, respectively; $t = 1.61$ $n.s.$). All subjects were investigated by interviewers three years after the flood at their homes in southern Poland (Racibórz).

Measures

To measure the symptoms of post-traumatic stress disorder (PTSD) a new instrument known as the PTSD-F inventory was developed (Strelau et al., 2002), which was applied in different samples of trauma victims (flood survivors, survivors of a coal mine catastrophe). In this study only the general score of the PTSD-F inventory was applied, reflecting the intensity of PTSD symptoms (30 items). It should be mentioned also that the PTSD-F general score correlates highly with the Mississippi PTSD Scale (0.71, $p < 0.05$; Norris and Perilla, 1996; adapted by Kaniasty) as well as with the MHI inventory (distress: 0.69 and well-being -0.52, $p < 0.05$; Cupas, 1997; Veit and Ware, 1983). Data showing high convergent and discriminant validity are presented elsewhere (see Zawadzki et al., 2004).

The trauma intensity was assessed by an interview comprising 14 questions referring to threat of life during the flood, the amount of material damage, prolonged financial problems, housing problems, as well as decline in socio-economic status after the flood. The total trauma index comprises all five aspects. Data for each aspect of trauma were dichotomized in a rational way into an indicator of non-trauma and trauma (present threat of life vs absent threat of life; no or only minor material damage vs substantial or very serious material damage; no or only minor financial and domestic problems vs substantial or serious problems, etc.). Finally, the total trauma score was calculated, indicating the intensity of trauma experience and prolonged objective trauma consequences (based on the number of trauma components, the scores range from 0 to 5 points).

The temperamental dimensions were assessed by the FCB-TI inventory as in the first study and only two scales were selected: Emotional Reactivity and Activity.

Procedure

The statistical analysis was based on hierarchical regression analysis (Aiken and West, 1991). The impact of age and gender on all variables was removed by linear regression – the data were stored in the form of standardized residuals. Then, all interactions were computed as products of independent variables.

The elaboration of data was based on hierarchical regression analysis, starting from the highest level interactions (the top-down model), as in the first study. The final model retained effects of trauma intensity, emotional reactivity, activity (insignificant effect) and two interactions: trauma x emotional reactivity and trauma x activity (both in disordinal form; see Pedhazur and Pedhazur-Schmelkin, 1991). The effect of the interaction between emotional reactivity and activity was not significant and was excluded from the analysis, as well as an interaction between all independent variables.

Results and discussion

Basic statistics of the applied scales (means, standard deviations, Cronbach's alphas, intercorrelations, and initial correlations with gender and age) are presented in Table 2.3.

The results of the hierarchical regression analysis are presented in Table 2.4. The data are in line with our hypotheses, with the exception of the interaction of all independent variables and the interaction between emotional reactivity and activity.

First of all, it may be demonstrated that trauma influences PTSD symptoms as well as emotional reactivity does. This trait generally increases PTSD symptoms, which is especially evident when the individual experiences the most dramatic trauma (high threat of life, serious material damage, domestic and financial problems following the flood). Emotionally low-reactive people

Table 2.3 Matrix of correlations among all variables with basic statistics of scales

Scale	No of items	Alpha	M	SD	Gender	Age	Trauma	RE	AC
Trauma	5	–	2.71	1.55	−0.04	0.25*			
ER	20	0.83	11.22	4.76	−0.36*	0.05	0.23*		
AC	20	0.83	9.72	4.55	0.09	−0.50*	−0.08	−0.44*	
PTSD	30	0.96	20.27	17.08	−0.24*	0.28*	0.46*	0.41*	−0.10

Notes
PTSD = PTSD total factor version score; ER = emotional reactivity, AC = activity; correlations significant at $p < 0.05$ (two-tailed) are marked by an asterisk (correlations were calculated on the basis of standardized variables). Correlations between PTSD and components of trauma index: threat for life (0.28*), material damage (0.26*), financial problems (0.48*), housing problems (0.41*) and decline in socio-economical status (0.35*); trauma index comprises 5 aspects based on 14 items.

Table 2.4 Results of the hierarchical regression analysis with trauma index and temperamental traits as a predictor of PTSD

Dependent model	PTSD total factor score – three years after the flood					
	F	F_{change}	R	R^2	Predictor	Partial correlation
TR, ER, AC, all 2-way interactions + 3-way interactions	19.09[a]*	1.78	0.57	0.33	–	–
TR, ER and AC + all 2-way interactions	21.90[b]*	2.57*	0.57	0.33	–	–
TR, ER and AC + selected 2-way interactions (final model)	26.36[c]*	3.83*	0.57*	0.33	TR ER AC TR × ER TR × AC	0.41* 0.36* 0.09 0.16* 0.12*

Notes
a – *df* = 7/271, b – *df* = 6/272, c – *df* = 5/273; * *p* < 0.05. TR – trauma index; for other symbols see Table 2.3.

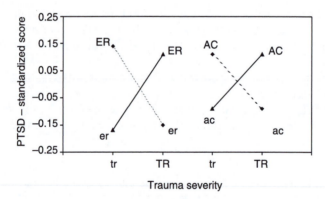

Figure 2.1 Impact of interactions between trauma and emotional reactivity, and trauma and activity on PTSD (standardized effects).

TR = high trauma, tr = low trauma, ER = high emotional reactivity, er = low emotional reactivity, AC = high activity, ac= low activity.

are able to better tolerate trauma and are less prone to PTSD when the trauma is more severe (see interaction presented in Figure 2.1). Thus, emotional reactivity may be seen as a risk factor for emotional disorders, because it probably leads to higher emotional arousal. Curiously enough, this effect changed when the experience was not extremely dramatic – the intensity of PTSD symptoms is higher in less reactive people. This effect might be due to the 'sensitization' of even weak negative emotions in low-reactive people and the greater ability of high-reactive individuals to cope with negative emotions, especially when they are not too intense ('inoculation' effect; Eysenck, 1983).

As in the first study, the role of activity seems to be more complex. It has no simple influence on PTSD symptoms (the zero-order correlation is negative, but not significant; the partial correlation is positive, but also not significant). The activity probably influences the PTSD in two ways, as was suggested in the discussion of the data from the first study. This is expressed in the interaction effect (see Figure 2.1). When the trauma is not very serious, activity plays a positive role. It decreases the intensity of PTSD symptoms, probably because people are more able to manage life problems following the flood. However, in the case of extreme trauma the more active people suffer from more intensive PTSD symptoms: higher activity leads to overstimulation and increases the level of arousal (high activity is an additional source of stimulation to trauma).

Finally, the data speak in favour of the two-dimensional model explaining the PTSD symptoms. Trauma by itself predicts PTSD. However, the prediction is much more accurate when temperamental traits are introduced into the model (from 21 per cent up to 31 per cent and 33 per cent for the model with interactions, data not presented in Table 2.4). This model seems to be especially valid if we consider the impact of trauma and temperament in terms of arousal level and PTSD as an arousal disorder (Everly, 1990). It must also be stressed that these data support the RTT postulates. Temperamental traits moderate the influence of stressors and the individual's arousal level. Besides the interactions, we have to remember about the correlations between trauma and temperament. Although a natural disaster may be considered a stressor independent of the individual, some people may overestimate the effect of trauma, experience more dramatic events, or the trauma may lead to changes in temperament. In Study 1 it was suggested that very active subjects may search for some life changes and experience more stressors than less active people. A similar person–environment correlation may be found in the data from the study on PTSD. The correlation between emotional reactivity and trauma (see Table 2.3) indicates that trauma may increase emotional reactivity or, more probably, highly reactive people experience/report more stressors or extremely dramatic trauma. This finding needs verification in a longitudinal study. However, the relationships between stressors, temperament and emotional disturbances seem to be more complex as was described in simple models. Temperament influences not only emotional disturbances, but is also tied with environmental stressors and its function may be regarded not only as a moderator, but also probably as a mediator of the environmental causes of stress.

STUDY 3: TEMPERAMENT AS A RISK FACTOR OF SOMATIC DISEASES

The idea that personality is the cause of somatic illnesses such as coronary heart disease (CHD) or cancer for many researchers seems to be humorous. However, a series of studies has been undertaken to examine the relationship between the Eysenckian temperament dimensions, especially neuroticism and extraversion, and both illnesses (see Kissen, 1967; Kissen and Eysenck, 1962; Eysenck, 1983, 1985). Among the determinants of these diseases, which may be interpreted as consequences of interactions between a variety of factors such as immune system regulation, neuroendocrine and biochemical factors, genetically determined vulnerability and environmental risk factors, an important role was found for temperament and other personality dimensions.

The most impressive studies on the relationship between personality variables, stress and physical illness, i.e. cancer and coronary heart disease, are those of Grossarth-Maticek and coworkers (Grossarth-Maticek, Bastiaans and Kanazir, 1985; Grossarth-Maticek and Eysenck, 1990, 1991). Three independent prospective studies were conducted over a ten-year period. Subjects in all three samples were diagnosed by means of inventories into four different personality types:

- Type I (equivalent to Type C) – cancer-prone, over-cooperative, unassertive, unexpressive of negative emotions, avoiding conflicts, over-patient and defensive in response to stress
- Type II (equivalent to Type A) – CHD-prone, chronically irritated and angry, failing to establish stable emotional relations, showing aggression and hostility responses
- Type III – hysterical, oscillating between inadequacy and anger
- Type IV (equivalent to Type B) – mentally healthy.

At the end of the ten-year period, mortality and cause of death were recorded. The results disclosed that in all three samples cancer mortality was highest in Type I and CHD mortality in Type II. It was also shown that a group of subjects diagnosed by relatives and friends as being permanently stressed showed significantly higher mortality rates (cancer and CHD) as compared with the non-selected (normal) group.

A replication of the Grossarth-Maticek studies conducted by Smedslund (1995) in which only Type I (cancer-prone), Type II (CHD-prone) and Type IV (healthy) were distinguished, has shown that individuals representing Type IV reported significantly less heart disease as compared with Types I and II. There were, however, no significant differences between the three types as regards cancer. The relationship between heart disease and personality type was blurred by such variables as age, smoking, diet and exercising. Types I and II were older and smoked more, and Type IV persons had a healthier diet and exercised more.

The literature also reports plenty of research in which CHD has been related to the Eysenckian temperament dimensions. Findings from several studies (see Thomas and Greenstreet, 1973; Eysenck, 1983, 1985, 1988: for a review see Booth-Kewley and Friedman, 1987; Friedman and Booth-Kewley, 1987) suggest that high neuroticism and high psychoticism (in terms of hostility and aggressiveness) interact with stressors to raise the risk of developing CHD. In a review comprising over 40 years of studies, Whiteman, Deary and Fowkes (2000) when searching for personality cardiovascular disease relationships found that Type A and hostility-related traits account for approximately 2 per cent of the variance in this disease.

A five-year follow-up study was conducted by Whiteman and coworkers (2000) in which two categories of incident CHD – angina and myocardial infarction – were related to submissiveness and hostility. It turned out that submissiveness is protective against myocardial infarction but not angina. Increased dominance, the opposite pole to submissiveness, considered as a component of Type A behaviour was associated with higher risk of coronary disease. Curiously enough, hostility was not related to any of the two categories of CHD. In this study a variety of demographic and SES variables were under control.

The meta-analytic studies (see Booth-Kewley and Friedman, 1987; Friedman and Booth-Kewley, 1987; McGee, Williams and Elwood, 1994; Miller, Smith and Turner, 1996) suggest that certain personality traits seem to be a common risk factor for both CHD and cancer, but some of them may be illness specific. We hypothesized that depression (depressiveness) is a general risk factor for many different illnesses (including lung cancer and myocardial infarction). Hostility may be treated as a myocardial infarction risk factor, but submissiveness (as a part of Type C; see Temoshok and Dreher, 1992) as a risk of lung cancer. Regarding the temperamental traits, it was expected that emotional reactivity may be considered a common risk factor, strongly related to depressiveness. In turn, activity is illness specific: high activity is related to hostility and myocardial infarction; low activity is related to submissiveness and lung cancer. Additionally, temperamental traits are regarded rather as an indirect risk factor of both illnesses with direct effects of personality factors (and direct relationships between temperament and other personality traits). It was assumed also that smoking is influenced by temperament (see Eysenck, 1988).

Method

The model applied in the analysis required the assessment of temperamental traits and other personality risk factors in groups of healthy subjects and patients suffering from myocardial infarction and lung cancer. Additionally, the smoking status was under control.

Subjects

The sample was composed of 329 subjects. Among them 135 persons suffered from lung cancer (39 females and 96 males, ranging in age from 27 to 72 years; $M = 54.62$; $SD = 8.57$; 119 smokers). Information about medical diagnosis was obtained from physicians, with the consent of the patients. The investigation was done prior to the cancer diagnosis and the data of six individuals were not introduced into the study because they suffered from other lung diseases. The next group was composed of 74 persons suffering from myocardial infarction (24 females and 50 males, ranging in age from 31 to 75 years; $M = 54.91$ $SD = 10.01$; 44 smokers). The investigation was done from one to three months after myocardial infarction and, again, information about the medical diagnosis was obtained from physicians by patient's agreement. The last group was composed from 120 healthy individuals (41 females and 79 males, ranging in age from 30 to 77 years; $M = 52.56$; $SD = 10.19$; 63 smokers). Those people indicated that they were healthy and did not suffer from CHD and cancer (and also other serious diseases). All groups did not differ with regard to age ($F = 1.97$, $df = 3/325$, $p = 0.14$) and gender ($chi^2 = 0.84$, $df = 2$, $p = 0.65$).

Measures

For measuring depressiveness, hostility and submissiveness, a new instrument was developed – the Inventory of Personality Syndromes (IPS; Zawadzki, 2001). The IPS enables us to measure three factors, which were derived by factor analysis (Principal Components, scree test and Varimax) in a group of more than 400 healthy persons and subjects suffering from myocardial infarction and lung cancer. The scales of IPS demonstrate satisfactory reliability and construct validity (Zawadzki, 2001). For instance: the Depressiveness scale (20 items) correlates – 0.60 with Type 4 (scale 4B) from the Short Interpersonal Reactions Inventory (SIRI; Grossarth-Maticek and Eysenck, 1990, adapted by Zawadzki, 2001), 0.37 with Type 1 and 0.48 with Type 2. The Submissiveness scale (15 items) correlates 0.59 with Type 1 from SIRI and the Hostility scale (15 items) 0.63 with Type A assessed by Kwestionariusz do Badania Wzoru Zachowania (Type A Inventory), developed by Wrześniewski (1990) and 0.42 with Type 2 from SIRI. It was also shown that the depressiveness score differentiates healthy subjects from patients of both groups, but higher level of hostility occurs only in myocardial infarction subjects, whereas higher level of submissiveness occurs in lung cancer patients.

Smoking status was examined via interview. Several questions were asked about the smoking rate and duration. Based on the data, the smoking status was dichotomized into smokers and non-smokers. Individuals, who had quit smoking more than two years before the study were rated as non-smokers. Healthy people were also asked during the interview about their health status. The health–illness variable was coded as a dichotomous variable with value '1' for all patients and value '0' for healthy individuals. Finally, the temperamental dimensions were assessed by the FCB-TI as in the first study and only two scales were selected: Emotional Reactivity and Activity.

Procedure

The statistical analysis was based on path analysis (Pedhazur and Pedhazur-Schmelkin, 1991). First of all, two subgroups were composed on which the independent analyses were conducted: the first comprised healthy and lung cancer people ($N = 255$) and the second healthy and myocardial infarction people ($N = 194$). In both subgroups independently, the impact of age and gender on all personality variables (except for smoking and health status) was removed by linear regression – the data were stored in the form of standardized residuals. Then, each variable was dichotimized over the mean and tetrachoric correlations as well as asymptotic covariances for all variables were calculated by PRELIS2.

The path analysis was applied independently in both subgroups, based on the Weighted Least Squares method by LISREL 8.0 (Jöreskog and Sörbom, 1993). Temperamental traits were treated as exogenous variables, smoking status, depressiveness and hostility/submissiveness as intermediate and illness as an endogenous variable. Analysis started from the full model with all paths, and the model then was trimmed (non-significant paths were discarded). The analysis was stopped when all paths were significant and the model indicated a good fit (based on the chi^2 test; see Pedhazur and Pedhazur-Schmelkin, 1991). Also two other models were tested: a model with no smoking status and a model with other than temperament personality variables as exogenous variables and temperamental traits as intermediate ones. The data obtained by the first model were very similar to the basic final one and are also presented. The second model showed that non-temperamental personality variables have direct and indirect effects on illness (via temperament), whereas the basic model comprises only indirect effect of temperament on illness (via non-temperamental personality traits). Following the assumption that temperament is an indirect risk factor of somatic diseases, this model was accepted as a basic and final one.

Results and discussion

Basic statistics of the personality scales (means, standard deviations, Cronbach's alphas, intercorrelations, and initial correlations with gender and age) are presented in Table 2.5 for each group separately. Because a substantial correlation was found between depressiveness and hostility, the impact of depressiveness was removed from hostility (in Table 2.5 the correlations of the corrected hostility scale are given in parentheses).

The data based on the final model for lung cancer are presented in Figure 2.2. As predicted, depressiveness and submissiveness are related to illness, although the main predictor of lung cancer is the smoking status. Temperamental traits predict all intermediate variables: depressiveness is mainly related to emotional reactivity, whereas submissiveness and smoking but also depressiveness to activity.

The data for the final model of myocardial infarction are presented in Figure 2.3. As expected depressiveness and hostility are related to illness, but surprisingly the smoking status does not predict myocardial infarction. Temperamental traits, as in the previous analysis, predict all intermediate variables: emotional reactivity is related to depressiveness, hostility and smoking, whereas activity to hostility and smoking.

The results of both analyses are summarized in Table 2.6 (the *chi*² value as an indicator of the fit of the model) illustrating that most of the results obtained in both analyses are in line with our predictions.

Depressiveness seems to be a common risk factor for both diseases. Hostility is an additional risk factor of myocardial infarction and submissiveness of lung cancer. All of them are reasonably related to temperamental traits: depressiveness in both subgroups to emotional reactivity, hostility and submissiveness to activity (although emotional reactivity is related to hostility too). It seems that both temperamental traits may be considered a basis for other personality risk factors of somatic diseases. Emotional reactivity

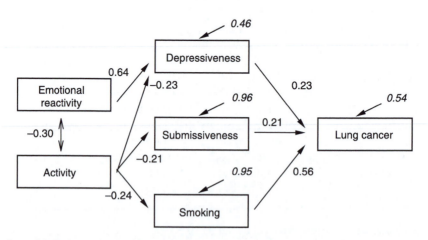

Figure 2.2 Path model for relationships between temperamental traits: emotional reactivity and activity, personality characteristics: depressiveness and submissiveness, smoking habit (status) and somatic health (lung cancer).

Table 2.5 Matrix of correlations among all variables with basic statistics of scales

Scale	Group	Alpha	M	SD	Gender	Age	Dp	Ho	Su	RE
Dp	H	0.87	6.73	5.06	-0.13	0.00				
	LC	0.86	8.72	4.91	-0.26*	-0.01				
	MI	0.88	8.55	5.59	-0.11	0.21				
Ho	H	0.79	5.79	3.54	-0.11 (-0.05)	0.04 (0.05)	0.50* (0.00)			
	LC	0.79	6.46	3.54	-0.02 (0.03)	0.03 (0.04)	0.23* (0.01)			
	MI	0.79	7.28	3.64	0.16 (0.21)	0.02 (-0.06)	0.35* (0.02)			
Su	H	0.73	9.88	2.99	0.00	0.01	0.05	-0.20* (-0.26*)		
	LC	0.73	11.06	2.78	-0.24*	0.09	0.13	-0.15 (-0.19*)		
	MI	0.73	10.14	3.22	-0.03	0.00	0.09	-0.24* (-0.29*)		
ER	H	0.88	10.02	5.27	-0.19*	-0.02	0.71*	0.52* (0.19*)	0.09	
	LC	0.79	11.61	4.26	-0.29*	0.01	0.56*	0.50 (0.39*)	0.15	
	MI	0.82	12.07	4.73	-0.15	0.13	0.74*	0.43* (0.19)	0.21	
AC	H	0.83	8.09	4.55	0.00	-0.05	-0.46*	-0.04 (0.23*)	-0.37*	-0.39*
	LC	0.72	6.76	3.66	0.17*	-0.16*	-0.28*	0.12 (0.18*)	-0.07	-0.11
	MI	0.79	7.29	4.20	0.08	-0.20	-0.53*	-0.15 (0.04)	0.04	-0.47*

Notes

Dp = depressiveness (20 items), Ho = hostility (15 items), Su = submissiveness (15 items), ER = emotional reactivity, AC = activity; correlations significant at p < 0.05 (two-tailed) are marked by an asterisk (correlations were calculated on the basis of standardized variables). H = healthy subjects (N = 135), LC = lung cancer patients (N = 120), MI = myocardial infarction patients (N = 74).

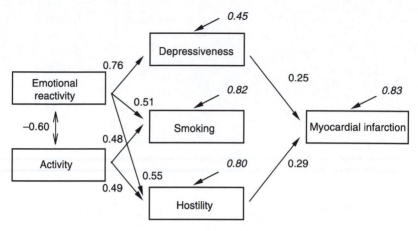

Figure 2.3 Path model for relationships between temperamental traits: emotional reactivity and activity, personality characteristics: depressiveness and hostility, smoking habit (status) and somatic health (myocardial infarction).

Table 2.6 Results of the path analysis for relationships between temperamental traits (emotional reactivity and activity), personality characteristics (depressiveness, submissiveness and hostility), smoking and lung cancer, and myocardial infarction

Lung cancer (chi² = 7.15 df = 7 p = 0.41)

Variable	Emotional reactivity	Activity	Lung cancer
Lung cancer	0.15* (0.18*)	−0.23* (−0.13*)	
Smoking		−0.24*	0.56*
Depressiveness	0.64*	−0.23*	0.23*
Submissiveness		−0.21*	0.21*

Myocardial infarction (chi² = 4.70 df = 7 heart infarct p = 0.70)

Heart infarct	0.35* (0.32*)	0.15 (0.13)	
Smoking	0.51*	0.48*	
Depressiveness	0.76*		0.25*
Hostility (corrected)	0.55*	0.49*	0.29*

Notes
Correlations significant at *p* < 0.05 (two-tailed) are marked by an asterisk. Hostility (corrected) – the hostility score, which has a partialled out effect of depressiveness. In parenthesis are correlations between temperament and illness, when the smoking status was not included into the model.

predicts, however, the risk factor common for both diseases, whereas activity is rather the illness-specific personality risk factor. Temperamental traits are also related to both diseases. High emotional reactivity is related to lung cancer and myocardial infarction, but high activity only to myocardial infarction, whereas low activity to lung cancer (this effect was not significant). However, temperamental traits demonstrated only the indirect effect via other personality risk factors with no significant direct influences. Studies conducted by Eliasz (2001) and Klonowicz and Eliasz (2004) have shown that misfit between temperament and other personality traits taking part in the system of regulation of stimulation control may result in different consequences of experienced stressors.

The role of smoking status and its relationships to temperament is less clear. In the first subgroup the smoking status was negatively related to activity and positively in the second subgroup. The same refers to emotional reactivity (positive correlation in the myocardial infarction study) and to the prediction of illness (only relationships with lung cancer). Although it may be suggested that smoking is related mainly to emotional reactivity (Zawadzki, 2001) with no clear prediction for activity, the data obtained in this study are unequivocal. It is surprising that smoking does not predict myocardial infarction. This may be due to the fact that the rate of smokers in the whole sample was very high (53 per cent among healthy subjects, 59 per cent among persons suffering from myocardial infarction and 88 per cent among lung cancer patients).

Finally, some comments regarding the role of temperament as a risk factor of somatic diseases are needed. The data indicate that temperament is not a direct risk factor of somatic illnesses. Rather it should be considered as a risk factor of pathology-prone personality traits that may directly lead to somatic disease. If an individual is not resistant to stress (emotionally reactive) and very active at the same time, she or he may develop a 'fighting spirit'. It enables him to cope with life problems, but the cost of this tendency is over-stimulation and overarousal leading to hostility and myocardial infarction. If the individual is trying to protect against a high level of arousal by low activity, but cannot successfully avoid environmental stressors, the result is a 'peaceful spirit', accompanied by the stoic tendency, low self-efficacy and submissiveness. The only way in which arousal may be released is visceral activity (or smoking), which might be a risk factor of lung cancer. Those hypotheses, however, should be verified in psychophysiological studies as well as by introducing a more complex model in prospective investigations.

CONCLUSIONS

The data obtained in all three studies indicate that the main assumptions of RTT are valid: temperamental traits themselves and with life stress increase the risk for emotional disorders and somatic diseases (see Strelau, 1995, 1998). The clearest finding refers to the emotional reactivity. This trait seems to be a risk factor of emotional disturbances and the more general tendency to react to life stress by depression, which may lead to somatic diseases. The role of temperamental activity is more complex. Activity may have a beneficial effect because it leads to effective coping with life stress and self-efficacy, but may result in overstimulation and overarousal as well, especially in the presence of environmental stressors. Low activity does not lead to overarousal, but at the same time it has no beneficial effects in the form of individual efficacy. Depending on environmental circumstances and the level of emotional reactivity, both low and high activity may be a risk factor of emotional disorders and somatic diseases.

The findings of our study indicate also that the models explaining mental and somatic disorders should comprise temperamental and environmental factors. However, not only interactional effects of both determinants should be considered, but also correlations of both factors. Individuals may select their environment according to temperament, but the environment may also lead to changes in temperament. The more complex model, comprising the interactional and correlational effects, is necessary and should be verified in longitudinal studies. The challenge is ahead.

ACKNOWLEDGEMENTS

Study 1 was supported by Grants No 1 H01 F06609 and No 1 H01 F00516 from the National Committee for Scientific Research and by Subsidies for Scientists (N-2/1998) awarded to Jan Strelau by the Foundation of Polish Science.

Study 2 was supported by Grant PZB-KBN 001/H01 from the National Committee for Scientific Research.

Study 3 was supported by Grants BST 571/97 and BST 601/98 from Warsaw University.

REFERENCES

Aiken, L. S. and West, S. G. (1991) *Multiple Regression: Testing and Interpreting Interactions*. Newbury Park, CA: Sage.

Antonovsky, A. (1979) *Health, Stress, and Coping: New Perspectives on Mental and Physical Well-Being*. San Francisco, CA: Jossey-Bass.

Booth-Kewley, S. and Friedman, H. S. (1987) 'Psychological predictors of heart disease: A quantitative review', *Psychological Bulletin* 101: 343–362.

Brown, G. W. and Harris, T. (eds) (1989) *Life Events and Illness*. London: Guilford Press.

Buss, A. H. and Plomin, R. (1984) *Temperament: Early Developing Personality Traits*. Hillsdale, NJ: Lawrence Erlbaum Associates Inc.

Chess, S. and Thomas, A. (1989) 'Temperament and its functional significance', in S. I. Greenspan and G. H. Pollock (eds) *The Course of Life*, vol. 2, pp. 163–227. Madison, CT: International Universities Press.

Cloninger, C. R. (1986) 'A unified biosocial theory of personality and its role in the development of anxiety states', *Psychiatric Developments* 3: 167–226.

Cloninger, C. R., Svrakic, D. M. and Przybeck, T. R. (1993) 'A psychobiological model of temperament and character', *Archives of General Psychiatry* 50: 975–990.

Cupas, M. (1997) *Adaptacja Inwentarza Zdrowia Psychicznego MHI Clarice Veit i J. Ware do warunków polskich* [Adaptation of the Mental Health Inventory (MHI), constructed by Clarice Veit and J. Ware, to Polish conditions]. Unpublished master's thesis, University of Warsaw, Warsaw, Poland.

Davidson, J., Kudler, H. and Smith, R. (1987) 'Personality in chronic post-traumatic stress disorder: A study of the Eysenck inventory', *Journal of Anxiety Disorders* 1: 295–300.

Eliasz, A. (2001) 'Temperament, type A, and motives', in H. Brandstätter and A. Eliasz (eds) *Persons, Situations and Emotions: An Ecological Approach*, pp. 55–73. New York: Oxford University Press.

Everly, G. S. (1990) 'PTSD as a disorder of arousal', *Psychology and Health: An International Journal* 4: 135–145.

Eysenck, H. J. (1970) *The Structure of Human Personality*, 3rd edn. London: Methuen.

Eysenck, H. J. (1983) 'Stress, disease, and personality: The "inoculation effect" ', in C. L. Cooper (ed.) *Stress Research*, pp. 121–131. London: Wiley.

Eysenck, H. J. (1985) 'Personality, cancer and cardiovascular disease: A causal analysis', *Personality and Individual Differences* 6: 535–556.

Eysenck, H. J. (1988) 'The respective importance of personality, cigarette smoking and interaction effects for the genesis of cancer and coronary heart disease', *Personality and Individual Differences* 9: 453–464.

Eysenck, H. J. and Eysenck, M. W. (1985) *Personality and Individual Differences: A Natural Science Approach*. New York: Plenum Press.

Eysenck, S. B. G., Eysenck, H. J. and Barrett, P. (1985) 'A revised version of the Psychoticism scale', *Personality and Individual Differences* 6: 21–29.

Folkman, S. and Lazarus, R. S. (1988) 'Coping as a mediator of emotion', *Journal of Personality and Social Psychology* 54: 466–475.

Friedman, H. S. and Booth-Kewley, S. (1987) 'The "disease-prone personality": A meta-analytic view of the construct', *American Psychologist* 42: 539–555.

Gray, J. A. (1964). 'Strength of the nervous system and levels of arousal: A reinterpretation', in J. A. Gray (ed.) *Pavlov's Typology*, pp. 289–364. Oxford: Pergamon Press.

Grossarth-Maticek, R. and Eysenck, H. J. (1990) 'Personality, stress and disease: Description and validation of a new inventory', *Psychological Reports* 66: 355–373.

Grossarth-Maticek, R. and Eysenck, H. J. (1991) 'Personality, stress, and motivational factors in drinking as determinants of risk for cancer and coronary heart disease', *Psychological Reports* 69: 1027–1093.

Grossarth-Maticek, R., Bastiaans, J. and Kanazir, D. T. (1985) 'Psychosocial factors as strong predictors of mortality from cancer, ischaemic heart disease and stroke: The Yugoslav prospective study', *Journal of Psychosomatic Research* 29: 167–176.

Holmes, T. H. and Rahe, R. H. (1967) 'The Social Readjustment Rating Scale', *Journal of Psychosomatic Research* 11: 213–218.

Jöreskog, K. G. and Sörbom, D. (1993) *LISREL 8. User's Reference Guide*. Chicago, IL: SPSS.

Kagan, J. (1983) 'Stress and coping in early development', in N. Garmezy and

M. Rutter (eds) *Stress, Coping and Development in Children*, pp. 191–216. New York: McGraw-Hill.

Kagan, J. (1994) *Galen's Prophecy: Temperament in Human Nature*. New York: Basic Books.

Kissen, D. M. (1967) 'Psychological factors, personality and lung cancer in men aged 55–64', *British Journal of Medical Psychology* 40: 29–34.

Kissen, D. M. and Eysenck, H. J. (1962) 'Personality in male lung cancer patients', *Journal of Psychosomatic Research* 6: 123–137.

Klonowicz, T. and Eliasz, A. (2004) 'Traumatyczny stres w zawodowym doświadczeniu pracowników pogotowia: Rola niedopasowania osobowościowych regulatorów zachowania' [Traumatic occupational stress in medical emergency sevices: The effect of a misfit between personality characteristics], in J. Strelau (ed) *Osobowość a ekstremalne stres*, pp. 167–182. Gdańsk: Gdańskie Wydawnictwo Psychologiczne.

Kohn, P. M., Lafreniere, K. and Gurevich, M. (1991) 'Hassles, health, and personality', *Journal of Personality and Social Psychology* 61: 478–482.

Kretschmer, E. (1944) *Körperbau and Charakter: Untersuchungen zum Konstitutionsproblem and zur Lehre von den Temperamenten* [Physique and character: Research concerning problems of constitution and knowledge on temperaments], 17–18th edn. Berlin: Springer.

Lauterbach, D. and Vrana, S. (2001) 'The relationship among personality variables, exposure to traumatic events, and severity of posttraumatic stress symptoms', *Journal of Traumatic Stress* 14: 29–45.

Lazarus, R. S. and Folkman, S. (1984). *Stress, Appraisal, and Coping*. New York: Springer Verlag.

Lee, K. A., Vaillant, G. E., Torrey, W. C. and Elder, G. H. (1995) 'A 50-year prospective study of the psychological sequelae of World War II combat', *American Journal of Psychiatry* 152: 516–522.

McFarlane, A. C. (1989) 'The etiology of post-traumatic morbidity: Predisposing, precipitating and perpetuating factors', *British Journal of Psychiatry* 154: 221–228.

McFarlane, A. C. (1992) 'Avoidance and intrusion in post-traumatic stress disorder', *Journal of Nervous and Mental Disease* 180: 439–445.

McGee, R., Williams, S. and Elwood, M. (1994) 'Depression and the development of cancer: A meta-analysis', *Social Sciences and Medicine* 38: 187–192.

Miller, T., Smith, T. W. and Turner, C. (1996) 'A meta-analytic review of research on hostility and physical health', *Psychological Bulletin* 119: 322–348.

Nebylitsyn, V. D. (1972) *Fundamental Properties of the Human Nervous System*. New York: Plenum Press.

Norris, F. and Perilla, J. (1996) 'The Revised Civilian Mississippi Scale for PTSD: Reliability, validity, and cross-language stability', *Journal of Traumatic Stress* 9: 285–298.

Pavlov, I. P. (1927) *Conditioned Reflexes*. London: Oxford University Press.

Pedhazur, E. J. and Pedhazur-Schmelkin, L. (1991) *Measurement, Design, and Analysis: An Integrated Approach*. Hillsdale, NJ: Lawrence Erlbaum Associates Inc.

Rahe, R. H. (1987) 'Recent life changes, emotions, and behaviours in coronary heart disease', in A. Baum and J. E. Singer (eds) *Handbook of Psychology and Health*, vol. 5, pp. 229–254. Hillsdale, NJ: Laurence Erlbaum Associates Inc.

Selye, H. (1975) *Stress without Distress*. New York: New American Library.

Sheldon, W. H. and Stevens, S. S. (1942) *The Varieties of Temperament: A Psychology of Constitutional Differences*. New York: Harper and Brothers.

Smedslund, G. (1995) 'Personality and vulnerability to cancer and heart disease: Relations to demographic and life-style variables', *Personality and Individual Differences* 19: 691–697.

Sobolewski, A., Strelau, J. and Zawadzki, B. (1999) Kwestionariusz Zmian Życiowych (KZŻ) – Polska *Adaptacja kwestionariusza 'Recent Life Changes Questionnaire (RLCQ) R. H. Rahe'a'* [Polish adaptation of Rahe's Recent Life Changes Questionnaire (RLCQ)], *Przegląd Psychologiczny* 42: 27–49.

Sobolewski, A., Strelau, J. and Zawadzki, B. (2001) 'The temperamental determinants of stressors as life changes: A genetic analysis', *European Psychologist* 6: 287–295.

Strelau, J. (1983) *Temperament, Personality, Activity*. London: Academic Press.

Strelau, J. (1995) 'Temperament and stress: Temperament as a moderator of stressors, emotional states, coping, and costs', in C. D. Spielberger and I. G. Sarason (eds) *Stress and Emotion: Anxiety, Anger, and Curiosity*, vol. 15, pp. 215–254. Washington: Hemisphere.

Strelau, J. (1998) *Temperament: A Psychological Perspective*. New York: Plenum Press.

Strelau, J. (2001a) *Psychologia temperamentu* [Psychology of temperament], 2nd edn. Warszawa: Wydawnictwo Naukowe PWN.

Strelau, J. (2001b) 'The place of the construct of arousal in temperament research', in R. Riemann, F. M. Spinath and F. Ostendorf (eds) *Personality and Temperament: Genetics, Evolution, and Structure*, pp.105–128. Lengerich: Pabst Science Publishers.

Strelau, J. and Zawadzki, B. (1993) 'The Formal Characteristics of Behaviour – Temperament Inventory (FCB-TI): Theoretical assumptions and scale construction', *European Journal of Personality* 7: 313–336.

Strelau, J. and Zawadzki, B. (1995) 'The Formal Characteristics of Behavior – Temperament Inventory (FCB-TI): Validity studies', *European Journal of Personality* 9: 207–229.

Strelau, J., Zawadzki, B., Oniszczenko, W. and Sobolewski, A. (2002) 'Kwestionariusz PTSD – wersja czynnikowa (PTSD-C): konstrukcja narzędzia do diagnozy głównych wymiarów zespołu stresu pourazowego' [The factorial version of the PTSD Inventory (PTSD-F): The development of a questionnaire aimed at assessing basic dimensions of post-traumatic stress disorder], *Przegląd Psychologiczny* 45: 149–176.

Temoshok, L. and Dreher, H. (1992) *The Type C Connection*. New York: Random House.

Thomas, A. and Chess, S. (1977) *Temperament and Development*. New York: Brunner/Mazel.

Thomas, C. B., and Greenstreet, R. L. (1973) 'Psychological characteristics in youth as predictors of five disease states: Suicide, mental illness, hypertension, coronary heart disease and tumor'. *Johns Hopkins Medical Journal* 132: 16–43.

Ursin, H. (1980) 'Personality, activation and somatic health: A new psychosomatic theory', in S. Levine and H. Ursin (eds) *Coping and Health*, pp. 259–279. New York: Plenum Press.

Veit, C. T. and Ware, J. E. Jr. (1983) 'The structure of psychological distress and well-being in general populations', *Journal of Consulting and Clinical Psychology* 51: 730–742.

Wachs, T. D. (1992) *The Nature of Nurture*. Newbury Park, CA: Sage.

Whiteman, M.C., Deary, I. J. and Fowkes, F. G. R. (2000) 'Personality and health: Cardiovascular disease', in S. E. Hampson (ed.) *Advances in Personality Psychology*, vol. 1, pp. 157–198. Hove, UK: Psychology Press.

Wrześniewski, K. (1990) 'Badanie Wzoru zachowania A przy użyciu polskiego kwestionariusza' [Diagnosis of the Type A behaviour pattern by the Polish inventory], *Przegląd Lekarski* 47: 538–542.

Zawadzki, B. (2001) 'Temperamentalny czynnik ryzyka chorób somatycznych: raka płuca i zawału serca' [Temperament as risk factor of somatic diseases: Lung cancer and myocardial infarction], in W. Ciarkowska and A. Matczak (eds) *Różnice indywidualne: Wybrane badania inspirowane Regulacyjną Teorią Temperamentu Profesora Jana Strelaua*, pp. 27–52. Warszawa: Interdyscyplinarne Centrum Genetyki Zachowania UW.

Zawadzki, B. and Strelau, J. (1997) *Formalna Charakterystyka Zachowania – Kwestionariusz Temperamentu (FCZ-KT): Podręcznik* [Formal Characteristics of Behaviour – Temperament Inventory (FCB-TI): Manual]. Warszawa: Pracownia Testów Psychologicznych PTP.

Zawadzki, B., Strelau, J., Oniszczenko, W., Sobolewski, A. and Bieniek, A. (2004) 'Diagnoza zespołu stresu pourazowego: charakterystyka psychometryczna wersji czynnikowej i wersji klinicznej kwestionariusza PTSD' [Assessment of the post-traumatic stress disorder: Psychometric properties of the factorial and clinical form of the PTSD inventory], in J. Strelau (ed.) *Osobowość a ekstremalny stres*, pp. 220–237. Gdańsk: Gdańskie Wydawnictwo Psychologiczne.

Zuckerman, M. (1979) *Sensation Seeking: Beyond the Optimal Level of Arousal*. Hillsdale, NJ: Lawrence Erlbaum Associates Inc.

Zuckerman, M. (1994) *Behavioural Expressions and Biosocial Bases of Sensation Seeking*. New York: Cambridge University Press.

Chapter 3

Personality and information processing

Biological foundations of thought and action

Joop Hettema

In this chapter personality is explored at different levels of inquiry. The major contention is that individual differences in social information processing are based on biological structures that, ultimately, are rooted in the individual's genotype. First, a biological model is proposed emphasizing the energetic rather than the cognitive aspects of information processing. In this framework energetics can be described as three independent bipolar dimensions, each opposing emotional and volitional processing. Some major findings with this model include conceptualization, measurement, consistency across situations and construct validation of the dimensions. Behaviour genetics research has indicated a high degree of genetic contribution in each of the dimensions. Subsequently evidence is provided suggesting direct links between scores on the three dimensions and some major elements (goals, beliefs) proposed in social information processing. The conclusion is drawn that thoughts and actions have biological as well as social foundations. As a second major conclusion, on the basis of the energetical patterns identified a limited number of information-processing types are proposed. Each type can be characterized with specific goals and beliefs. At the behavioural level information-processing types may provide a basis for explaining different styles identified earlier in teaching, designing, and leadership. Our findings are discussed in the general framework of multilevel research as well as the study of information processing.

INTRODUCTION

A recent development affecting personality theory and research comes from behaviour genetics. Overwhelming success in the behaviour genetic analysis of personality traits has urged personality psychologists to redefine their object as well as to reconsider the most expedient ways to study it. Particularly the assessment and explanation of individual differences may benefit from the new frame of reference offered by behaviour genetics. Recent studies suggest considerable genetic contributions in several personality traits including altruism, empathy, nurturance, aggression and assertiveness (Rushton *et al.*, 1986), the Big Five personality dimensions (Bouchard, 1993), interest patterns (Nichols, 1978; Lykken *et al.*, 1993; Waller *et al.*, 1995), vocational interests (Moloney *et al.*, 1991; Betsworth *et al.*, 1994), religious interests

(Waller *et al.*, 1990), work values (Keller *et al.*, 1992), and special mental abilities (Nichols, 1978; Bouchard *et al.*, 1990). From a behaviour genetics point of view, traits are to be seen as phenotypes, i.e. manifestations of genotypic propensities. Underlying traits are physiological, biochemical and neurological processes, ultimately genes at the most distal level. Classical biological approaches to personality have proposed a rather direct relationship between biological structures and processes on the one hand and traits like neuroticism, extraversion (Eysenck, 1967), or impulsivity and anxiety (Gray, 1991) on the other. Those approaches have been among the foremost exponents of the hypothesis that personality traits provide a window on individual differences in brain functioning. However, recent comments have concluded that the assumptions of the biological approach to personality are in need of reassessment. In particular it has been suggested that trait research should place more emphasis on the social-cognitive bases of personality (Matthews and Gilliland, 1999). A more systematic ordering of the diverse conditions underlying personality has been proposed in Zuckerman's (1993) seven turtles model. According to this model personality traits are based on social behaviour that, in turn, is the fruit of learning. Physiological conditions underlie learning but are based on biochemical processes that rest on neurological conditions themselves. Finally, the major foundations of neurology are genes, controlling the production of proteins, which in turn exert profound effects on behavioural structures and processes via the nervous system and production of behaviourally relevant hormones and neurotransmitters. Thus, summarizing, traits, social behaviour, learning, physiology, biochemistry, neurology and genes are the stations along which genotypes are translated into phenotypes. To explore the ways in which the different levels exert their influence is a major task for current personality psychology.

Recent attempts to study personality from a biosocial multilevel perspective may be noted in different domains like sexuality (Jansen *et al.*, 2000), criminality (Magnusson, 1988), sensation seeking (Zuckerman, 1993), stress (Lensvelt-Mulders and Hettema, 2001) and depression (Kenrick, *et al.*, 1985; Hettema, 1995). For instance, Kenrick *et al.* (1985) have pointed out a number of different conditions that have to be fulfilled before a person will become depressed. They argued that a person would not become depressed unless he or she has an unpleasant experience of some kind. However, not everyone who has an argument with his or her spouse becomes clinically depressed. Unless a person devotes cognitive attention to that unpleasant experience, it will not bother him or her. On the other hand, if the person mentally rehearses the argument, recalling evidence that their own faults have always broken up previous relationships, tells themselves that he or she will never be able to get along with others, and convinces himself or herself that their spouse is probably going to leave, then the event will be more likely to lead to depression. However, even a series of negative events that an individual accepts blame for may not lead to depression if that individual has a high physiological threshold for depression. Antisocial individuals are not very likely to experience depression under any circumstances, while some individuals experience depression at the drop of an unkind word.

Before starting multilevel studies it is wise to be aware and keep in mind some rules derived from other fields of science looking for explanations at several levels. Simon (1992) assumes that for psychology as for other sciences it is essential to explain complex phenomena at different levels. First of all, different levels should be defined and conceived as complementary rather than competing. Different levels of resolution use different constructs or units emphasizing different processes along which they operate. Units will have to be defined at the different levels. While defining units it should be kept in mind that units with optimal explanatory power at one level of inquiry may be less relevant at another level. As Simon proposes, higher level theories may use aggregates of the constructs at lower levels to provide parsimonious explanations of phenomena. However, it would be naive to assume that the units at one level exhibit a strict isomorphism with the elements studied at another level. Instead, for each level separate rules will have to be specified for connecting its elements to the elements at a higher level. Finally, each level should be connected with the lowest level: genes. Only if a level exhibits higher genetic influence can it be taken to provide an explanation of the higher levels.

A crucial and recurrent problem in any multilevel approach to personality is the question where biological and social determinants meet. The classical biological approaches to personality have particularly emphasized conditioning and motivation. However, as yet the results have not been unequivocal. A viable alternative may be to look for information processing as the most likely place where biological and social determinants meet. The information-processing approach assumes that in the same environment individuals may show different behaviours to the extent that they differ in the way they process the available information. Not only are most current multilevel approaches centred on information processing, but for this choice there are historical reasons as well. In the study of personality and individual differences, information processing has always occupied a special position. Explanations based on information processing may be found already in Freud's defence mechanisms and Jung's archetypes. After World War II information processing has been studied in perceptual styles, like e.g. levelling versus sharpening (Klein) and field dependence versus field independence (Witkin). Information-processing notions underlie cognitive styles like impulsivity versus reflexivity (Kagan), cognitive complexity versus simplicity (Bieri), repression versus sensitization (Byrne). Other approaches have used information-processing concepts to explain differences in performance (Broadbent) and problem solving (Newell and Simon). The information-processing approach has obtained special urgency in the context of recent developments in evolutionary psychology. David Buss (1991) defined the major aim of evolutionary psychology as: 'To identify psychological mechanisms and behavioural strategies as evolved solutions to adaptive problems our species has faced over millions of years' (pp. 459–460). In the same context Tooby and Cosmides (1990) outlined a modern adaptationist framework proposing the view that the mind consists of a collection of evolved function-specific, information-processing mechanisms organizing actions appropriate to situations. At the core of this approach are tangible and inheritable ways to process the information available in our habitat, existing currently as well as many years ago.

SOCIAL-COGNITIVE INFORMATION PROCESSING

One may wonder why most classical approaches to information processing in personality are abandoned nowadays. A major reason can be found in the dominant tendency to study information processing in the laboratory and trying to connect the outcomes with traits like field dependence. Information processing was studied apart from the environment supplying the information in the first place. For most current approaches to personality based on information processing this is not very well possible. The modern information-processing approach can best be understood as a reaction against dispositional theory. In the late 1960s dispositions became discredited as major personality units because accumulating evidence indicated that one of their main features – consistency across situations – could not be warranted (Mischel, 1968). As a reaction personality theorists started to work with interactionist models based on the assumption that an individual's behaviour can only be properly explained as a result of complex interactions between the person and the situation. Between the person, the situation and behaviour so-called triadic reciprocal causality was assumed to be present: the person affects behaviour, behaviour affects the situation and vice versa. Clearly, this picture needed further elaboration before the interactionist position could provide a basis for the study of personality. The reciprocal relationship between situation and behaviour has obtained special attention in learning. The other two are assumed to be the province of personality psychology. Accordingly, special attention is paid to the reciprocal relationships of persons with situations and with behaviours. Most current approaches are based on the assumption that information processing plays a crucial role in person–environment relationships. In those relationships the part of the person is an active-structuring one. Individual thoughts and actions are to a considerable extent based on social considerations, thus closely reflecting the concrete circumstances of daily life. Bandura (1986) argued that people no longer need to be viewed as responders to environmental stimuli but as causal agents whose personal agendas and capabilities shape the conditions of their lives and the course of their development. Person–environment relations are governed by the person's intention to exert a certain amount of control over the environment. People select and shape their environments and give meaning to events by interpreting them according to their personal beliefs. In dealing with their environment people not only perform responses but also notice the effects they produce. If the effects confirm pre-existing goals or expectancies, the person experiences competence, self-efficacy, or control. What people think, believe and feel affects how they behave.

A comprehensive framework with the capacity to study all the relations mentioned is information processing. Cognitive information processing is the cornerstone of many current approaches to personality (like e.g. Carver and Scheier, 1981; Bandura, 1986; Cantor and Kihlstrom, 1987; Dweck and Leggett, 1988; Cervone, 1991; Mischel and Shoda, 1995). Cognitive information-processing models are mediating process models including hypotheses about the mental activities or decisions regulating behaviour in the context of daily life. Those mental activities rest on knowledge acquired through modelling, observation, upbringing, education, learning, i.e. social conditions enhancing learning. Central concepts used in social information-processing theories include, e.g. declarative and procedural knowledge concerning the world and the self, expectancies, schemas, constructs, attributions, encoding strategies, values, appraisals, plans, scripts, intentions, goals, beliefs, self-efficacy and control. Although there is no complete consensus on the major elements of information processing, three major classes are usually acknowledged. First there are knowledge structures including a person's beliefs about the world and the situations in it. Second, there are goals and intentions providing direction to a person's behaviour. Finally, there are self-regulatory mechanisms helping the person to maintain control over himself and the world around him. Individuals can and will usually differ in the ways in which the different structures and mechanisms are organized. Within this framework personality may be defined as an individual's ways to process information in the context of different situations.

CRITIQUE OF THE SOCIAL COGNITIVE APPROACH TO PERSONALITY

Do current social-cognitive information-processing approaches have the capacity to offer a major contibution to the explanation of individual differences? Several objections can be made here. I will mention four types of objection that have been raised before: the range of convenience of the models, the definition of elements and the dealing with the central issues of consistency and origination of personality.

The range of convenience

As a major improvement of information processing over trait models it is generally stated that information-processing models take into account the actual environment or context in which behaviour occurs. No doubt this is a major advantage enlarging the range of convenience of the personality model and improving the precision of statements concerning personality. However, much of the advantage is lost if the environment is represented only in inner structures like beliefs, expectancies, goals or self-efficacy. Like the person, the environment has its own structure and dynamics that are not always in line with the person's beliefs and expectancies. As a major innovation and essential enlargement of current information-processing approaches together with many current authors I propose the introduction of control as a central concept. Control is not meant to replace concepts like self-efficacy, achievement motive, or competence motive. Rather it serves to connect those concepts with events in the real world. Control is currently recognized as a basic aspect of personality underlying physical as well as mental health, achievement, optimism, persistence, motivation, coping with stress, self-esteem, personal adjustment, and success and failure in a variety of life domains (Skinner, 1996). An underlying assumption of all control theories is that humans want to produce behaviour–event contingencies and thus exert control over the environment (White, 1959; Heckhausen and Schulz, 1995). Primary control is present as long as and to the extent that a person manages to affect the world in service of his/her well-being. However, control is not always warranted. Environmental influences may affect persons as when thoughts and feelings are modified through modelling, tuition or social persuasion. At times, environmental influences may interfere with ongoing behaviour causing a state of uncontrollability in the person. In that case secondary control may give meaning to otherwise uncontrollable events and have the effect to minimize the loss of control. While primary control is almost always characterized in terms of ongoing behaviour engaging the external world, secondary control is predominantly characterized with cognitive processes residing within the individual. To obtain, maintain, or restore control, people use two basically different modes of responding: primary and secondary control (Rothbaum et al., 1982). Primary control refers to behaviours directed at the external environment and involves attempts to change the world and to fit the needs and desires of the individual. Secondary control is targetted at internal processes and serves to minimize loss in existing levels of control. This type of control includes cognitions; for example, biased expectations, shifts in goal values, attributions of success and failure, illusions, and so forth. Secondary control is generally assumed to become active after primary control has failed. Primary versus secondary control is related to major dichotomies like operants versus respondents (Skinner, 1953), action versus thought (Bandura, 1986), problem-oriented versus emotion-oriented coping (Folkman *et al.*, 1986), approach versus avoidance during stress (Roth and Cohen, 1986), action orientation versus state orientation (Kuhl, 1994), assimilation versus accommodation (Brandstaedter and Renner, 1990), mastery versus helplessness (Dweck, 1991), transformations of environment by persons versus transformations of persons by environments (Hettema and Kenrick, 1992). Primary versus secondary control may provide a major framework for further study of information processing.

The definition of elements

A second problem concerns the definition of elements: there is little or no consensus on the major information-processing elements to be studied. A major benefit of the social cognitive approach to personality is its potential to describe information processing in everyday behaviour. However, in exploring and documenting the complexity and richness of personality, social cognitive theorists have often sacrificed the parsimony typically present in the more static approaches to personality like traits. Instead, there is a proliferation of concepts including, for example, scripts, goals, encoding strategies, self-regulation mechanisms, expectancies, beliefs, etc. Take, for instance, Mischel and Shoda's (1998) cognitive-affective personality system (CAPS). The personality elements in this model include the following:

1   Encoding categories for the self, people, events, and situations.
2   Expectancies and beliefs about the social world, about outcomes of behaviour in particular situations, about self-efficacy; affects: feelings, emotions and affective responses (including physiological reactions).
3   Goals and values, desirable outcomes, aversive outcomes; goals, values and life projects.
4   Competencies and self-regulatory plans: potential behaviours and scripts that one can do, and plans and strategies for organizing action and for affecting outcomes and one's own behaviour and internal states.

Do we really need all these fine-grained distinctions? Are there no overlaps and redundancies within and across categories? For instance, affects are treated separately from expectancies, beliefs, goal values, although a vast literature suggests they are related. Not only is the conceptual/empirical ratio far from favourable, but, as yet, neither is there a concise generally accepted conceptual framework. Based on the control conception outlined earlier, such a framework should at least entail separate classes for transformational elements underlying primary control and representational elements underlying secondary control. Examples of transformational elements are competencies, plans, strategies, values, and goals. Representational elements might entail, for example, encoding categories, expectancies, beliefs.

Within both categories many different types of elements have been proposed. For instance, current goal theories emphasize life tasks (Cantor and Kihlstrom, 1987), personal projects (Little, 1989), personal strivings (Emmons, 1989), current concerns (Klinger, 1977). Each goal concept may have its own range of convenience. Yet, as Grant and Dweck (1999) have stressed, a case can and should be made to define an optimal set of goals to be studied. Ideally, goal constructs should enable us to predict specific behaviours in specific situations, however without being confined to a specific situation domain. Thus, goals should be classified into meaningful categories that cut across content areas. Grant and Dweck (1999) consider, for example, goals to attain favourable judgements of one's competence, goals to acquire new knowledge, goals to acquire intimacy, goals to acquire social power.

A recent overview of goal constructs suggests that goals are hierarchically organized (Austin and Vancouver, 1996). Traditionally, personality psychologists have favoured high-level goal constructs like, for example, to become happy or to lead a meaningful life. More recently middle-level constructs include goals such as to pass an exam or to have a nice vacation. However, even at that level many different actions may be undertaken to materialize the goals. It is the special merit of script theory to have identified cognitive structures organizing procedural knowledge underlying sequences of very concrete actions. A limited set of low-level goals is usually sufficient to describe actions in a wide array of situations. The low-level goals may be inserted as building blocks in scripts aimed at the fulfilment of widely divergent middle-level and even high-level goals (Schank and Abelson, 1977).

Primary control

In the context of primary control, goal constructs should emphasize some kind of alteration intended to be brought about. Primary control is present to the extent that the intended alteration is effected. Finally, as personality elements the constructs should be stable and consistent across situations. In the study of scripts a general set of goal concepts answering the requirements mentioned has been derived in the shape of delta goals (Schank and Abelson, 1977). A major feature of delta goals is their unique intention for specific alterations to be accomplished. Several studies in our lab suggest that delta goals are generally applicable, have the capacity to act as building blocks for most higher order goals, and are rather consistent across time and situations (Hettema, 1989; Van Heck, *et al.*, 1993; Hol, 1994; Hettema, 1996; Hettema and Hol, 1998; Riteco 1998; Lensvelt-Mulders, 2000). Our set of delta goals includes:

- *Delta social control*: the intention to gain power or authority
- *Delta control*: the intention to gain control over resources
- *Delta proximity*: the intention to reduce the distance to another person

- *Delta knowledge*: the intention to increase knowledge
- *Delta agency*: the intention to get someone else to pursue a goal on one's behalf
- *Delta support*: the intention to help other people
- *Delta preparation*: the intention to prepare the attainment of other goals.

Secondary control

Secondary control is based on representational elements instead of transformational elements. Those elements are directed at maintaining or restoring control. They include, for example, beliefs, values, attributions to self or the environment, social comparisons, goal preferences, optimistic or pessimistic expectancies, self-blaming, outcome appraisals. Not every reaction will be equally rational or effective. Ellis (1962) has identified a number of frequently occurring irrational beliefs such as: one must be loved by everyone, or one must be extremely competent in all undertakings, or one must support everyone who is in trouble. While considering different belief systems we argued that secondary control is always preceded by control loss. Thus, it seems obvious to look for beliefs in the area of coping behaviour. Coping is frequently mentioned as a key example of secondary control. A major system is the coping style system proposed by Folkman and Lazarus (1980). It could be objected that coping styles may not be the proper choice here because research on coping styles has revealed a notorious lack of cross-situational consistency. Information-processing models can explain inconsistency because people differ as regards the situations causing stress. Clearly, inconsistency is a major problem in personality research. However, our studies of coping suggest that if individuals experience stress then they tend to react with the same coping style (Geenen, 1991; Hettema and Geenen, in preparation; Van Heck and Vingerhoets 1989; Vingerhoets 1985; Vingerhoets and Flohr, 1984). Thus, we feel assured that coping styles reflect at least stable individual differences.

Van Heck and Vingerhoets (1989) analysed a great number of overt and covert reactions to stressful situations. Using factor analysis they identified seven oblique factors reflecting coping styles: planning, self-blaming, distancing, fantasizing, seeking support, positive thinking, wishful thinking. Underlying coping styles are persons' beliefs regarding themselves or the outside world:

- *Planning*: the belief that an active planful and rational approach is the best way to proceed.
- *Self-blaming*: the belief that problems are caused by one's own shortcomings.
- *Distancing*: the belief that problems usually solve themselves.
- *Fantasizing*: the belief in extraordinary events like miracles.

- *Seeking support*: the belief that company in stress makes sorrow less.
- *Positive thinking*: the belief that all experiences are enriching, including the negative ones.
- *Wishful thinking*: the belief that things may turn out better next time.

The consistency issue

For many years personality theorists have had to face the 'personality paradox' (Mischel and Shoda, 1995), or the inability to reconcile the stable consistent nature of personality with the variation of individuals' behaviour across different situations. Different solutions have been proposed. Trait theorists emphasized the more stable elements of personality by focusing on individual differences in average levels of behaviour. Evolutionary psychologists posited psychological mechanisms that are of use only in very specific domains. In this context, most individual differences are quite unimportant for inclusive fitness in the environment of evolutionary adaptedness. Social cognitive theorists have chosen an intermediate position while emphasizing coherence instead of consistency. Personality coherence is explained as stable connections among cognitive and affective units underlying behaviour that may give rise to different behaviours given the nature of the situation acting as a context (Mischel and Shoda, 1995, 1998). It follows that if the situation changes behaviour may change as well, but the nature of the change conforms to the stable underlying cognitive and affective units. A major problem with this conception is that unless one is able to indicate precisely which system governs behaviour at any given moment it is hard to provide evidence pro or con. This leads to the suspicion that the nature of the behaviour studied is crucial for the amount of consistency observed. Many years ago Mischel (1973) argued that social emotional behaviours such as anxiety, depression, dominance, hostility, conformity are less consistent than abilities, cognitive competencies and academic achievement. More recent research has largely confirmed this view. Funder and Colvin (1991) explained the difference in terms of operant versus respondent behaviour. In an observational study they found that consistent behaviours tended to have the character of operants, whereas inconsistent behaviours looked like respondents. Based on this result relationships with primary versus secondary control seemed obvious. This relationship was tested and confirmed in three subsequent studies in our laboratory (Hettema and Van Bakel, 1997; Hettema and Hol, 1998; Riteco, 1998). We concluded that as major elements of primary control goals are relatively consistent across situations. As parts of secondary control we expect beliefs to be less consistent. The reason for this is that information processing not only underlies the beliefs that a person will cherish but also the situations in which that person will lose control and experience stress.

The origination issue

A final major problem with the social cognitive approach is that it does not provide an exhaustive explanation of why individuals differ. As a major basis for individual differences the individual learning history is frequently advanced. The underlying assumption is that if different behaviours are reinforced (either directly or vicariously) individuals will tend to learn different things. However, on this explanation it is hard to understand why individuals raised in the same environment, even in the same families, may show such tremendous differences. Only sizable genetic influences may provide a proper explanation here. Behaviour geneticists have forwarded gene–environment correlations to explain selective exposition to different environments (Plomin, DeFries and Loehlin, 1977). This notion implies that individuals tend to grow up in environments that fit their genotypes. Gene–environment correlations may be either passive, reactive or active. Passive correlations occur because parents not only pass on their genetic material to their children but also control much of the enviromental conditions in which they are raised. Reactive correlations occur because the environment tends to select children for school, sports, etc. on the basis of their appearance that is at least to some extent based on their genes. Finally, active gene–environment correlations occur because children tend to seek out environments that fit their genotypes.

Endorsing this explanation does not mean that learning processes like imitation, modelling and observation learning are ineffective. However, it does mean that there are biological constraints on learning. Individuals differ in biological preparedness, taking up what fits with their genetic endowment and rejecting what does not fit.

THE BIOLOGICAL APPROACH TO INFORMATION PROCESSING

Thus far the emphasis was on social information-processing models. The focus of this chapter is the identification and testing of biological systems on which social information processing is based. As Zuckerman (1993) argued, most previous attempts to identify biological structures underlying personality have been of the top-down type. In a top-down approach research starts with some personality trait. Subsequent research is aimed at the identification of neurological, biochemical and physiological processes underlying them. Finally, behaviour genetic studies are used to identify the contribution of genetics to the trait. Our approach has been different using a bottom-up rather than a top-down strategy. First, on theoretical grounds we identified biological systems presumably underlying social information processing. Subsequently, we addressed the behaviour genetics of information processing using the MZ-DZ design to test the genetical basis of the physiological systems involved. Finally, we studied the connections between the biological systems and some major elements derived from the social cognitive tradition of information processing.

The choice of a model

Several biological models of information processing have been proposed. Those models have a common focus emphasizing formal aspects rather than cognitive contents of information processing. A major class of formal models are energetic models. Those models are based on the idea that the processing of information requires energetic resources, mental or attentional capacity. Most current energetic models are multiple resource models according to which the human processing system is composed of several relatively independent resources. Relatively early in the study of information-processing energetics the attention was confined to the output regulating activation system (Duffy, 1957). Later on, research of the orienting reflex emphasized the input regulating arousal system (Sokolow, 1960). Finally, studies of the co-ordination between input and output drew the attention to a third system: effort (Kahneman, 1973). Accordingly, in several current models three kinds of processing systems are proposed. Examples are Pribram and McGuinness (1975, 1992), Wickens (1984) and Gray (1991). The model used in this study is based on one of them: the Pribram and McGuinness (1975, 1992) model of attentional control. In this model one control system is connected with arousal regulating input processes. The arousal system is particularly sensitive to novelty. With increasing novelty arousal tends to become more controlled, with increasing familiarity arousal becomes more automatic. A second system regulates the preparation of actions through *activation*. Controlled activation underlies tonic readiness, i.e. maintaining a set to continue ongoing behaviour. A third system co-ordinates the arousal and activation systems through *effort*. A major activity of the effort system is to uncouple output processes from input processes.

The arousal, activation and effort systems are independent processing systems. They may act serially or in parallel and there is no fixed order in their functioning. Each system may be represented as a bipolar dimension ranging from controlled processing to automatic processing (Hettema et al., 2000). The dimensions should not be taken to represent merely affectively neutral processing systems underlying intellectual task performance. Instead, intimate connections are assumed of the processing systems with emotion, motivation and volition (McGuinness and Pribram, 1980; Hettema, 1991). Recent developments in the study of emotions and volition suggest that the distinction between automatic and controlled processing may be connected (Kuhl, 1994; Ledoux, 1996). Summarizing then, the Pribram-McGuinness model proposes different processing systems for input, output and input–output co-ordination. Each system has the capacity to process information in a more automatic or more controlled way, suggesting that emotional and volitional processing may be involved in each.

Operationalization and measurement

Biological models of information processing have been studied almost invariably in laboratory settings. A major aim of our research has been to study information processing in daily life situations. The situations were derived from an extensive taxonomy of situations developed by Van Heck (1989), in which over 200 situations have been defined meticulously in terms of cues and features. For the experimental study of information processing 25 situations were selected and cast in films (Hettema *et al.*, 1989; Hettema, 1994). During the films seven psychophysiological reactions presumably relevant for the Pribram-McGuinness model were measured continuously. Reactions included heart interbeat intervals (HIV), pulse transit time (PTT), T-wave amplitude (TWA), galvanic skin response level (GSL), finger temperature (FTT), diastolic blood pressure (DBP), and systolic blood pressure (SBP). The pattern of physiological reactions was taken to reflect information processing at each moment in time. This claim was tested in different studies (Hettema *et al.*, 2000). Our analyses included several thousands of reaction patterns. First, after proper standardization correcting for time trends as well as for base levels, on the basis of covariations among the measures we derived three dimensions, interpreted as arousal, activation and effort. Subsequently, the specific characteristics of each dimension were tested. As expected, the arousal dimension was particularly sensitive to novelty induced with films mismatching existing expectancies. The activation dimension was sensitive to evaluative aspects, i.e. good versus bad. Evaluations were induced with positive versus negative explanations of the films' content prior to exposition. The effort dimension reflected involvement versus detachment on the side of our subjects, induced through instructions emphasizing involvement versus detachment. Finally, in a separate study we found evidence on the nature of each dimension to reflect controlled versus automatic processing. We concluded that our three dimensions represented arousal, activation and effort as proposed by Pribram and McGuinness (1975, 1992).

Individual differences

A major problem yet to be solved is individual differences in information-processing energetics. Since the Pribram-McGuinness model was neither intended nor ever used to study individual differences this was a major question to be answered. We were especially interested in the consistency of individual reactions across different situations. To that effect for each dimension we analysed the reactions of our Ss during seven different films and tested for consistency across situations. Intraclass correlations were 0.80 for arousal, 0.84 for effort, and 0.84 for activation indicating high levels of consistency across situations (Hettema *et al.*, 2000). These results suggest that in each dimension the ordering of subjects remains about the same no matter the situation in which testing is done. It should be stressed here that situations have sizable overall effects upon reactivity as well so that reactions actually observed within the same subject tend to show variation across situations as well.

Behaviour genetics

To my knowledge and surprise, our attempts to find direct behaviour genetics data on information processing were not successful. True, behaviour genetics has studied variables like mental abilities and personality traits, and interpreted the outcomes to reflect inheritable differences in information processing. However, in those studies no direct processing indices were collected. The recent work of Lensvelt-Mulders (2000; Lensvelt-Mulders and Hettema, 2001) has changed this picture. Using the experimental design explained earlier she studied the reactions of 100 MZ and DZ twins to eight films and analysed scores on the three dimensions identified earlier with quantitative genetic analysis. As a result heritability estimates (h^2) revealed values of 0.79 for arousal, 0.81 for effort and 0.82 for activation. Interestingly, the heritability estimates (h^2) for the single variables were much lower ranging from 0.28 for GSL to 0.42 for SBP. Heritability estimates for the three dimensions are among the highest ever found for personality measures of individual differences. The heritability of information-processing energetics appears to be firmly established.

Emotion–volition interactions

A central contention of this chapter is that part of the individual differences observed in social information-processing elements are due to inheritable differences in information-processing energetics. Our first hypothesis states that all three energetic dimensions are involved. However, rather than a linear additive model we expected the dimensions to interact as regards the different elements of social information processing. Our second hypothesis states that specific patterns of emotional and volitional information processing underlie goals and beliefs. For instance, in primary control delta goals are central elements. People with a tendency to react with a specific energetic pattern are expected to pursue the corresponding delta goal rather than people with a tendency to react with other energetic patterns. For primary control the hypotheses were tested in a recent study in which 87 female twins were observed in eight different situations (Hettema and Lensvelt-Mulders, in preparation). The situations were presented in two different modes: films and verbal descriptions. During the films physiological reactions on seven variables were registered continuously and cast into dimension scores using the procedures given before. Each S obtained scores on each dimension in each situation. Delta goals were measured with an SR questionnaire in which brief descriptions of the situations were followed by 28 action descriptions. The actions were prototypical actions each representing one of the delta goals of social control, control, proximity, knowledge, agency, or preparation. The actions were obtained from four domains – the mental, social, physical and instrumental domains. In each situation offered the Ss indicated in how far they would consider acting like described. Delta goal scores were averages across domains. Our first analysis was directed at identifying the basic model underlying the relations. Two models were considered: the linear additive model and the interactive model. To test the models we obtained average dimension scores and average delta goal scores across the eight situations. First for the prediction of each delta goal the linear model was tested using multiple regression analysis as a tool. The resulting multiple Rs ranged from 0.08 for delta preparation to 0.15 for delta social control. Subsequently, we tested the interaction model by inserting two-way and three-way interaction terms in the regression model. The multiple Rs increased to values ranging from 0.20 for delta preparation to 0.26 for delta social control. In addition, for each analysis the regression coefficients for interactions were compared with those for the main effects. For the main effects the median (absolute) coefficient was 0.15, for first order interactions 0.21, and for second order interactions we found 0.38. We concluded that underlying delta goals are interactive energetic patterns rather than global differences in overall activity. The patterns were conceived as information-processing types emphasizing either controlled or automatic processing in each dimension. With dichotomies on the three dimensions there are eight different patterns (Table 3.1). Inspection of the regression coefficients led to hypotheses about the precise form of the patterns involved in each delta goal. The hypotheses were tested on relatively independent data using differences in situations rather than persons as a tool. First of all, we divided our sample into two equivalent subsamples of twin halves. For each subsample in each situation two scores were obtained: the number of patterns predicted to underlie a delta goal and the average delta goal preference score. Correlations between these two indices for the two samples separately are presented in Table 3.1.

Table 3.1 shows sizable correlations between most information processing types and delta goal preferences. The correlations obtained with the two samples are almost identical. Thus, the data suggest that delta goals have unique underlying energetic patterns. It appears that one delta goal – delta knowledge – is based exclusively on volitional processing. None of the other delta goals is based only on emotional processing, although there are differences in emphasis. Delta preparation, delta proximity and delta control seem

Table 3.1 Correlations between information processing types and delta goal preferences across eight situations.

IP type	Delta goal	Sample I	Sample II
CCC	Delta Knowledge	0.52	0.60
CCA	Delta Preparation	0.77	0.75
CAC	Delta Proximity	0.32	0.38
ACC	Delta Control	0.76	0.86
CAA	Delta Support		
ACA	Delta Agency	0.42	0.58
AAC	Delta Social control	−0.06	0.03

Notes

In the information processing types the dimensions are arranged in the order arousal-effort-activation.

C = controlled processing, A = automatic processing. Thus, for instance, CAC implies that delta proximity is characterized by controlled arousal, automatic effort, and controlled activation. Delta support was not studied here.

'more volitional' whereas delta agency and delta social control are 'more emotional'. Clearly, there are also differences in the specific systems emphasized. For instance controlled effort, sometimes connected with general intelligence, is related with delta knowledge, delta preparation, delta control and delta agency, but not with delta proximity or delta social control. As a whole these results are promising, although it should be kept in mind that the correlations reflect differences among situations, not individual differences.

Secondary control

A major difference between primary and secondary control is that primary control is proactive whereas secondary control is reactive. Primary control includes actions to maintain or increase control. For primary control no specific eliciting situation is required. Secondary control on the other hand includes reactions elicited by an uncontrollable situation. The prototype of uncontrollable situations are stress situations. Thus our central hypothesis regarding secondary control states that part of individual differences observed in coping reactions to stressful situations are due to inheritable differences in reactivity on the three energetic dimensions. Secondary control in general and coping in particular serves to give meaning to otherwise uncontrollable events. However, individuals show vast differences in the ways they provide meaning to the situation prevailing. Connected with those differences are the beliefs of individuals. In our view, beliefs are based on specific forms of processing emotional and volitional information. People with a tendency to react with those forms are expected to use the corresponding coping style rather than people tending to react with other forms.

This hypothesis was tested in a recent study (Hettema and Geenen, in preparation) in which 43 male Ss were observed while being confronted with an accident presented on film. This particular film was chosen because, as earlier research had shown, watching other people suffering is a potent stressor. The film contains a quiet household situation interrupted with an accident in which a person is hurt. The film was presented five consecutive times and physiological reactions were monitored continuously. All Ss completed a coping inventory based on the work of Folkman and Lazarus. The results indicated that when the actual stressor was met there was an increase in automatic reactivity in all systems reflecting emotion. As a reaction there was an increase of controlled activity in all systems reflecting volition. During the replications, previous to meeting the stressor all systems gave an increase of volitional activity interpreted as coping. Correlations were computed between energetic dimension scores in those phases and coping styles. The results are summarized in Table 3.2.

Table 3.2 shows that the multiple correlations of dimensions with coping styles are generally lower than the correlations obtained with delta goals. It should be kept in mind, however, that the delta goal correlations were computed across situations. While coping styles were studied in a single situation this procedure could not be followed here. It is quite possible that the conditional nature of secondary control underlies the lower correlations found. Unlike primary control, secondary control is activated only when a situation tends to become uncontrollable, as with stress. However, the amount of stress experienced in a given situation is not necessarily equal for different persons. Our approach assumes differences in experience to occur as a function of the ways in which the information is processed. While the same situation is more stressful for some Ss than for others, coping behaviour will be more pronounced for those Ss. Therefore, clearly, this study needs replication with other stressors. Nevertheless we did find correlations between information-processing dimensions and some of the coping styles. These outcomes suggest that, like delta goals, coping styles may be characterized by specific patterns of information processing. Restricting ourselves to the significant correlations found the data suggest that two styles – planful/rational and daydreams/fantasies are predominantly volitional. Two other styles –

Table 3.2 Correlations between information processing dimensions and coping styles

	Plan	Selfbl	Dist	Fant	Supp	Pos	Wish
Arousal	0.30*	0.21	−0.34*	0.30*	0.24	0.08	−0.03
Effort	−0.07	−0.32*	0.35*	0.00	−0.24	−0.01	−0.10
Activation	−0.04	0.41*	−0.25	0.29	0.12	−0.12	0.07
Multiple R	0.33	0.45	0.44	0.39	0.30	0.19	0.13

Note
*$p < 0.05$

self-blame and distancing – are mixed types involving emotion as well as volition.

Discussion

The results of our two studies are positive while confirming some existing expectations. What makes these findings rather extraordinary is the fact that connections between physiological indices and the *content* of human behaviour were obtained. In past research those correlations are rare. What has been obtained with some regularity are connections with formal aspects such as relaxation, startle, orienting, defence, vigour, tiredness, or rather global emotional states like anger, anxiety, grief and tenseness. Here we found connections of physiological measures with specific types of goals and thoughts obtained with self-reports. In view of the weak measures employed we were rather surprised. As mentioned before, replication of both studies is urgently wanted. However, if these findings can be replicated, there is every reason to paraphrase Bandura (1986) and study the 'biological foundations of thought and action'.

Information-processing types

It is rather generally assumed that information processing is a major basis for most behaviours which humans demonstrate in daily life conditions. Individual differences in the ways people process information are major candidates for defining personality. However, what type of model is best suited to accommodate individual differences based on information processing? Our contribution to answering that question is based on the results of our studies. The physiological measures scrutinized here have found an almost natural fit in three independent dimensions. Formally speaking, those dimensions come up to all requirements that are usually imposed on personality traits. Our earlier studies of the energetic dimensions have invariably revealed a great deal of consistency across time and across situations. Furthermore energetics have revealed a great deal of genetic influence. Accordingly, if one intends to study personality at the energetics level, information-processing traits are the obvious choice. However, if one is interested in overt behaviour the picture changes drastically. As regards overt behaviour the energetic dimensions interact. This implies that a given score on one dimension may underlie behaviours that are qualitatively different depending on the individual's scores on the other dimensions. Accordingly, rather than three different trait dimensions regarding overt behaviour we must think in terms of eight different types. Personality can be defined as the intra-individual organization of information-processing dimensions. Personality types are persons with similar intra-individual organizations of the information-processing dimensions. If our information-processing variables occupy the central position we think they do, persons of the same type may be expected to behave in similar ways. Information processing is directly connected with the presence or absence of control in a variety of situations. I expect information processing to become manifest in the behaviours that people show in daily life. In domains of a recurrent nature they will obtain the character of 'styles'.

Examples are the styles that people demonstrate in major professional activities like teaching, sports, arts, selling and managing. For a long time, psychologists have successfully explored and mapped styles in those areas. However, why and how they are connected with personality has never been sufficiently explained. Our information-processing approach may provide a new framework here. An assumption to be tested first is that information processing provides a basis for job control in a more general sense. Direct evidence bearing on this question has been obtained in a recent study of job control (Riteco, 1998). Riteco asked 180 workers at a Dutch university to indicate how far they were able to control a number of key situations in teaching and research. He also asked them to indicate to what extent they pursued the different delta goals in their work. Correlations between both data sets are presented in Table 3.3.

As Table 3.3 shows, preference for each of the delta goals is connected with job control. This finding suggests that in the same university jobs different delta goals may be emphasized all having a positive effect on control in key situations. This is tantamount to saying that it may be useful to distinguish among different occupational styles. The information-processing types proposed here may provide an explanation.

To study the capacity of the information-processing types to explain occupational styles we addressed the domains of teaching, designing and leadership. For teaching we re-analysed the data of a now classical study of teaching styles (Hettema, 1972). In that study lessons given by 100 high school teachers in the areas of English and mathematics were observed. Detailed observation of teacher behaviour included technical acts, like explaining, asking questions, giving feedback, using the blackboard, but also social behaviours like

Table 3.3 Correlations between delta goal preferences and perceived control in work situations

Delta goal	
Social control	0.38*
Control	0.30*
Proximity	0.25*
Knowledge	0.25*
Agency	0.28*
Preparation	0.29*

Note
*$p < 0.05$

cracking jokes, addressing pupils, giving support, maintaining order, gesticulating, punishing, etc. Based on long-term behaviour observation, we found clear differences in the ways teachers dealt with subject matter, with classroom activities and with student social behaviour. Teacher behaviour could be classified as reflecting one of six different styles. The styles were labelled the normative, structuring, accepting, stimulating, directive and supportive style of teaching. For the different styles we identified the dominant delta goal present in the behaviours defining the style and found some clear relationships with delta social control, control, proximity, knowledge, agency and support (cf. Table 3.4).

A completely different area is architectural designing. Van Bakel (1995; Hettema and Van Bakel, 1997) studied information processing in reports of 52 experienced architects while designing new buildings. As a major tool he used an S-R inventory containing ten typical designing situations. In each situation the architects reported on the decisions they would make when confronted with such a task. Decisions could be based mainly on the building site S, the program or design brief P, or pre-existing conceptions C of what the building should look like. The results showed clear individual differences in information processing that were rather consistent across different designing tasks. The different ways of processing information could be allocated to six designing styles. The feasability style is dominated by making inventories to be aware of all the problems to be met, emphasizing delta knowledge. Typical for the pragmatic style are trial and error to improve the existing conditions before designing starts: delta preparation. A primary concern in the convergent style is turn to the building site and study the natural environment as a major prerequisite. Delta proximity may be the underlying delta goal. In the analogic style the design is derived analogically from forms existing before in the head of the architect. This rather conservative approach might reflect delta control. In the iconic style a fixed mental image is adopted as a powerful guideline and all other data are subordinate to that image. Delta agency might be the underlying goal. In the syntactic style geometrical proportions and modular grids are employed as shape decision rules. This type of designing provides the designer with authority for a great many

Table 3.4 Occupational styles based on information processing

IP type	Deltagoal	Copingstyle	Teachingstyle	Designstyle	Leaderstyle
CCC	Knowledge	Fantasies	Stimulating	Feasability	Democratic
CCA	Preparat	Planful	——	Pragmatic	——
CAC	Proximity	Expression	Accepting	Convergent	Participat
ACC	Control	Wishful	Structuring	Analogic	Performance
CAA	Support	Positive	Supportive	——	Supporting
ACA	Agency	Distancing	Directing	Iconic	Directive
AAC	Soccont	Self blame	Normative	Syntactic	Authoritar.
AAA					

decisions that are otherwise left to his own judgement: delta social control. Clearly, to some extent the goals governing architectural designers agree with the delta goals proposed here (cf. Table 3.4).

An area where styles have obtained special attention is leadership. In earlier work the main objective of leadership research was to provide means for selecting good managers. This approach put special emphasis on authoritarian versus democratic leadership, sometimes completed with laissez-faire. However, in recent work more refinement has been obtained. Thus, for instance, House and Mitchell (1974) made a distinction into six different styles: authoritarian, performance-oriented, participating, democratic, directive and supporting styles of leadership. In this model, rather than criteria used by selectors the goals of the leaders are emphasized. Democratic leaders are primarily interested in knowing what their co-workers want. Participating leaders want to work in close connection with the others. Performance-oriented leaders are interested in production or output, no matter how this is attained. Supporting leaders on the other hand, are especially concerned with underachievers, for whom they provide help whenever necessary. The main objective of directive leaders is to have others behave according to their own preferences. Finally, authoritarian leaders will impose norms, pass judgement and punish co-workers not living up to company standards. There are some clear relationships between the leader goals and the delta goals proposed here. Table 3.4 gives a summary.

Table 3.4 suggests that information processing may have the potency to provide an explanation of individual differences in styles of functioning in different occupations. Hitherto, styles like these have been proposed without much theory guiding them. Particularly, the question why styles are so hard to be altered has always remained enigmatic. Now it can be seen why and how persons functioning in the same environment emphasizing the same company goals use different stylistic means for goal attainment. Clearly much work remains to be done in the area of occupational styles. First of all, the classification proposed in Table 3.4 needs further confirmation. One way to test this categorization is to study people with divergent styles observed in the same occupational settings. Their information-processing types may be crystallized in the delta goals emphasized. A further step would be to assess the dominant energetic patterns of those people confronted with films representing those settings.

DISCUSSION

In this study we have explored personality at different levels of inquiry. Major considerations to start research of this type are the results of behaviour genetic research suggesting that personality traits exhibit considerable genetic effects. On the other hand, however, trait heritability is far from perfect. This may be taken to suggest that between genes and traits there are more levels at which individual differences can be fruitfully studied. Zuckerman (1993) has indicated the different levels that may be taken into account. His seven turtles model provides an agenda for further research into the type of variables not only describing but also explaining individual differences. Meanwhile some progress may be noted in the direction of completing the agenda. There have been successful attempts to explain trait scores on the basis of the frequencies of specific social behaviours shown in daily life conditions (Buss and Craik, 1980). Workers in the social cognitive tradition have explained individual differences in social behaviours on the basis of cognitive information processing, enabling them to exert a certain amount of control over their environment. There are two modes of control. Primary control reflects active goal-directed behaviour affecting the environment. Goals are the major elements of primary control. Secondary control includes a dynamic system of beliefs about oneself and the environment providing control in situations where primary control fails. Goals and beliefs are acquired through social learning, imitation and modelling. In terms of the seven turtles model, the boundaries of the social approach to personality have now been reached. The present contribution is an attempt to make the next step and study the biological determinants underlying individual differences. To explain information processing we proposed a biological model studying the energetic aspects of information processing. The model emphasizes different energetic systems, indicated here as arousal, effort and activation. In each system information is processed according to a dimension ranging from controlled/volitional processing to automatic/emotional processing. Our findings suggest that individuals have their own positions on each dimension and that those positions are highly consistent across different situations. Our research has also shown that the positions occupied are to a great extent determined through heredity. Finally, we found evidence suggesting connections between the dimensions of arousal, effort and activation on the one hand and goals and beliefs on the other. As our work satisfies some major conditions of multilevel research we believe this contribution may help in finding our way in the lower parts of the Zuckerman model.

However, multilevel research not only maps out the ways overt 'phenotypic' behaviours are connected with underlying genes. As Simon (1992) has pointed out, this approach may also provide support for those working at the different levels. First of all, there is the cognitive information-processing approach. A major issue in that approach is the kind of variables underlying cognitive information processing. In Mischel and Shoda's cognitive-affective personality system (CAPS) cognition and affect are specially emphasized as underlying systems. However, Bandura's concepts of self-efficacy and agency as well as the strong emphasis on goal directedness in social information processing more generally suggest basic volitional tendencies to be typically involved. However, when it comes to defining systems underlying those tendencies the concept of volition appears to be notoriously absent. Our studies suggest that this is a major shortcoming that may be profitably restored in future work on social information processing. Can individuals henceforth be characterized as either emotional or volitional? Our findings point in another direction. In our studies we have attempted to predict some major information-processing variables – goals and beliefs – using energetic dimension scores as predictors. Predictions according to a linear additive model yielded no results. Instead, complex interactions between emotion and volition appeared to underlie individual differences. Our data suggest that goals and beliefs rest on their own patterns of emotional and volitional information processing. Accordingly, as Mischel and Shoda (1995, 1998) expected, it is not the variables per se but the organization within the individual that seems to underlie individual differences. A major conclusion drawn from our research is that individual differences in information processing obtain the character of types rather than traits. Although the underlying energetics have all the features of a dimensional trait model, when it comes to predicting cognitive information-processing variables, the dimensions exhibit strong interactions. The types ensuing can be characterized with their own coherent patterns of goals and beliefs, and their own styles of behaving in a social context. The type of model suggested by our outcomes may explain why in social information processing coherence instead of consistency is a major characteristic of personality (Cervone and Shoda, 1999).

Not only are our studies connected with information processing but also with classical biological approaches to personality as exemplified in the work of Eysenck (1967) and Gray (1991). Especially the work of Gray seems of interest here. As we noted earlier, like ours Gray's model includes three different brain systems. The behaviour approach system (BAS) is a reward system. The behaviour inhibition system (BIS) is a punishment system. The third system is the fight/flight system, organizing behaviour in response to actually existing punishment or pain. Although far from coinciding, the neural structures underlying Gray's model do show some connections with the Pribram-McGuinness model forwarded here. However, while we proposed information processing as a major outflow of those systems Gray posited traits like impulsivity and anxiety, or the traits of extraversion and neuroticism. A major question cropping up is: whence those differences? First of all, although the energetical systems may be comparable to some extent, Gray was mainly interested in the emotional parts of the systems, whereas we emphasized emotions as well as volitions. Furthermore, the fight/flight system has played little or no part in Gray's discussion of personality. Thus, compared with our approach, Gray's model is based on a double reduction: one system is kept outside the discussion and in the other systems only one pole is acknowledged. Our results suggest that only through this double reduction is it possible to make the systems directly underlie the traits of impulsivity and anxiety.

REFERENCES

Austin, J. T. and Vancouver, J. G. (1996) 'Goal constructs in psychology: Structure, process, and content', *Psychological Bulletin* 120, 3: 338–375.

Bandura, A. (1986) *Social Foundations of Thought and Action: A Social Cognitive Theory*. Englewood Cliffs: Prentice-Hall.

Betsworth, D. G., Bouchard, T. J. Jr, Cooper, C. R. and Grotevant, H. D. (1994) 'Genetic and environmental influence on vocational interests assessed using adoptive and biological families and twins reared apart and together', *Journal of Vocational Behavior*, 44: 263–278.

Bouchard, T. J. Jr (1993) 'Genetic and environmental influences on adult personality', in P. J. Hettema, and I. J. Deary (eds) *Foundations of Personality*, pp. 15–44. Dordrecht: Kluwer.

Bouchard, T. J. Jr, Segal, N. L. and Lykken, D. T. (1990) 'Genetic and environmental influences on special mental abilities in a sample of twins reared apart', *Acta Genetica Medicae et Gemellologiae* 39: 193–206.

Brandstaedter, J. and Renner, G. (1990) 'Tenacious goal pursuit and flexible goal adjustment: Explication and age-related analysis of assimilative and accommodative strategies of coping', *Psychology and Aging* 5: 58–67.

Buss, D. M. (1991) 'Evolutionary personality psychology', *Annual Review of Psychology* 42: 459–491.

Buss, D. M. and Craik, K. H. (1980) 'The frequency concept of disposition: Dominance and prototypical dominance acts', *Journal of Personality* 48: 379–392.

Cantor, N., and Kihlstrom, J. F. (1987) *Personality and Social Intelligence*. Englewood Cliffs: Prentice-Hall.

Carver, C. S. and Scheier, M. F. (1981) *Attention and Self-regulation: A Control-Theory Approach to Human Behavior*. New York: Springer.

Cervone, D. (1991) 'The two disciplines of personality psychology', *Psychological Science* 2: 371–377.

Cervone, D. and Shoda, Y. (1999) *The Coherence of Personality: Social-Cognitive Bases of Consistency, Variability, and Organization*. New York: Guilford Press.

Duffy, E. (1957) 'The psychological significance of the concept of "arousal" or "activation" ', *Psychological Review* 64: 265–275.

Dweck, C. S. (1991) 'Self-theories and goals: Their role in motivation, personality and development', in R. A Dienstbier (ed.) *Nebraska Symposium on Motivation*, vol. 38, pp. 199–235. Lincoln: University of Nebraska Press.

Dweck, C. S. and Leggett, E. L. (1988) 'A social-cognitive approach to motivation and personality', *Psychological Review* 95: 256–273.

Ellis, A. (1962) *Reason and Emotion in Psychotherapy*. Secaucus: Lyle Stuart.

Emmons, R. A. (1989) 'The personal striving approach to personality', in L. A. Pervin (ed.) *Goal Concepts in Personality and Social Psychology*, pp. 87–126. Hillsdale, NJ: Lawrence Erlbaum Associates Inc.

Eysenck, H. J. (1967) *The Biological Basis of Personality*. Springfield: Thomas.

Folkman, S. and Lazarus, R. S. (1980) 'An analysis of coping in a middle-aged community sample', *Journal of Health and Social Behavior* 21: 219–239.

Folkman, S., Lazarus, R. S., Dunkel-Schetter, C., DeLongis, A. and Gruen, R. (1986) 'The dynamics of stressful encounter: Cognitive appraisal, coping, and encounter outcomes', *Journal of Personality and Social Psychology* 50: 992–1003.

Funder, D. C. and Colvin, C. R. (1991) 'Explorations in behavioural consistency: Properties of persons, situations, and behavior', *Journal of Personality and Social Psychology* 60: 773–794

Geenen, R. (1991) *Psychophysiological Consistency and Personality*. Tilburg: Tilburg University Press.

Grant, H. and Dweck, C. S. (1999) 'Goal analysis of personality and personality coherence', in D. Cervone and Y. Shoda (eds) *The Coherence of Personality: Social-Cognitive Bases of Consistency, Variability, and Organization*, pp. 345–371. NewYork: Guilford Press.

Gray, J. A. (1991) 'Neural systems, emotion and personality', in J. Madden IV (ed.) *Neurobiology of Learning, Emotion and Affect*. New York: Raven Press.

Heckhausen, J. and Schulz, R. (1995) 'A life-span theory of control', *Psychological Review* 102: 284–304.

Hettema, P. J. (1972) *Teaching Styles: An Explorative Study in High School*. Nijmegen: NIVOR.

Hettema. P. J. (1989) 'Transformation rules: Towards a taxonomy of everyday behavior', in P. J. Hettema (ed.) *Personality and Environment: Assessment of Human Adaptation*, pp. 71–85. Chichester: Wiley.

Hettema, P. J. (1991) 'Emotions and adaptation: An open-systems perspective', in C. D. Spielberger, I. G. Sarason, Z. Kulcsar and G. L. Van Heck (eds) *Stress and Emotion: Anxiety, Anger, and Curiosity*, pp. 47–63. New York: Hemisphere.

Hettema, P. J. (1994) 'Psychophysiological assessment of personality using films as stimuli', *Personality and Individual Differences* 16: 167–178.

Hettema, P. J. (1995) 'Personality and depression: A multilevel perspective', *European Journal of Personality* 9: 401–412.

Hettema, P. J. (1996) 'Cross-situational consistency and temporal stability of biological and social personality variables', paper presented at the XXIVth International Congress of Psychology, Montreal.

Hettema, P. J. and Hol, D. P. (1998) 'Primary control and the consistency of behavior across different situations', *European Journal of Personality* 12: 231–248.

Hettema, P. J. and Geenen, R. (in preparation) *Physiological Reactions in Stress and Coping*.

Hettema, P. J. and Lensvelt-Mulders, G. J. (in preparation) *The Psychophysiology of Goal-directed Behavior*.

Hettema, P. J. and Kenrick, D. T. (1992) 'Models of person-situation interactions', in G. V. Caprara and G. L. Van Heck (eds) *Modern Personality Psychology: Critical Reviews and New Directions*, pp. 393–417. New York: Harvester-Wheatsheaf.

Hettema, P. J. and van Bakel, A. P. (1997) 'Cross-situational consistency in a mastery condition', *Journal of Research in Personality* 31: 222–239.

Hettema, P. J., Leidelmeijer, K. C. and Geenen, R. (2000) 'Dimensions of information processing: Physiological reactions to motion pictures', *European Journal of Personality* 14: 39–63.

Hettema, P. J., Van Heck, G. L. and Brandt, C. (1989) 'The representation of situations through films', in P. J. Hettema (ed.) *Personality and Environment: Assessment of Human Adaptation*, pp. 113–127. Chichester: Wiley.

Hol, D. P. (1994) *Persoon–situatie interacties: Operationalisering, gedragsvoorspelling en modelvergelijking*. Tilburg: Tilburg University Press.

House, R. J. and Mitchell, T. (1974) 'Path–goal theory of leadership', *Journal of Contemporary Business* 3: 81–97.

Jansen, E., Everaerd, W., Spiering, M. and Jansen, J. (2000) 'Autonomic processes and the appraisal of sexual stimuli: Toward an information processing model of sexual arousal', *Journal of Sex Research* 37, 1: 8–23.

Kahneman, D. (1973) *Attention and Effort*. Englewood Cliffs: Prentice-Hall.

Keller, L. M., Bouchard, T. J. Jr, Arvey, R. D., Segal, N. L. and Dawis, R. V. (1992) 'Work values: Genetic and environmental influences', *Journal of Applied Psychology* 77: 79–88.

Kenrick, D. T., Montello, D. R. and McFarlane, S. (1985) 'Personality, social learning, social cognition, or sociobiology?', in R. Hogan and W. H. Jones (eds) *Perspectives in Personality*, vol.1, pp. 201–234. Greenwich: JAI Press.

Klinger, E. (1977) *Meaning and Void: Inner Experience and the Incentives in People's Lives*. Minneapolis: University of Minnesota Press.

Kuhl, J. (1994) 'A theory of action and state orientation', in J. Kuhl and J. Beckman (eds) *Volition and Personality: Action versus State Orientation*, pp. 9–56. Seattle: Hogrefe.

Ledoux, J. (1996) *The Emotional Brain*. New York: Simon and Schuster.

Lensvelt-Mulders, G. J. (2000) *Personality at Different Levels: A Behavior Genetic Approach*. Tilburg: Tilburg University Press.

Lensvelt-Mulders, G. J. and Hettema, P. J. (2001) 'Genetic analysis of autonomic reactivity to psychologically stressful situations', *Biological Psychology* 58: 25–40.

Little, B. R. (1989) 'Personal project analysis: Trivial pursuits, magnificent obsessions, and the search for coherence', in D. M. Buss and N. Cantor (eds) *Personality Psychology: Recent Trends and Emerging Directions*. New York: Springer.

Lykken, D. T., Bouchard, T. J. Jr, McGue, M. and Tellegen, A. (1993) 'Heritability of interests: A twin study', *Journal of Applied Psychology* 78: 649–661.

McGuinness, D. and Pribram, K. H. (1980) 'The neuropsychology of attention: Emotional and motivational controls', in M. C. Wittrock (ed.) *The Brain and Psychology*, pp. 95–139. New York: Academic Press.

Magnusson, D. (1988) *Individual Development from an Interactional Perspective: A Longitudinal Study*. Hillsdale, NJ: Lawrence Erlbaum Associates Inc.

Matthews, G. and Gilliland, K. (1999) 'The personality theories of H. J. Eysenck and J. A. Gray: A comparative review', *Personality and Individual Differences* 26: 583–626.

Mischel, W. (1968) *Personality and Assessment*. New York: Wiley.

Mischel, W. (1973) 'Toward a cognitive social learning reconceptualization of personality', *Psychological Review* 80: 252–283.

Mischel, W. and Shoda, Y. (1995) 'A cognitive-affective system theory of personality: Reconceptualizing situations, dispositions, dynamics, and invariance in personality structure', *Psychological Review* 102: 246–268.

Mischel, W. and Shoda, Y. (1998) 'Reconciling processing dynamics and personality dispositions', *Annual Review of Psychology* 49: 229–258.

Moloney, D. P., Bouchard, T. J. Jr and Segal, N. L. (1991) 'A genetic and environmental analysis of the vocational interests of monozygotic and dizygotic twins reared apart', *Journal of Vocational Behavior* 39: 76–109.

Nichols, R. C. (1978) 'Twin studies of ability, personality and interests', *Homo* 29: 158–173.

Plomin, R., DeFries, J. C. and Loehlin, J. C. (1977) 'Genotype–environment interaction and correlation in the analysis of human behavior', *Psychological Bulletin* 84: 309–322.

Pribram, K. H. and McGuinness, D. (1975) 'Arousal, activation and effort in the control of attention', *Psychological Review* 82: 116–149.

Pribram, K. H. and McGuinness, D. (1992) 'Attention and para-attentional processing: Event-related brain potentials as tests of a model', in D. Friedman and G. Bruder (eds) *Annals of the New York Academy of Sciences* 658: 65–92.

Riteco, Ch. R. (1998) 'Job control, personality and health: An explorative study at a Dutch university', PhD thesis, Tilburg University.

Roth, S. and Cohen, L. (1986) 'Approach, avoidance, and coping with stress', *American Psychologist* 41: 813–819.

Rothbaum, F., Weisz, J. R. and Snyder, S. S. (1982) 'Changing the world and changing the self: A model of perceived control', *Journal of Personality and Social Psychology* 42: 5–37.

Rushton, J. P., Fulker, D. W., Neal, M. C., Nias, D. K. B. and Eysenck, H. J. (1986) 'Altruism and aggression: The heritability of individual differences', *Psychological Review* 88: 582–589.

Schank, R. C. and Abelson, R. (1977) *Scripts, Plans, Goals and Understanding: An Inquiry into Human Knowledge Structures*. Hillsdale, NJ: Lawrence Erlbaum Associates Inc.

Simon, H. A. (1992) 'What is an explanation of behavior?', *Psychological Science* 3: 150–161.

Skinner, B. F. (1953) *The Analysis of Behavior*. New York: Macmillan.

Skinner, E. A. (1996) 'A guide to constructs of control', *Journal of Personality and Social Psychology* 71: 549–570.

Sokolov, E. N. (1960) 'Neuronal models and the orienting reflex,' in M. A. B. Brazier (ed.) *The Central Nervous System and Behavior*, pp. 187–276. New York: Josiah Macy Jr Foundation.

Tooby, J. and Cosmides, L. (1990) 'The past explains the present: Emotional adaptations and the structure of ancestral environments', *Ethology and Sociobiology* 11: 375–424.

Van Bakel, A. P. (1995) 'Styles of architectural designing', PhD thesis. Eindhoven: TUE.

Van Heck, G. L. (1989) 'Situation concepts: Definition and classification', in P. J. Hettema (ed.) *Personality and Environment: Assessment of Human Adaptation*, pp. 53–69. Chichester: Wiley.

Van Heck, G. L. and Vingerhoets, A. J. J. M. (1989) 'Copingstijlen en persoonlijkheidskenmerken', *Nederlands Tijdschrift voor de Psychologie* 44: 73–87.

Van Heck, G. L., Hettema, P. J. and Leidelmeijer, K. C. (1993) 'Personality and the selection and transformation of situations', in D. L. Palenzuela and A. M. Barros (eds) *Modern Trends in Personality Theory and Research*, pp. 25–42. Porto: Apport.

Vingerhoets, A. J. J. M. (1985) *Psychological Stress: An Experimental Approach*. Lisse: Swets and Zeitlinger.

Vingerhoets, A. J. J. M. and Flohr, P. (1984) 'Type A behaviour and self-reports of coping preferences', *British Journal of Medical Psychology* 57: 15–21.

Waller, N. G., Kojetin, B. A., Bouchard, T. J. Jr, Lykken, D. T. and Tellegen, A. (1990) 'Genetic and environmental influences on religious interests, attitudes, and values: A study of twins reared apart and together', *Psychological Science* 1: 138–142.

Waller, N. G., Lykken, D. T. and Tellegen, A. (1995) 'Occupational stress, leisure time interests, and personality: Three domains or one? Findings from the Minnesota Twin Registry', in D. J. Lubinski and R. V. Dawis (eds) *Assessing Individual Differences in Human Behavior: New Concepts and Findings*, pp. 233–259. Palo Alto: Davies-Black.

White, R. (1959) 'Motivation reconsidered: The concept of competence', *Psychological Review* 66: 297–333.

Wickens, C. D. (1984) 'Processing resources in attention', in R. Pasuraman and D. R. Davies (eds) *Varieties of Attention*, pp. 63–102. Orlando: Academic Press.

Zuckerman, M. (1993) 'Personality from top (traits) to bottom (genetics) with some stops at each level between', in P. J. Hettema and I. J. Deary (eds) *Foundations of Personality*, pp. 73–100. Dordrecht: Kluwer.

Chapter 4

Three superfactors of personality and three aspects of attention

Błażej Szymura and Edward Nęcka

The aim of this chapter is to describe and explain the relationships between basic personality dimensions and efficiency of visual attention. The hypotheses concerning these relationships are based on two assumptions. First, we assume that personality-related individual differences in attention are detectable only if the attentional task is demanding enough. Second, we assume that what is demanding for one person may be not so for another. According to Hans J. Eysenck's biological theory of personality, it is hypothesized that: (a) quick alternation in selection conditions should be demanding for neurotic people; (b) necessity to divide attentional resources in dual-task conditions should be demanding for introverts; (c) prolonged concentration over time should be demanding for persons scoring high on psychoticism. Hence, different personality traits are connected with the efficiency of different aspects of attention: neuroticism is related to performance on selective attention tasks, introversion is connected with the efficacy of divided attention, and psychoticism is related to performance on the sustained attention tasks. These hypotheses are validated on the basis of empirical data. Although we concentrate on our own research, these findings are also complemented by supporting data from other studies.

INTRODUCTION

Apart from many other things, people differ in the way they pay attention to stimuli. Individual differences in attention are interesting as such but also as correlates of intellectual and personality traits. We can look at differences between people concerning selectivity, dual-task performance, endurance, and other aspects of attention, asking ourselves how salient these differences are and to what extent do they account for human performance in the variety of cognitive tasks. Also, we can ask ourselves whether people characterized by different levels of intelligence, extraversion, neuroticism and other dimensions of individual differences also differ in the specificity of functioning of their attentional mechanisms. Knowledge of such relationships should increase our understanding of the cognitive mechanisms of human intelligence and personality. It should also be helpful in creation of integrated models of performance, which take into account both general rules of cognition and their interindividual variability.

In this chapter we have adopted the latter approach. First, we will review in brief the most important aspects of attention as a fundamental cognitive mechanism. Second, we will formulate hypotheses concerning the relationships between extraversion, neuroticism, and psychoticism, on the one hand, and three aspects of attention, on the other. These hypotheses result from the three-dimensional theory of personality developed by Hans J. Eysenck. In the next section, these hypotheses will be validated on the basis of empirical material available in the literature. We concentrate on the research conducted in our own research group, although these findings will be complemented by supporting data from other studies as well. Finally, we will provide some conclusions concerning possible practical applications of the knowledge about relationships between personality and attention.

THREE ASPECTS OF ATTENTION

At the most general level of analysis, attention is a mechanism responsible for reduction of the surplus of data overwhelming the information-processing system at the given moment (Reed, 1988). First of all, there is a surplus of sensory information that has to be reduced substantially so that the remaining portion of data be processed efficiently. For that reason, attention is sometimes defined as the mechanism of selectivity of sensory input (Broadbent, 1958). Humans (and animals) cannot deal properly with the entire stimulation attacking their sensory organs. Besides, a great part of such stimulation is useless or irrelevant. In order to avoid chaos at the input level of cognition, we have to cut off what is irrelevant, unnecessary, or not interesting at the moment. We do so thanks to the mechanisms of *selective attention*, although it may not be certain in advance what is relevant and what is not. However, the fundamental nature of selectivity results in the fact that this aspect of attention is relatively well known and thoroughly investigated. A popular paradigm of research in this field amounts to the dichotic presentation of two different channels of verbal information to each ear. Thanks to selective attention, people can efficiently screen off one source of information in order to concentrate on the other. However, some fragments of the ignored channel can sometimes appear in the attended[1] one (Treisman, 1960). Such intrusions are interpreted as an indication of temporary failures of the otherwise rather efficient system of selective attention.

Reduction of the surplus of information refers not only to the early stages of sensory input but also to the execution of final responses. The information-processing system usually has to choose among many potentially available ways of responding. Since it is even more difficult to respond in two ways at the same time than to pay attention simultaneously to different stimuli, the system has to deploy the resources of attention carefully in order to give way to the response that is most suitable in the given situation. Sometimes the system cannot avoid deployment of attention among two or even more simultaneous responses, provided that they are technically possible to execute (e.g. a verbal response accompanied by a manual one). In such cases, we speak about a phenomenon called dual-task performance (Kahneman, 1973). Experimental paradigms used for the assessment of the individual capacity of attentional resources usually require that participants are completing two tasks simultaneously. The magnitude of detrimental effects of the so-called primary task due to the necessity to execute the secondary task is interpreted in terms of the amount of resources of attention that a person is losing due to the necessity to disperse his or her resources. So *divided attention* is as important an aspect of the discussed phenomenon as is the selectivity aspect.

Apart from selectivity and division of resources, attention is also responsible for the continuous vigilance to certain stimuli, as well as for the continuous search for the stimuli of certain characteristics (Mackworth, 1970). Selection of the important stimulation may be a trivial task if it is performed either on one occasion or several times but during a short period of time. The same task usually gets rather demanding if it has to be done continuously during several hours. This is why the job of guards and air traffic controllers is so difficult. *Prolonged concentration* on a given stimulation is usually investigated with the use of continuous performance tasks. Participants are asked to focus their attention on a long series of stimuli, most of which being irrelevant (distraction or noise). Ignoring the irrelevant stimuli is a proper mode of functioning. However, it should not lead to the omission of very important signals, even if they are rather infrequent. People usually do not differ in such tasks at the initial phases of performance. They start to differ later on, for example, during the second half of the experimental session or during the most recent of a number of time slots. The extent to which a participant's performance is deficient in the ending phases, as compared to the initial ones, is a measure of an individual ability to concentrate attention over time in spite of fatigue and distraction.

PERSONALITY AND ATTENTION

Hypotheses

Our hypotheses concerning the relationships between personality and attention are based on two assumptions. First, we assume that individual differences turn out to be visible only when a cognitive task is *demanding* enough. If the task is rather simple, the variance of human performance is at least mildly restricted, and sometimes such a restriction is so severe that the ceiling effect appears. Restriction of variance causes two important consequences: it reduces the salience of individual differences in cognitive performance and it conceals the correlations between such performance and the chosen dimensions of individual differences, like intelligence, personality and temperament. In other words, if a task is quite easy, various people deal with it at almost equal levels of efficiency, so we cannot observe differences between them concerning how good they are at such a task. We are also unable to discern relationships between cognitive efficiency and various dimensions of human individuality, because if everybody performs at a comparable level of effectiveness there is no way to check whether, say, extraverts do better than introverts, or intelligent people perform better than less intelligent ones. Only when the task at hand becomes more demanding can individual differences in cognition be related to individual differences in personality or intelligence.

Second, we assume that what is demanding for one person may be not demanding at all for another. Specifically, we postulate the existence of systematic differences between people characterized by different scores on the dimensions of extraversion/introversion, neuroticism, and psychoticism, concerning the task's characteristics that are supposed to be rather demanding, quite demanding, or not so demanding. Such differences are most likely rooted in the biological mechanisms of personality traits, as hypothesized by Eysenck (1952; see also Eysenck and Eysenck, 1985).

Neuroticism is defined as an emotional instability probably caused by hyperactivity of the limbic system. A neurotic person quickly responds to emotional stimuli, and his or her responses are rather intense. Specifically, such a person easily gets anxious, particularly if some external causes of negative emotions, such as time pressure, are present. Neurotic persons cope with their predisposition through careful planning, orderly behaviour, and the use of feedback information concerning their performance. They also show hypervigilance to threatening stimuli: that is, they are able to discern even the slightest signals of possible negative events (Eysenck, 1992, 1997). For that reason, neurotic persons often experience anxiety and depressed mood, although such states rarely reach the level of clinical disturbance. According to the above stated assumptions concerning the biological mechanisms of neuroticism, we are entitled to hypothesize that what is really demanding for neurotic people amounts to

- novelty of the task's conditions
- quick alteration of the task's conditions
- time pressure.

Hence, we should look for the relationships between neuroticism and attention in the mechanisms of selective attention. Specifically, we suppose that neurotic persons should demonstrate substantial deficits in the selective attention tasks, particularly in such versions of these tasks where either time pressure would exist or the criterion of selection would change rapidly. We do not assume any relationships between neuroticism and attention if the task is routine (prolonged concentration) or if simultaneous tasks are to be performed (divided attention), unless time pressure or another source of negative affect is involved in such tasks.

Extraversion is usually linked to weaker cortical activation, whereas introversion, as an opposite pole of the same dimension, is associated with stronger cortical activation (Gale, 1981, 1983; Stenberg, Wendt and Risberg, 1993). Permanent differences of this nature produce specific differences between introverts and extraverts concerning their temperament, general level of activity and social life. Overly activated introverts prefer quiet settings and well-practised tasks, whereas insufficiently activated extraverts usually seek external stimulation, no matter if it comes from physical, intellectual or social activity. As to the modes of attentional functioning, introverts should present decreased performance in the dual-task situations because such tasks bring about too much stimulation. Extraverts, on the other hand, should outperform introverts in the dual-task settings, because such settings offer more stimulation, which is preferred and sought after. There is no justification to formulate any hypotheses concerning other aspects of attention. In particular, we do not assume any differences between extraverts and introverts concerning selectivity and prolonged concentration.

Psychoticism is the least investigated dimension as compared to neuroticism and extraversion. At the behavioural level, this dimension refers to the inclination to violate the rules, social as well as intrapsychical. Hence, a person scoring high on the P scale is usually nonconformist and radical in his or her actions and attitudes. He or she is typically more creative than people scoring low on this scale. In social life, a psychotic person is a bit aloof, sometimes unsympathetic and hostile. Such a person is also predisposed to certain forms of personality disorders (e.g. psychopathic disorders or schizotypy), and even to mental diseases. The biological bases of psychoticism are rather unclear. Eysenck (1967; see also Eysenck, Eysenck and Barrett, 1985) believed that this trait should be associated with diminished inhibition of neural impulses resulting from the excessive production of dopamine by the nervous system. Lack of inhibition makes a psychotic person more creative, on the one hand, but also more susceptible to various forms of disorders on the other. Lack of inhibition may also cause increased susceptibility to distraction in tasks and situations that require concentration of mental energy. Hence, we hypothesize that psychoticism should be related to decreased performance in such tests of attention that require prolonged concentration over time. There are no solid grounds to postulate relationships between the P dimension and other aspects of attention, like selectivity and dual-task control.

As we can see, our theoretical analyses, based on the biological theory of personality, allowed formulation of three specific hypotheses concerning the relationships between personality and attention. These hypotheses are rooted in the assumption that individual differences appear only if the task at hand is demanding enough. They are also based on the assumption that what is demanding for one person may be not demanding for another. These hypotheses are listed below:

- *H1: Neuroticism is related to efficiency of selective attention.* For neurotics, the necessity to select valid signals under the time pressure is probably really demanding. Therefore, neurotic persons should perform at a lower level than stable ones if the selectivity task is difficult and associated with time pressure.
- *H2: Extraversion is related to efficiency of divided attention.* For introverts, the necessity to control two (or more) tasks simultaneously seems really demanding. Hence, introverts should perform worse than extraverts in dual-task conditions, because such situations make them overly aroused.
- *H3: Psychoticism is related to efficiency of sustained attention.* For psychotic persons, the necessity to concentrate their attention during prolonged periods of time seems rather demanding. This is because they are susceptible to distraction and cannot inhibit unwanted responses with required effectiveness. Hence, there should appear differences between people scoring high and low on the psychoticism scale in the attentional tasks that involve the aspect of prolonged concentration.

Although the biological theory of personality, developed by H. J. Eysenck served as the groundwork for these three hypotheses, our predictions are in consent with other theoretical models as well. According to Gray (1978, 1981, 1982), the behaviour inhibition system (BIS) is typically switched on in the case of high-anxiety persons, particularly if they have to deal with new situations. Subjective feelings of novelty may result from quick appearance of stimuli. The experimental manipulation with increased speed of stimuli presentation probably prevents anxious and neurotic person from habitual application of routine modes of dealing with novelty. These routine modes usually facilitate coping with the stress involved in novel situations.

Moreover, our hypotheses obtained partial support in some empirical results. For instance, the data obtained by Revelle and his co-workers (Revelle, 1993; Revelle and Anderson, 1992; Humphreys and Revelle, 1984; Anderson and Revelle, 1994), as well as by Matthews and his colleagues (Matthews, 1986, 1987; Matthews and Amelang, 1993; Matthews, Jones and Chamberlain, 1989) clearly suggest that people differing in extraversion also differ in their cognitive functioning. These relationships are possible to account for in terms of the theory of individual differences in optimal stimulation and also in terms of the arousal theory of extraversion. According to these findings, extraverts do better than introverts if a cognitive task is rich in stimulation. However, a number of intermediate factors, like caffeine or time of day, tend to mediate this relationship but these mediating factors are not of interest here.

Furthermore, the findings gathered by Kaiser and his collaborators (Kaiser, Beauvale and Bener, 1997; Kaiser, Barry and Beauvale, 2001) suggest that the factor of psychoticism is related to characteristic patterns of cardiac phasic response. People scoring high on the P scale usually demonstrate smaller effects of deceleration and acceleration in the phasic response to novel stimuli. These results suggest that psychotic persons pay less attention in 'stimulus intake' (deceleration phase) and stimulus elaboration (acceleration phase). These mechanisms may be responsible for the effects of negative priming, which are found to be less salient in psychotic persons in comparison to less psychotic ones (Bullen and Hemsley, 1984; Stavridou and Furnham, 1996). To sum up, our hypotheses seem justified not only by Eysencks's biological theory of personality but also by a number of empirical findings gathered by other researchers. These hypotheses will now be validated on the basis of available data.

PERSONALITY AND ATTENTION: SOME EMPIRICAL EVIDENCE

Neuroticism

Some studies on the relationships between neuroticism and attention have been conducted with the use of a paper-and-pencil test of selective attention developed by Marciusz Moroń (Nęcka and Szymura, 2001; Szymura and Słabosz, 2002). This test consists of a sheet of A4 paper on which small icons of a clock are arranged line by line. Participants are supposed to detect and mark with a cross as many instances of five o'clock as possible in the pre-arranged time period (usually varying between one to two minutes). The icons representing four o'clock serve as distractors, whereas all other icons serve as noise. The number of hits, misses and false alarms are registered as dependent variables. Using this test, Szymura, Waluszko and Stachów (2003) found that neurotic participants committed significantly more errors than stable persons. The number of misses, as opposed to false alarms, was particularly high in the neurotic subgroup. In another study, Nęcka and Szymura (2001) found significant differences between neurotics and stable persons concerning the tempo of automatization of the detection processes. Participants carried out the Moroń test three times so the beneficial effects of learning and automatization could be observed. It appeared that stable persons gained much at the beginning, that is, between the first and the second series, and relatively less at the end, that is between the second and the third series. Neurotic persons, on the other hand, benefitted from learning at a stable rate, without any particular preference to the initial stages of learning.

Another approach to the problem has been adopted by Szymura and Wodniecka (2003), who used the DIVA test of attention. This test consists in presentation of several letters on the screen, which have to be matched to the centrally located probe letter. Participants are supposed to rapidly detect letters that are semantically identical with the probe, but differ in size (lowercase and uppercase letters are used). The number of letters simultaneously appearing on the screen varies from three to five (the set size variable). Apart from that, distractive letters may appear or not appear on the screen. For instance, if the probe letter is capital F, a participant is supposed to detect as quickly as possible all instances of a small letter f. In this case, a capital letter F among the test letters is a distractor. Moreover, participants could be asked to do a simultaneous psychomotor task, consisting in the control of the location of a small horizontal bar on either the left or right side of the screen. Thus, the DIVA test allows assessment of the efficiency of selective and divided attention at different levels of difficulty (set size, the presence or absence of distraction). Szymura and Wodniecka (2003) found that neurotic people committed more errors, including false alarms and misses, than the stable participants. This difference was particularly visible in the dual-task condition. As we can see (Figure 4.1), there is no significant difference between these two groups in the single-task condition. In the dual-task condition, however, the stable persons even increased their accuracy to some extent, whereas the neurotic persons obtained exceptionally high error rates.

The effects shown in Figure 4.1 refer to the experiment in which the rate of presentation of the stimuli was quite fast: 650 ms per letter. In another experiment, the authors lengthened the rate of presentation to 850 ms per letter. In this way, the task became easier and the differences between the neurotic and stable persons concerning the error rate were less salient. Neurotics committed more false alarms than stable persons, but there were no differences concerning the number of misses (Szymura and Wodniecka, 2003). Moreover, the significance of the variables of distraction and series has been demonstrated. As we can see (Figure 4.2), both groups were less accurate in the presence of distractive stimuli than without any distraction. However, the neurotic participants were significantly less accurate, as compared to the stable ones, particularly in the first series with no distraction and in the last two series with distraction. The main effect of neuroticism is also shown in Figure 4.2.

Thus, the results obtained by Szymura and his colleagues (Nęcka and Szymura, 2001; Szymura and Wodniecka, 2003; Szymura et al., 2003) justify the opinion that a high level of neuroticism is associated with decreased accuracy in the situations requiring selective attention. These differences are particularly noticeable if more difficult versions of the task are used (e.g. dual-task condition, the presence of distractors) or if time pressure is imposed. Hence, we can conclude that neuroticism is related to relatively poor performance in the selective attention tasks.

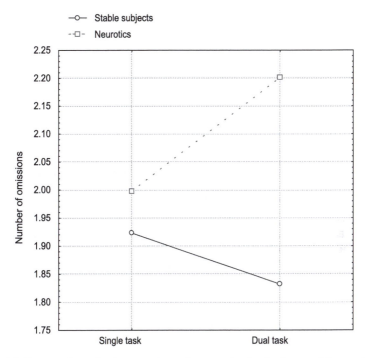

Figure 4.1 The number of misses as dependent on the level of neuroticism and single versus dual-task condition in the quicker version of the DIVA task (Szymura and Wodniecka, 2002). © Pergamon Press (reprinted with permission).

Extraversion

In the study by Szymura and Nęcka (1998) two experiments are reported, in which the easy and difficult versions of the DIVA task were employed. In the easy version of the DIVA task, participants were supposed to detect letters that would be identical with the probe both in meaning and in size (e.g. F and F). In the difficult version of this task, they were supposed to detect letters that were similar to the probe in meaning but not in size (e.g. F and f).

There were systematic differences between the groups in the easy version of the DIVA task, to the effect that introverts performed generally better than extraverts regardless of condition (Figure 4.3). However, the differences between extraverts and introverts were most noticeable in the easiest condition of the task (set size 3).

In the difficult version of the DIVA task, such differences appeared only in the most demanding conditions (dual-task, set size 4 and 5). This time, how-ever, extraverts performed significantly better than introverts (Figure 4.4). It seems that the easy version of the DIVA task was not stimulating enough for extraverts, whereas the difficult version of this task produced too much

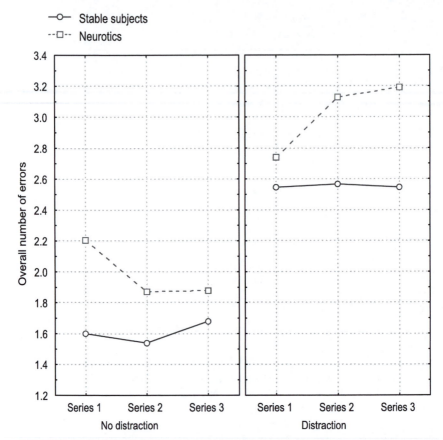

Figure 4.2 Overall number of errors as dependent on the level of neuroticism, distraction, and series in the slower version of the DIVA task (Szymura and Wodniecka, 2002). © Pergamon Press (reprinted with permission).

stimulation for introverts. Hence, the arousal theory of extraversion obtained substantial empirical support as far as the mechanisms of attention are regarded.

Nęcka and Szymura (2001) also found that extraverts differed from introverts in the magnitude of the Stroop (1935) effect. Stroop interference refers to the difficulty with which people ignore the meaning of the word in order to name the colour of ink that was used to write this word. In the case of 'conflicting' stimuli (e.g. the word 'green' written in red ink) time needed to name the colour of ink is usually much longer than in the case of regular stimuli (e.g. the word 'green' written with green ink). It appeared that, at the average, extraverts needed 943 ms to process a conflicting stimulus, whereas introverts needed as much as 1061 ms to do the same task. In the control condition (coloured patches instead of words) there were no significant

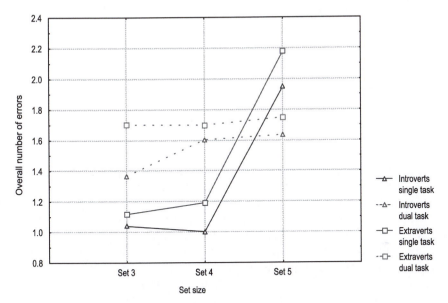

Figure 4.3 Overall number of errors as dependent on the level of extraversion, single/dual task, and set size in the easy version of the DIVA task (Szymura and Nęcka, 1998). © Pergamon Press (reprinted with permission).

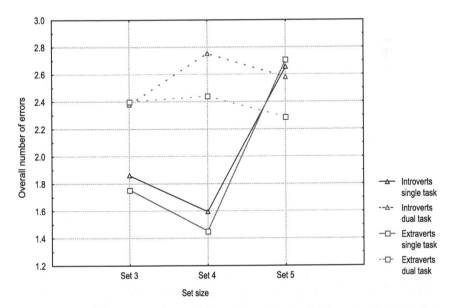

Figure 4.4 Overall number of errors as dependent on the level of extraversion, single/dual task, and set size in the difficult version of the DIVA task (Szymura and Nęcka, 1998). © Pergamon Press (reprinted with permission).

differences between extraverts (517 ms) and introverts (530 ms) in the pace of colour naming. It also appeared that the difference of time between conflicting and regular stimuli, interpreted as the index of magnitude of the Stroop Effect, was significantly greater in the case of introverts (531 ms) than in the case of extraverts (426 ms). Magnitude of the Stroop Effect reflects the efficiency of the processes of selective attention.

It is worth pointing out that selectivity in the Stroop interference task is particularly demanding, since it requires not only focusing on what is relevant but also active inhibition of what is irrelevant albeit suggestive. The superiority of extraverts over introverts is therefore rather interesting for our search for the attentional correlates of personality dimensions. These findings suggest that extraversion is associated with increased efficiency of attentional functioning not only in reference to the divided attention paradigm but also concerning the Stroop interference task, which is regarded as a measure of selectivity. The dual-task findings are interpretable in terms of the arousal theory of extraversion. Extraverts, who are not aroused at the optimal level, perform quite well if the task settings are abundant in some extra stimulation. The Stroop data are not easily interpretable in a similar way, unless it will be demonstrated that conflicting stimuli produce more activation than regular Stroop words.

Psychoticism

Rawlings (1985) employed the dichotic listening task that consisted in mental shadowing of one of two simultaneously presented auditory channels while ignoring the other one. The number of intrusions from the unattended channel served as a measure of inefficiency of the attentional mechanism to screen out irrelevant information. The author found positive correlations between psychoticism and intrusion rate but only in the divided attention condition. In the focused attention condition, a negative correlation occurred. These results may suggest that psychotic persons cannot concentrate on the relevant information, particularly if they have to divide their attention among several stimuli. However, in the study by Szymura and Nęcka (1998) participants scoring high on the psychoticism scale obtained better results in a divided attention test (DIVA), particularly in the more demanding dual-task conditions.

The contradictory nature of data reported by Rawlings (1985), on the one hand, and Szymura and Nęcka (1998), on the other, prompted Aleksandra Gruszka (1999) to investigate this problem in a new way. The author employed two experimental procedures: the negative priming task (McDowd and Oseas-Kreger, 1991) and the Navon (1977) task. The first procedure allows measurement of the strength of cognitive inhibition, whereas the second serves as a measure of the susceptibility to interference. The author found that psychotic persons were characterized by increased susceptibility to interference, particularly if the global aspects of stimulation were supposed to be neglected. However, she was unable to prove that high levels of psychoticism were associated with decreased cognitive inhibition.

Scarcity of data concerning the cognitive aspects of psychoticism makes it rather difficult to validate the formerly stated hypotheses. The data obtained by Rawlings (1985), Szymura and Nęcka (1998) and Gruszka (1999) are not conclusive enough to validate the hypothesis that psychoticism reveals systematic relationships with the concentration of attentional effort. They are intriguing enough, however, to suggest the existence of cognitive mechanisms of this dimension of personality. Further research should make this relationship more understandable.

CONCLUSIONS

Let us conclude this chapter with two remarks. First, there is a problem of the direction of causation. In the field of intelligence research, it is customary to account for complex traits, for example, IQ level, in terms of certain elementary cognitive mechanisms, for example, attention (Hunt and Lansman, 1982; Nęcka, 1996). According to this line of reasoning, behavioural traits are rather complex and heterogeneous in nature, so they do not work properly as explanatory factors. Elementary cognitive mechanisms seem much more convenient from this point of view. Hence, it is frequently stated that somebody presents high level of intelligence because he or she has capacious working memory or resourceful attention. However, the correlational nature of the relationship between intelligence and attention allows the opposite explanation as well, which assumes that the efficiency of elementary cognitive mechanisms depends on the level of intelligence.

This kind of explanation is much more easy to maintain in the case of personality dimensions. Such dimensions, particularly the 'superfactors' of neuroticism, extraversion and psychoticism, seem elementary enough to serve quite well as explanatory factors for the cognitive mechanisms of attention. According to such a view, our attention is more or less vulnerable to specific failures due to the biological mechanisms underlying the PEN traits. However, the problem of direction of causation cannot be solved easily on empirical grounds.

Second, there is a question of practical implications of the discussed relationships because research on attention is as much purely theoretical as it is applied in nature. Should air traffic controllers be selected on the basis of their selectivity skills, dual-task control and ability to concentrate mental energy? Or should they be picked on the basis of their emotional stability, extraversion and lack of psychotic tendencies? The review provided in this chapter suggests that cognitive and personality mechanisms, as well as a variety of other factors (e.g. social, environmental), may interact in determination of successful performance on difficult and highly stressful jobs, like air traffic control or stock exchange brokerage. Moreover, this review suggests that there may exist certain typical ways of attentional functioning, systematically associated with personality dimensions. From the practical point of view, every major personality dimension has its specific weaknesses concerning the mechanism of attention, which could perhaps be compensated through careful training. For that reason, neurotic persons should be helped with development of their selective attention skills, whereas introverts may need some coaching in dual-task performance. As to psychotic individuals, the situation is not clear enough to suggest specific modes of training, although we believe that such recommendations will be possible thanks to new research in the field.

NOTES

1 'Attended channel' and 'ignored channel' are terms used in the attention literature to denote the relevant and irrelevant sources of stimulation.

REFERENCES

Anderson, K. J. and Revelle, W. (1994) 'Impulsivity and time of day: Is rate of change in arousal a function of impulsivity?', *Journal of Personality and Social Psychology* 67: 334–344.

Broadbent, D. E. (1958) *Perception and Communication*. London: Pergamon Press.

Bullen, J. G. and Himsley, D. R. (1984) 'Psychoticism and visual recognition threshold', *Personality and Individual Differences* 5: 633–648.

Eysenck, H. J. (1952) 'The organization of personality', *Journal of Personality* 20: 101–117.

Eysenck, H. J. (1967) *The Biological Basis of Personality*. Springfield: Thomas.

Eysenck, H. J. and Eysenck, M. W. (1985) *Personality and Individual Differences: A Natural Science Approach*. New York: Plenum Press.

Eysenck, M. W. (1992) *Anxiety: The Cognitive Perspective*. Hove, UK: Lawrence Erlbaum Associates Ltd.

Eysenck, M. W. (1997) *Anxiety and Cognition: A Unified Theory*. Hove, UK: Psychology Press.

Eysenck, S. B. G., Eysenck, H. J. and Barrett, P. (1985) 'A revised version of the Psychoticism scale', *Personality and Individual Differences* 6: 21–29.

Gale, A. (1981) 'EEG studies of extraversion-introversion: What is the next step?', in R. Lynn (ed.) *Dimensions of Personality*, Ch. 8, pp. 181–207. Oxford: Pergamon Press.

Gale, A. (1983) 'Electroencephalographic studies of extraversion–introversion: A case study in the psychophysiology of individual differences', *Personality and Individual Differences* 4: 371–380.

Gray, J. A. (1978) 'The neuropsychology of anxiety', *British Journal of Psychology* 69: 417–434.

Gray, J. A. (1981) 'A critique of Eysenck's theory of personality', in H. J. Eysenck (ed.) *Model of Personality*, pp. 124–276. Berlin: Springer-Verlag.

Gray, J. A. (1982) *The Neuropsychology of Anxiety: An Enquiry into the Functions of the Septohippocampal System*. Oxford: Oxford University Press.

Gruszka, A. (1999) 'Relationships between basic personality dimensions and the attentional mechanism of cognitive inhibition', *Polish Psychological Bulletin* 30: 129–142.

Humphreys, M. S. and Revelle, W. (1984) 'Personality, motivation, and performance: A theory of the relationship between individual differences and information processing', *Psychological Review* 91: 153–184.

Hunt, E. B. and Lansman, M. (1982) 'Individual differences in attention', in R. J. Sternberg (ed.) *Advances in the Psychology of Human Intelligence*, vol. 1, pp. 207–254. Hillsdale, NJ: Lawrence Erlbaum Associates Inc.

Kahneman, D. (1973) *Attention and Effort*. New Jersey: Prentice Hall.

Kaiser J., Barry, R. J. and Beauvale, A. (2001) 'Evoked cardiac response correlates of cognitive processing and dimensions of personality: Eysenck's concept of psychoticism revisited', *Personality and Individual Differences* 30: 657–668.

Kaiser J., Beauvale, A. and Bener, J. (1997) 'Evoked cardiac response as a function of cognitive load differs between subjects separated on the main personality dimensions', *Personality and Individual Differences* 22: 241–248.

McDowd, J. M. and Oseas-Kreger, D. M. (1991) 'Aging, inhibitory processes, and negative priming', *Journal of Gerontology* 46: 340–345.

Mackworth, J. F. (1970) *Vigilance and Attention*. Baltimore: Penguin.

Matthews, G. (1986) 'The interactive effects of extraversion and arousal on performance: Are creativity tests anomalous?', *Personality and Individual Differences* 7: 751–761.

Matthews, G. (1987) 'Personality and multidimensional arousal: A study of two dimensions of extraversion', *Personality and Individual Differences* 8: 9–16.

Matthews, G. and Amelang, M. (1993) 'Extraversion, arousal theory and performance: A study of individual differences in the EEG', *Personality and Individual Differences* 14: 347–363.

Matthews, G., Jones, D. M. and Chamberlain, A. G. (1989) 'Interactive effects of extraversion and arousal on attentional task performance: Multiple resources or encoding processes?', *Journal of Personality and Social Psychology* 56: 629–638.

Navon, D. (1977) 'Forest before trees: The precedence of global features in visual perception', *Cognitive Psychology* 9: 353–383.

Nęcka, E. (1996) 'The attentive mind: Intelligence in relation to selective attention, sustained attention, and dual-task performance', *Polish Psychological Bulletin* 27: 3–24.

Nęcka, E. and Szymura, B. (2001) 'Who has the temperament to attend? Neuroticism, extraversion, and the mechanisms of attention', *Polish Psychological Bulletin* 32: 159–166.

Rawlings, D. (1985) 'Psychoticism, creativity, and dichotic shadowing', *Personality and Individual Differences* 6: 737–742.

Reed, S. K. (1988) 'Attention', in S. K. Reed *Cognition: Theory and Applications*, Ch. 3, pp. 35–54. California: Brooks/Cole.

Revelle, W. (1993) 'Individual differences in personality and motivation: "Non-cognitive" determinants of cognitive performance', in A. Baddeley and

L. Weiskrantz (eds) *Attention: Selection, Awareness, and Control. A Tribute to Donald Broadbent*, pp. 346–373. Oxford: Clarendon Press.

Revelle, W. and Anderson, K. J. (1992) 'Models for the testing of theory', in A. Gale and M. W. Eysenck (eds) *Handbook of Individual Differences: Biological Perspectives*, pp. 81–113. Chichester: Wiley.

Stavridou, A. and Furnham, A. (1996) 'The relationship between psychoticism, trait creativity and the attentional mechanism of cognitive inhibition', *Personality and Individual Differences* 21: 143–153.

Stenberg, G., Wendt, P. and Risberg, J. (1993) 'Regional cerebral blood flow and extraversion', *Personality and Individual Differences* 16: 547–554.

Stroop, J. R. (1935) 'Studies on interference in serial verbal reactions', *Journal of Experimental Psychology* 18: 643–662.

Szymura, B. and Nęcka, E. (1998) 'Visual selective attention and personality: An experimental verification of three models of extroversion', *Personality and Individual Differences* 24: 713–729.

Szymura, B. and Słabosz, A. (2002) 'Uwaga selektywna a pozytywne i negatywne konsekwencje automatyzacji czynności' [Selective attention and positive and negative consequences of automatization of information processing], *Studia Psychologiczne* 40: 161–183.

Szymura, B. and Wodniecka, Z. (2003) 'What really bothers neurotics? In search for factors impairing attentional performance', *Personality and Individual Differences* 34: 109–126.

Szymura, B., Waluszko A. and Stachów, D. (2003) 'Neurotyzm i lęk jako determinaty procesów poznawczych' [Neuroticism and anxiety as determinants of cognitive processes], *Przegląd Psychologiczny* 46: 197–200.

Treisman, A. M. (1960) 'Contextual cues in selective listening', *Quarterly Journal of Experimental Psychology* 12: 242–248.

Chapter 5

Personality, trait complexes and adult intelligence

Phillip L. Ackerman

To a substantial degree, modern personality theory and assessments have developed largely independent of other trait families (such as intelligence and interests). I provide a brief review of the history of such developments, and a justification for re-examination of the common variance among trait families. In a meta-analysis and review, Ackerman and Heggestad (1997) demonstrated that there are important communalities across personality, intelligence and other trait families (e.g. self-concept and interests). Many significant correlations can be found, but there appear to be several major 'trait complexes' (where trait complexes refer to sets of traits that are sufficiently interrelated to suggest exploration of mutually causal interdependencies). The existence of these complexes indicates that, for adults, various personality, interest and ability traits cluster together in a way that suggests mutually supportive roles among the different domains. For example, two trait complexes (Social and Clerical/Conventional) represent individuals whom we expect to be *less* likely to pursue intellectual development opportunities, while the other two trait complexes (Science/Math and Intellectual/Cultural) appear to be closely identified with an orientation toward learning and knowledge acquisition. In a review of empirical investigations, I discuss how these trait complexes are associated with individual differences in the breadth and depth of knowledge across a wide adult age span. In addition, I will discuss how these trait complexes suggest potentially critical gaps in our representation of personality constructs, as they relate to intelligence and interests. This research perspective provides a substantial impetus for reinvigorating both theory and application of trait research in personality and other domains.

INTRODUCTION AND BACKGROUND

Personality trait theory has changed markedly over the last century, partly in concert with 100 years of developments in personality assessment and application (e.g. see Kanfer *et al.*, 1995, for a review). Early developments at personality assessment focused mainly on single traits such as Allport's (1928) Ascendence-Submission Test or the Pressey (Cross-Out) X-O Tests for Investigating the Emotions (Pressey and Pressey, 1919). Gradually, however, investigators sought to capture a broader representation of personality traits as multiple-trait inventories were created, such as the Bernreuter Personality

Inventory (Bernreuter, 1933a, 1933b) and the Humm-Wadsworth Temperament Scale (Humm and Wadsworth, 1933a, 1933b). Such approaches culmin-
ated in the development of the Minnesota Multiphasic Personality Inventory
for assessment of psychopathology (Hathaway and McKinley, 1940) and
multiple-trait personality inventories for normal populations (such as the
Personality Research Form, Jackson, 1967, and the California Personality
Inventory, Gough, 1957).

However, some theorists found relatively blurred lines between mainstream
views of personality traits and other trait families, such as abilities, interests
and attitudes. Guilford (1959) proposed that personality is composed of
seven different identifiable trait families, including: temperament, aptitudes,
attitudes, interests, needs, physiology and morphology. Cattell (1946) similarly proposed many sources of interaction among cognitive, affective and
conative traits. Nonetheless, most subsequent approaches to personality
assessment have largely eliminated consideration of non-temperament traits.
In doing so, theoretical developments for personality, intelligence and other
traits have developed independently.

Modern depictions of the respective nomological networks of intellectual
ability constructs and personality trait constructs find relatively few overlapping hypothetical constructs (with the exception of the personality trait of
openness to experience/intellectance/culture, about which more will be said
below). It is perhaps ironic, however, that several theoretical orientations have
been provided that cast this as a false separation, when it comes to the opera-
tionalizations for measurement of these respective domains. Cattell (1946),
for example, claimed that no single behaviour can be identified with a single
'modality'. Rather, behaviours are a function of three different modalities,
which generally correspond to Plato's depiction of trait families (cognitive,
affective and conative). Cattell referred to the three modalities as 'ability',
'temperament', and 'dynamic traits' (where dynamic traits include a somewhat broader domain of 'interests, attitudes, and sentiments' (Cattell, 1946,
p. 62).

In this sense, it is entirely reasonable to expect that criterion variables, such
as everyday behaviours, will have nontrivial communalities among traits
across these domains. For example, whether an individual shows up to work
on time or is substantially late will be dependent to a greater or lesser degree
on the interactive influences of ability, personality and motivational traits.
The individual's standing on Conscientiousness might capture a general preference of the person to be punctual in arriving to work, but the individual
might not have the requisite ability to efficiently remember where the car keys
were put the previous evening, or the person might also be attempting to
satisfy other competing goals (such as helping a child with an overdue home-
work assignment from school).

Cattell's (1946) thrust, though, also encompasses the measurement of
traits. As noted by Terman (1924), trait assessments can be thought of as

psychological experiments. As such, assessments can induce a relatively higher or lower number of constraints. Butler and Fiske (1955; Fiske and Butler, 1963) for example, noted that personality assessments can be highly constrained experiments, in an attempt to reduce or constrain the influence of traits that are not of direct interest. The constraints may or not be successful in reducing variance, say, of motivations to look good to the therapist or the organizational human resources professional, but it would be fair to say that no formal personality assessment can effectively eliminate the influence of cognitive and conative traits. Even such influences of reading ability or verbal fluency are bound to have some influence on the individual's level of under-standing or vocalizations, respectively, on a personality assessment instrument. Numerous other examples can be found for such influences with respect to personality assessment. Motivational traits may represent what the assessor is looking for (e.g. dependability in a context of selecting a security guard; extraversion in the context of selecting salespeople, lack of thrill seeking in selection of airline pilots, and so on). Much of the recent literature on response sets and 'faking' has attempted to quantify just how much variance in personality trait assessments may be accounted for by different motivational orientations or attitudes toward the test (e.g. see Rosse *et al.*, 1998).

Only with surreptitious naturalistic observation over an extended period can one hope to assess personality trait tendencies, by assuming that sufficient heterogeneity (with respect to cognitive and conative demands) in the situations observed will cancel one another out in the long run. Such would be the approach advocated by Humphreys (1962), within a facet-based assessment strategy. That is, the same trait would be assessed across a complete crossing of all other influences, so that the only common variance would be attributed to the trait in question. Although projective personality assessments are used with a lower frequency in the past 30 or 40 years, the inherent ambiguity of such measures increases the potential confounds of non-personality traits rather than decreases them. Given the low practicality of such assessments, it seems much more reasonable simply to accept that both personality trait assessments and behaviours outside the testing situation are jointly affected by cognitive, affective and conative influences. Once we accept this proposition, it becomes appropriate to inquire about the extent of the commonalities among these different trait families.

TYPICAL BEHAVIOURS VS. MAXIMAL PERFORMANCE

One important reason for the historical dissociation between personality trait assessments and at least some measures of intellectual ability is that there is a mismatch between the aims of the assessments. Such a mismatch is implied in that most ability assessments are aimed at eliciting maximal effort on the part of the examinee (see Ackerman, 1994, 1996). Starting as early as with the Binet-Simon intelligence scales, the examiner is instructed to establish rapport with the examinee and to encourage the examinee to give the task maximal attention and effort (e.g. Binet and Simon, 1911/1915). Such ability assessments are assumed to capture what the individual 'can do', which may or may not be what the individual will do, under circumstances outside the testing room. This approach makes sense for theoretical purposes, when the assessor is interested in inferring an individual's capabilities, independent of his or her day-to-day motivational state.

However, personality trait assessments aim at an entirely different construct: that is, how the individual *typically* behaves, rather than how the individual is capable of behaving (e.g. see Cronbach, 1949; Fiske and Butler, 1963). Thus, most personality assessment instruments ask the respondent what he or she enjoys doing, or how he or she typically responds to a situation.[1] Predictions from such assessments focus on the individual's behaviour across many situations. The principle of aggregation is key to the concept of trans-situational personality traits, in contrast to behaviours elicited in the presence of a strong external environmental press. As a side note, the distinction between specific situations and trans-situational tendencies is the key to the resolution of the trait – situation controversy which raged in the social psychology and personality psychology literatures 20 or 30 years ago (e.g. see Rushton, Brainerd, and Pressley, 1983).

Where does this mismatch of typical behaviours and maximal performance leave investigators interested in personality–intelligence relations? On one level, it suggests that correlations between personality trait measures and intelligence measures may not be all that large, given the lack of Brunswik Symmetry between one family of traits and the other (e.g. see Wittman and Süß, 1999).[2] However, this anticipates the results of a personality–intelligence relations meta-analysis, which will be discussed in a later section. On another level, the mismatch suggests that we should more closely differentiate the wide range of ability measures that underlie intelligence, in the hope of finding ability traits that are more or less likely to be associated with typical behaviours or maximal performance. This approach turns out to provide a useful means toward further examining personality–intelligence relations, but it requires a short review of extant ability theory.

Fluid intelligence and crystallized intelligence

In the early 1940s Cattell (1943) and Hebb (1942) separately introduced the notion that intelligence is not best considered a unitary construct (such as Spearman's *g*), but rather that adult intelligence is better considered as two related but distinct constructs – one that is more physiologically based (and is identified with abstract reasoning, immediate memory, and similar processes), and another that is more educationally or experientially based (and identified mostly with verbal abilities and general knowledge). Hebb called these intelligences A and B, respectively, but Cattell's terms of fluid intelligence (*gf*) and crystallized intelligence (*gc*) have become the standard referents for these different domains of intelligence. For present purposes, the most important aspect of these types of intelligence, is that *gf* is hypothesized to represent a set of abilities that is less influenced by environment, while *gc* is hypothesized to be mainly influenced by an individual's long-term investment of *gf* through educational and experiential activities. The only complicating factor is that while *gf* is relatively tractable with standard ability tests, there are as many facets of *gc* as there are domains of knowledge and skills (Cattell, 1957). Traditional measures of *gc* concentrate on verbal abilities or broad cultural knowledge, but domain-specific knowledge (such as academic, occupational, and avocational knowledge domains) also falls under the broad heading of *gc*.

Although there is no small amount of controversy about the finer points of Cattell's theory of intelligence (e.g. see Carroll, 1993; Guilford, 1980; Humphreys, 1967), the prospect of operationally separating these kinds of intelligence has important implications for differentiating personality–intelligence relationships. Theoretically *gc* is more associated with typical behaviours (such as intellectual effort in and out of school), and *gf* is less associated with any specific environmental influences. Thus, measures of *gf* will have the highest potential of association with personality traits that are more rooted in physiological processes, such as neuroticism (e.g. see Matthews and Deary, 1998). Conversely, measures of *gc* may be more highly associated with personality traits that capture typical behaviours in intellectual engagement or cultural openness.

Typical intellectual engagement

Based on the framework described above separating *gf* and *gc*, Goff and Ackerman (1992) attempted to test the notion that *gc* would be more highly related to intellectually oriented personality than would *gf* (see also Ackerman, 1994). We developed a personality scale called Typical Intellectual Engagement (TIE) that described intellectual behaviours and asked respondents whether they typically enjoyed and/or engaged in such behaviours: for example, 'I enjoy the challenge of reading a complicated novel.' 'I would rather study than watch television.' 'Sometimes I like to consider concepts even if they may be of no practical consequence.' We predicted that such a personality trait would be substantially associated with *gc*, which reflects an accumulation of intellectually oriented behaviour over a long time period. We also predicted that the TIE measure would be less associated with *gf*, as *gf* was expected to be relatively uninfluenced by such an intellectual orientation. Across several studies, both of these predictions were supported by empirical data. On average, TIE scores correlate $r = 0.30$ to 0.40 with estimates of *Gc*, but correlate $r = -0.23$ to 0.10 with estimates of gf (e.g. see Ackerman and Heggestad, 1997). In addition, TIE scores also correlate highly with individual differences in domain knowledge in the areas of humanities and social sciences (domains highly associated with verbal abilities and gc), but correlate less with domain knowledge in the physical sciences and mathematics (domains that are more associated with gf type abilities, such as abstract reasoning and working memory).[3]

TIE is also substantially, but not univocally, associated with more traditional personality traits of culture and openness to experience (Ackerman and Goff, 1994; Rocklin, 1994). By linking a set of intellectual abilities most highly associated with 'typical' behaviours with a personality trait measured in the same context, it seems clear that it is possible to obtain a greater Brunswik Symmetry (Wittmann and Süß, 1999), and thus higher correlations than are usually found between personality measures and omnibus intelligence tests. The next section reviews the broader corpus of data relating particular personality traits and particular intellectual abilities.

META-ANALYSIS OF PERSONALITY AND INTELLIGENCE RELATIONS

Although some theoretical orientations (e.g. Eysenck, 1995) have previously suggested that there are specific non-linear relations between particular personality traits and intelligence, there are several problems with empirically evaluating such claims. First, extreme scores on personality trait measures are often associated with psychopathology, which in turn is associated not just with intellectual deficits, but also a wide variety of other adjustment-related issues. It is thus not clear whether findings of lower intelligence associated with extreme personality traits can discriminate between a general relationship between traits or a common cause for pathology. In addition, non-linear relations found among normal populations cannot be readily generalized, because different assessment instantiations of the same or similar traits are not similarly scaled or similarly sensitive throughout the range of the trait. That is, in contrast to some standardized ability tests that discriminate equally well throughout the range-of-talent, different personality inventories tend to maximally discriminate at one or another point in the range of the trait expression. Thus, one measure may be capable of resolving a non-linear relationship, while another measure of the same trait may not, simply because it does not discriminate sufficiently at the inflection points of the underlying relationship.

Fortunately, for most intents and purposes, Pearson product-moment correlations are relatively robust even in the presence of modest non-linearity. So, even if one cannot adequately address non-linear relations in all but the largest sample size studies, it is possible to use Pearson correlations and meta-analytic procedures to get a rough idea of which personality traits over-lap with which intelligence traits. Ackerman and Heggestad (1997) performed such a meta-analysis, by examining 135 studies that reported correlations between at least one personality trait and at least one intellectual ability. The meta-analysis was performed on 188 independent samples, which yielded 2033 correlations and a total N of 64,592 individuals. The correlations were categorized by 10 different intellectual abilities and 19 different person-ality traits, for a total of 190 different intelligence–personality trait pairings.

Although some cells of the 10 × 19 matrix were empty (i.e. no studies that investigated specific pairings), there were several general findings. Personality traits that represent aspects of Neuroticism-Negative Emotionality and Psychoticism-Constraint (see Eysenck, 1970; Tellegen, 1982) tended to show negative correlations with a broad array of intellectual abilities. Personality traits of Extraversion and Positive Emotionality tended to have small, posi-tive correlations across many different intellectual abilities. In addition to general personality–intelligence relations, there were some specific relations. In particular, Openness to Experience, TIE, and Intellectance traits tended to be positively related to gc-type abilities, and unrelated to gf-type intellectual abilities. That is, consistent with the individual empirical studies of TIE and similar constructs, there appears to be a group of personality traits that is most highly associated with abilities reflective of cumulative investment in academic and intellectual pursuits.

Trait complexes

Demonstration that there are significant associations between some personal-ity traits and intellectual abilities is an important first step towards unifying previously divergent individual differences domains. It is possible to explore other trait families, such as vocational interests, self-concept, and motiv-ational traits, for common variance with personality and intelligence. In contrast to many personality–intelligence trait pairings, however, there are relatively few correlational studies that investigate commonality among these other families of traits. The most notable domain that lacks correlational data is that of vocational interests. This situation is largely due to the tra-ditional methodology for assessing vocational interests, starting with the work of the Carnegie Institute of Technology group (see Thurstone, 1952), which was followed by Cowdery and then Strong, resulting in the Strong Vocational Interest Blank (see Strong, 1952). In the view of these researchers, the best means for assessing vocational interests was to match a variety of personality, attitude, and interest questions to specific groups of occupational incum-bents. The principle underlying this work is that individuals are most suited to occupations where they share characteristics with most job incumbents. Moreover, several of the standard interest inventories are specifically designed so that they confound the intellectual demands of jobs with the content of the jobs (e.g. higher level work with physical objects, such as the occupation of scientist, or lower level work such as lab technician). So, traditional vocational interest inventories provide profiles, rather than scale scores. When scale scores are provided, few demonstrate substantial correlations with intellectual abilities.

The theoretical orientation of Holland (1959) and others (e.g. Roe, 1956; Guilford *et al.*, 1954) represented a partial shift away from the profile approach by identifying a small set of occupational themes (six, in the case of Holland). Although most applications of vocational interest assessment remain steeped in a typological approach, which does not lend itself to examination of trait correlations, it is possible to rework some measures to provide separate scale scores for each of the vocational themes (e.g. see Gottfredson, Jones and Holland, 1993; Randahl, 1991). When scale scores are correlated with personality and intelligence measures, clear sets of significant and substantial relations are found (for a review, see Ackerman and Heggestad, 1997). For example, Extraversion-related personality traits are highly associated with Enterprising and Social vocational interests. Conscientiousness and Traditionalism are substantially related to Conventional interests, which in turn, is related to perceptual speed and clerical abilities. Investigative and Artistic interests share communality with Openness to Experience and TIE, and thus with *gc*. Interestingly, Realistic interests, which are associated with spatial and mechanical abilities, do not show specific relations with any extant personality traits.

By integrating the meta-analysis of personality–intelligence relations with the data concerning relations between interests and both personality and intelligence traits, Ackerman and Heggestad (1997) found evidence for at least four broad groups of traits that had common variance, which they called Social, Clerical/Conventional, Science/Math and Intellectual/Cultural. The term applied to such combinations of traits is 'trait complexes' (Ackerman and Heggestad, 1997). The term has roots in what Snow (1963) called 'aptitude complexes' – which are combinations of traits that may be mutually supportive (or impeding) for learning. Snow was specifically interested in the potential for interactions between trait combinations and learning or instructional treatments (in the context of aptitude-treatment interactions). However, we can ask a more general question regarding such trait complexes. The question is whether such trait complexes are predictive of particular patterns of learning or behaviour, regardless of whether they have an independent or interactive role in such outcomes.

TRAIT COMPLEX RESEARCH

In recent years, we have completed studies that provide direct information on both the construct and criterion-related validity of the trait complexes that emerged from the meta-analysis. Below I describe a few of these studies, which also help shed light on the commonality among personality and intelligence. In keeping with the notion that the most likely place to find the effects of personality on intelligence is on *gc*, rather than *gf*, the focus of such research has been on the broader aspects of *gc*. Specifically we investigated the degree to which trait complexes are associated with domain knowledge – across areas of academic, current events and health areas. That is, when considering domain knowledge (in contrast to predicting individual differences in abilities per se), there is a greater potential role for mixtures of affective and conative traits to determine performance. The reason for this is that domain knowledge is much more dependent on typical intellectual investment over long time periods. Allocating maximal effort (trying harder, if you will) to a domain knowledge test is likely to yield relatively small increments in performance – simply because the examinee either knows or does not know the information prior to the examination, and cannot derive it during the administration of the test. Performance on a spatial analogy test, in contrast, is much more highly associated with maximal performance (and thus *gf*) than it is with typical performance, at least as traditionally assessed. Relatively few, if any, assessments of fluid abilities are constructed and administered in a fashion that encourages typical performance, rather than maximal performance (see Ackerman, 1994).

Trait complexes and domain knowledge

In two studies of adults between the ages of 18 and 70, we administered a large battery of trait measures, including personality, ability, interests, self-concept, and so on. The criterion measures were a set of nearly 20 domain knowledge tests, covering domains of physical sciences, civics, humanities and business (for details, see Ackerman and Rolfhus, 1999; Ackerman, 2000). The first sample (Ackerman and Rolfhus, 1999) included 143 college students and an older community sample ($N = 135$) between the ages of 30 and 59. The second sample ($N = 228$) minimized potential confounds of educational differences and age, by requiring that all participants had achieved at least a baccalaureate level of education (Ackerman, 2000). In both studies, trait complexes were evaluated by the use of factor analytic techniques, where personality, intelligence, interest and self-concept measures were simultaneously factored. The results of these factor analyses clearly show the replication of three of the previously suggested trait complexes, namely: Social, Science/Math and Intellectual Cultural (see Tables 5.1 and 5.2). Both factor solutions are orthogonal, meaning that the trait complexes are essentially uncorrelated. Thus, an individual's standing on one trait complex is not associated with the individual's standing on the other two trait complexes.

Scores on the trait complexes were formed by unit-weighted z-score composites of the variables with salient loadings on the trait-complex factors

Table 5.1 Factor analysis to reveal trait complexes (data from Ackerman and Rolfhus, 1999)

	Factor		
	Science/math	Intellectual/cultural	Social
Openness	−0.005	**0.803**	−0.046
Typical intellectual engagement (TIE)	0.135	**0.838**	0.109
Investigative interests	0.250	**0.638**	−0.033
Artistic interests	−0.085	**0.670**	0.040
Verbal self-concept	−0.070	**0.630**	0.066
Verbal ability	0.152	**0.608**	−0.373
Realistic interests	**0.390**	*0.320*	0.112
Math self-concept	**0.628**	*−0.339*	0.014
Mechanical self-concept	**0.653**	0.216	0.066
Spatial self-concept	**0.688**	0.211	0.141
Math ability	**0.502**	−0.190	−0.263
Spatial ability	**0.616**	0.034	−0.274
Extroversion	−0.075	−0.092	**0.662**
Social interests	0.047	0.234	**0.688**
Enterprising interests	0.004	−0.067	**0.586**

Note
Salient factor loadings shown in boldface.

Table 5.2 Factor analysis to reveal trait complexes (data from Ackerman, 2000)

	Factor		
	Science/math	Intellectual/cultural	Social
Social interests	−0.052	**0.314**	**0.703**
Enterprising interests	−0.084	0.130	**0.642**
Social potency	0.084	0.144	**0.569**
Social closeness	0.009	−0.088	**0.485**
Math self-concept	**0.772**	−0.218	−0.020
Spatial self-concept	**0.521**	−0.015	0.153
Science self-concept	**0.739**	−0.025	−0.029
Realistic interests	0.221	0.189	0.161
gf	**0.638**	0.116	**−0.313**
Artistic interests	−0.155	**0.671**	0.132
Absorption	−0.012	**0.533**	0.139
Typical intellectual engagement (TIE)	0.176	**0.709**	0.084
Verbal self-concept	−0.076	**0.580**	0.008
gc	**0.414**	**0.431**	−0.350

Note
Salient factor loadings shown in boldface. gf = fluid intelligence, gc = crystallized intelligence.

(excluding intelligence measures, which are already known to differentially correlate with domain knowledge). Then, the trait complex scores were correlated with domain knowledge. Correlations between trait complex scores and domain knowledge are shown in Figures 5.1 and 5.2). The correlations between trait complexes and domain knowledge are illuminating, with respect to understanding how different traits relate to where individuals presumably invest their cognitive effort over an extended period of their adult life. Scores on the Science/Math trait complex were associated with higher levels of domain knowledge, especially in the area of physical sciences. Scores on the Intellectual/Cultural trait complex were positively associated with most areas of domain knowledge, but most highly associated with Humanities knowledge. In contrast, scores on the Social trait complex were negatively associated with all of the measured knowledge domains.

In a follow-up study with college students (Ackerman *et al.*, 2001), a wider array of personality measures was administered, in conjunction with domain knowledge tests. In this study, the trait complexes were expanded, to generate

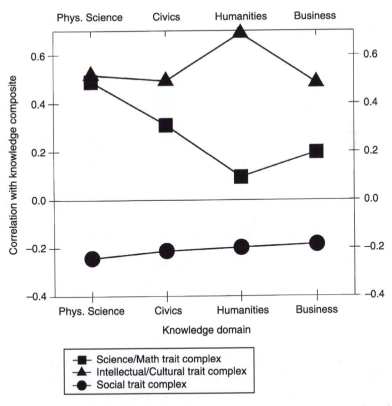

Figure 5.1 Correlations between trait complex scores and domain knowledge. Data from Ackerman and Rolfhus (1999).

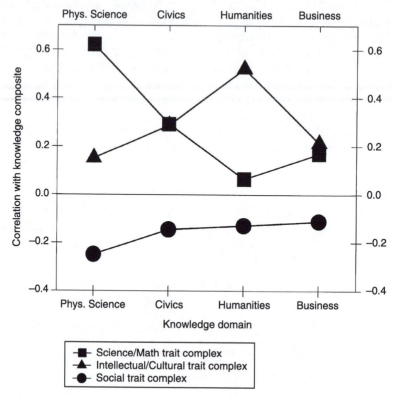

Figure 5.2 Correlations between trait complex scores and domain knowledge. Data from Ackerman (2000).

separate forms of the social trait complex (Social Closeness/Femininity and Social Potency/Enterprising), and an additional trait complex that included motivational traits along with a personality trait of Traditionalism. Consistent with the earlier results, these data indicated that the Science/Math and Intellectual/Cultural trait complexes are largely supportive of domain knowledge, but the other trait complexes were negatively associated (or impeding) of domain knowledge. A structural equation model of the results from this study is shown in Figure 5.3, illustrating both the positive and negative associations between trait complexes and domain knowledge.

Some of these identified trait complexes were also differentially and significantly associated with gender differences. Men had, on average, higher Science/Math/Technology trait complexes ($r = -0.22$ between dichotomously coded gender and trait complex scores). Women had, on average, higher scores on the Traditionalism/Worry/Emotionality trait complex ($r = 0.20$) and the Social Closeness/Femininity trait complex ($r = 0.28$). Together, these results suggest that an individual's standing on these trait complexes may be

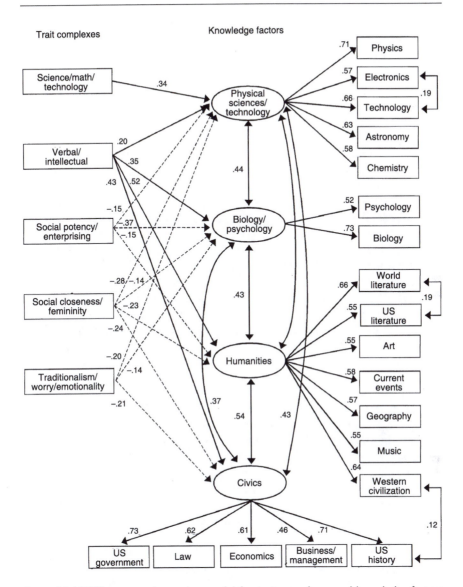

Figure 5.3 LISREL structural equation model for trait complexes and knowledge factors. Lines indicate significant path coefficients. Negative paths shown in dotted lines. From Ackerman, Bowen, Beier and Kanfer (2001). © American Psychological Association. Reprinted by permission.

intertwined with gender differences, that in turn determine both individual and group differences on domain knowledge tests, even when there is a high degree of commonality on motivation to perform well in acquisition of domain knowledge (see Ackerman, *et al.*, 2001, for a discussion of this issue).

WHAT'S MISSING?

The trait complexes identified so far represent only a small sampling of underlying cognitive, affective and conative communalities. Most of the research described to date has limited consideration to major trait families from each of these different domains. Expansion of the predictor space to include other somewhat narrower traits in each of these families, might be expected to both show other important sources of common variance, but also might help identify causal mechanisms underlying development and expression of adult intellect. One of the interesting aspects of the trait complexes resolved through the Ackerman and Heggestad (1997) meta-analysis is that there were no personality traits associated specifically with the Science/Math trait complex, nor were there any ability traits associated with the Social trait complex. Thus, it may very well be that personality theory and measurements could be usefully expanded to include traits that are associated with that which is common to math and spatial abilities and self-concepts, along with realistic and investigative interests. It may be that previously identified personality traits fit into this trait complex, such as Cattell's tough-minded personality trait, or some other trait that is not well represented in the literature correlating personality, interests and abilities. For the social trait complex, there is an abundance of extraversion-related personality traits that fit. However, there was not a substantive literature at the time comparing ability traits such as 'social intelligence' with extant personality and interest measures. It may be that aspects of so-called emotional intelligence may be fitted into this trait complex (e.g. see Zeidner, Matthews, and Roberts, 2001), or perhaps a new ability trait operationalization is needed.

CONTRACTION WITHIN TRAIT DOMAINS

It is interesting to observe that there have been serious attempts towards contraction of the construct space in each of the cognitive, affective and conative trait domains over the past 50 years. Although efforts to contract the cognitive ability domain started long before the middle of the last century (e.g. Spearman, 1904, 1927), the major controversies which focused on the number of important ability factors were prevalent through the 1930s and 1940s (e.g. Spearman, 1930; Thurstone, 1938). In the United States, the Primary Mental Ability orientation, offered by Thurstone and his colleagues (e.g. Thurstone and Thurstone, 1941; Thurstone, 1962), which specified at least seven major ability traits was prominent in both theory and practice through the 1970s. Such an approach is still quite popular in educational assessments, but there has been a disassociation between educational practice and both intelligence theory and industrial/occupational practice. In recent years, Spearman's view of an all-encompassing single general factor of intelligence (g) has gained a substantial following in both basic and applied research (e.g. Jensen, 1998; Hunter, 1986). For these adherents, there is little utility toward considering abilities that are narrower than a single broad dimension along which individuals can be ordered from intelligent to un-intelligent. Other approaches have focused on a more differentiated view (e.g. Horn, 1989; Carroll, 1993), thus there are more viewpoints on the nature of intelligence in modern ability theory.

Early efforts towards measurement of personality generated large taxonomies of personality traits (e.g. see Cattell, 1946). Dozens of different personality traits were hypothesized, and measures were developed to assess each of these traits. It should be noted, however, that many of these traits were examples of what Kelly (1927) called the 'jangle fallacy' – that is, different construct terms for the same trait. Nonetheless, there are parallels between the approach taken by personality researchers and ability researchers during this period. Where ability investigators like Guilford were proposing over 100 different separable, but relatively narrow intellectual abilities (Guilford, 1956), personality investigators were coming up with large lists of separable personality traits, such as the compendium of 49 personality factors identified by French (1953).

Although one can point to earlier influences, the major press towards contraction in the personality domain started in the 1960s, with the work by Tupes and Christal (1961), Norman (1963), and others (see Digman, 1990 for a review). However, a major source of influence in the adoption of a five-factor model of personality was the development and proliferation of the NEO Personality Inventory (Costa and McCrae, 1985). Hundreds if not thousands of studies concerning personality traits (and their correlates) have focused only on some or all of these five personality factors. Although many investigators still seek to expand the domain of personality by examination of other traits, and other investigators have called into question the adequacy and accuracy of the five-factor approach (e.g. Block, 1995), contraction in the field of personality trait research and application is a dominant theme for the field, at least as far as non-clinical personality assessment is concerned. That is, clinical applications tend to maintain a more differentiated view of psychopathic personality (e.g. the MMPI) than that adopted by researchers who study normal personality.

The vocational interest domain provides an interesting contrast to ability and personality trait theory. Specifically, early vocational interest assessments (such as the Strong, 1943) did not posit underlying traits at all, but rather approached interests in terms of empirically matching diverse interests and attitudes of individuals with those who were job incumbents in different occupations. Nonetheless, research in the 1950s converged on a relatively small set of replicable vocational interest factors (e.g. see Guilford, *et al.*, 1954; Roe, 1956), culminating in Holland's (1959) identification of six major interest themes. Holland's theory is one that still has prominence in the field, though others (e.g. Prediger, 1982) have suggested that even these six themes can be further contracted into two major interest dimensions: people/things and data/ideas (see Rounds and Tracey, 1993 for a contrast of these two approaches).

HOW MANY TRAITS?

If one were to take the reductionist approach from each of these three trait domains, we might only concern ourselves with only 12 traits to adequately describe individual differences across cognitive, affective and conative domains (one ability, five personality traits, and six interest themes). The advantage of such an approach is that each of the trait domains is refined to a level that is, for the most part, minimally associated with the other domains. For personality and intelligence, there are relatively few substantive correlations between general intelligence and three of the five dominant trait factors – Agreeableness, Conscientiousness and Extraversion. The trait complexes described earlier capture much of the common variance among abilities and Openness (positive correlations), and Neuroticism (negative correlations). Similarly, these trait complexes capture the higher associations between interest traits and personality traits, when considered from the Holland and five-factor model perspectives respectively (e.g. large correlations between Social and Enterprising interests and Extraversion). By using a reduced trait approach, the trait complex research described in this chapter provides a good 'first pass' toward finding communalities, and may serve as a starting point toward the development of integrative theory regarding the development of traits during childhood, adolescence and early adulthood.

It is important to note, however, that the five-factor approach to personality, the general ability framework for intelligence, and to some degree the six-theme framework for vocational interests, are poor theoretical vehicles for establishing a viable nomological network for understanding the wide range of cognitive, affective and conative traits. Each of these frameworks is at least partially drawn from the factor analytic approach to understanding intercorrelations of variables. While factor analysis is an obviously useful technique for data reduction, it remains somewhat controversial to maintain that factors represent something more than a convenient fiction. Moreover, one eventually retreats to the quagmire of the multiple determination of behaviour. Factor analysis can be used to statistically reduce a trait to what Allport

(1927) referred to as an 'independent statistical variable'. From this perspective, Allport suggested that 'a trait is a tendency to reaction which, when measured with reliability, demonstrates an independence with other variables'. But, as noted by Cattell (1946) and discussed earlier, behaviours are always a function of multiple influences across cognitive, affective and conative domains. For the purpose of theory development, unsophisticated use of factor analysis to refine traits to the lowest common denominator can result in either erroneous generalizations (e.g. see Block, 1995, for a discussion of this issue in personality research), or even mischaracterization of the functional relations among variables (e.g. see Armstrong, 1967, for a demonstration).

OBJECTIONS TO THE TRAIT COMPLEX APPROACH

A legitimate concern about the trait complex approach is that it attempts to combine traits at different levels of generality (such as gc on the ability domain, Investigative interests in the interest domain, and Openness to Experience in the personality domain). A few comments about this issue are appropriate. First, there is no inherent necessity of jointly considering traits at different levels of breadth – the history of the various individual research areas has resulted in approaches that minimize the number of underlying factors in each domain – but as noted earlier in this chapter, there are indeed alternative interpretations that have narrower or broader constructs in each of the respective domains of abilities, personality, interests, self-concept, and so on. Second, it is an empirical question whether the highest level of Brunswik Symmetry between, say, personality traits and intellectual abilities will be seen at different levels of respective generalities (e.g. general personality traits and specific intellectual abilities – though see Ackerman and Heggestad, 1997 for a meta-analysis and discussion of this issue). Third, in addition to data-reduction issues, there may be functional interactions between these various domains. For example, whether an individual is described as 'large' or 'small' is not usefully determined by either the person's height or weight, but by some combination of the two – similarly, judgements of physical attractiveness are based on the combination of related but different physical characteristics. Finding the optimal level of analysis for such considerations remains a task that requires an openness to different methods for weighting and combining disparate variables.

FINAL COMMENTS

The trait complex approach to finding underlying communalities among cognitive, affective and conative variables started as an inductive enterprise, which is certainly as acceptable as any other method within the context of discovery (Hanson, 1961). It is still early days in this domain, but without formal models and theory that seek to understand and predict how these communalities come about during human development, the approach will fail to satisfy the context of justification. It seems clear that such approaches will be based not on the highly reductionist models of ability, personality and interests, but rather on representations that have underlying genetic, bio-logical and environmental influences. In this fashion, we may come to understand why communalities are found between trait families, but also we may explain why the communalities within domains are found (such as the communalities that give rise to the five-factor model of personality). Providing the impetus for a more unified approach to trait interrelations across domains seems to yield promising results for both theory and applications. Rather than focusing on which trait family 'owns' the particular variance in behaviour that is accounted for, it appears to be more heuristically useful to orient toward potential synergies across trait families. For example, Holland (1959) speculated that interests and abilities develop during childhood in tandem, such that when a child encounters success in a particular domain (e.g. language or mathematics), both the interest to further engage in related activities and ultimately the ability perform in that domain will both show increments. Also, Kanfer, Ackerman and Heggestad (1996) showed that self-efficacy to perform a complex task was determined not by abilities *directly*, but rather the influence of objective abilities was mediated by individual differences in self-concept for those abilities. Decisions to engage in a particular task or even a decision to pursue a particular career are likely to be a complex function of such cognitive, affective and conative traits. The trait complex approach is one method for investigating these synergies that has been demonstrated to provide such an integrated perspective, that may in turn be useful for vocational counselling, occupational selection, and in the pursuit of optimal interventions for training. Applications may ultimately be based on profile interpretations of trait complexes, rather than separate interpretations and qualitative synthesis of individual assessments for cognitive, affective and conative traits.

NOTES

1 Although few studies have been conducted on performance-based tests of personality constructs, there do exist some attempts in this domain (e.g. see Willerman *et al.*, 1976; for a review, see Goldfried and Kent, 1972). Also, there have been some efforts aimed at developing self-estimates of personality-oriented competencies (e.g. see Paulhus and Martin, 1988).
2 According to Wittman and Süß (1999), Brunswik Symmetry refers to the degree of construct overlap between predictor traits and criterion traits. The overlap is a function of identifying the appropriate matching domains of each set of traits, and a function of matching the breadth of the constructs in both predictors and criteria

(e.g. matching broad criteria with broad traits and narrow criteria with narrow traits).

3 It may be useful to note that preferences for activities in the math and numerical domains (such as doing math puzzles in one's free time) have higher correlations with *gf* type abilities than the TIE scale does (Kanfer, 2003).

REFERENCES

Ackerman, P. L. (1994) 'Intelligence, attention, and learning: Maximal and typical performance', in D. K. Detterman (ed.) *Current Topics in Human Intelligence. Volume 4: Theories of Intelligence*, pp. 1–27. Norwood, NJ: Ablex.

Ackerman, P. L. (1996) 'A theory of adult intellectual development: process, personality, interests, and knowledge', *Intelligence* 22: 229–259.

Ackerman, P. L. (2000) 'Domain-specific knowledge as the "dark matter" of adult intelligence: gf/gc, personality and interest correlates', *Journal of Gerontology: Psychological Sciences* 55B, 2: P69–P84.

Ackerman, P. L. and Goff, M. (1994) 'Typical intellectual engagement and personality: Reply to Rocklin', *Journal of Educational Psychology* 86: 150–153.

Ackerman, P. L. and Heggestad, E. D. (1997) Intelligence, personality, and interests: Evidence for overlapping traits. *Psychological Bulletin* 121: 219–245.

Ackerman, P. L. and Rolfhus, E. L. (1999) 'The locus of adult intelligence: Knowledge, abilities, and non-ability traits', *Psychology and Aging* 14: 314–330.

Ackerman, P. L., Bowen, K. R., Beier, M. B. and Kanfer, R. (2001) 'Determinants of individual differences and gender differences in knowledge', *Journal of Educational Psychology* 93: 797–825.

Allport, G. W. (1927) 'Concepts of trait and personality', *Psychological Bulletin* 24: 284–293.

Allport, G. W. (1928) 'A test for ascendance-submission', *Journal of Abnormal and Social Psychology* 23: 118–136.

Armstrong, J. S. (1967) 'Derivation of theory by means of factor analysis or Tom Swift and his electric factor analysis machine', *American Statistician*, December: 18–21.

Bernreuter, R. G. (1933a) 'The theory and construction of the personality inventory', *Journal of Social Psychology* 4: 387–405.

Bernreuter, R. G. (1933b) 'The validity of the personality inventory', *Personnel Journal* 11: 383–386.

Binet, A. and Simon, T. (1911/1915) *A Method of Measuring the Development of the Intelligence of Young Children*, 3rd edn, trans. C. H. Town. Chicago, IL: Chicago Medical Book Co.

Block, J. (1995) 'A contrarian view of the five-factor model', *Psychological Bulletin* 117: 187–215.

Butler, J. M. and Fiske, D. W. (1955) 'Theory and techniques of assessment', *Annual Review of Psychology* 6: 327–356.

Carroll, J. B. (1993) *Human Cognitive Abilities: A Survey of Factor-analytic Studies*. Cambridge, MA: Cambridge University Press.

Cattell, R. B. (1943) 'The measurement of adult intelligence', *Psychological Bulletin* 40: 153–193.

Cattell, R. B. (1946) *Description and Measurement of Personality*. Yonkers-on-Hudson, NY: World Book Company.

Cattell, R. B. (1957) *Personality and Motivation*. New York: Harcourt, Brace.

Costa, P. T. and McCrae, R. R. (1985) *The NEO Personality Inventory Manual*. Odessa, FL: Psychological Assessment Resources.

Cronbach, L. J. (1949) *Essentials of Psychological Testing*. New York: Harper.

Digman, J. M. (1990) 'Personality structure: Emergence of the five-factor model', *Annual Review of Psychology* 41: 417–440.

Eysenck, H. J. (1970) *The Structure of Human Personality*, 3rd edn. London: Methuen.

Eysenck, H. J. (1995) *Genius: The Natural History of Creativity*. New York: Cambridge University Press.

Fiske, D. W. and Butler, J. M. (1963) 'The experimental conditions for measuring individual differences', *Educational and Psychological Measurement* 23: 249–266.

French, J. W. (1953) *The Description of Personality Measurements in Terms of Rotated Factors*. Princeton, NJ: Educational Testing Service.

Goff, M. and Ackerman, P. L. (1992) 'Personality–intelligence relations: Assessing typical intellectual engagement (TIE)', *Journal of Educational Psychology* 84: 537–552.

Goldfried, M. R. and Kent, R. N. (1972) 'Traditional versus behavioural personality assessment: A comparison of methodological and theoretical assumptions', *Psychological Bulletin* 77: 409–420.

Gottfredson, G. D., Jones, E. M. and Holland, J. L. (1993) 'Personality and vocational interests: The relation of Holland's six interest dimensions to five robust dimensions of personality', *Journal of Counseling Psychology* 40: 518–524.

Gough, H. G. (1957) *Manual for the California Psychological Inventory*. Palo Alto, CA: Consulting Psychologists Press.

Guilford, J. P. (1956) 'The structure of intellect', *Psychological Bulletin* 53, 4: 267–293.

Guilford, J. P. (1959) *Personality*. New York: McGraw-Hill.

Guilford, J. P. (1980) 'Fluid and crystallized intelligences: Two fanciful concepts', *Psychological Bulletin* 88: 406–412.

Guilford, J. P., Christensen, P. R., Bond, N. A. Jr. and Sutton, M. A. (1954) 'A factor analysis study of human interests', *Psychological Monographs: General and Applied* 68 (4 No. 375).

Hanson, N. R. (1961) 'Is there a logic of discovery?' in H. Feigl and G. Maxwell (eds) *Current Issues in the Philosophy of Science*, pp. 20–35. New York: Holt, Rinehart, and Winston.

Hathaway, S. R. and McKinley, J. C. (1940) 'A Multiphasic Personality Schedule (Minnesota): I. Construction of the schedule', *Journal of Psychology* 10: 249–225.

Hebb, D. O. (1942) 'The effect of early and late brain injury upon test scores, and the nature of normal adult intelligence', *Proceedings of the American Philosophical Society* 85: 275–292.

Holland, J. L. (1959) 'A theory of vocational choice', *Journal of Counseling Psychology* 6, 1: 35–45.

Horn, J. L. (1989) 'Cognitive diversity: A framework of learning', in P. L. Ackerman, R. J. Sternberg and R. Glaser (eds) *Learning and Individual Differences. Advances in Theory and Research*, pp. 61–116. New York: W. H. Freeman.

Humm, D. G. and Wadsworth, G. W. (1933a) 'The Humm-Wadsworth Temperament Scale Preliminary report', *Personnel Journal* 12: 314–323.

Humm, D. G. and Wadsworth, G. W. (1933b) 'A diagnostic inventory of temperament. A preliminary report', *Psychological Bulletin* 30: 602.

Humphreys, L. G. (1962) 'The organization of human abilities', *American Psychologist* 17: 475–483.

Humphreys, L. G. (1967) 'Critique of Cattell's "Theory of fluid and crystallized intelligence: A critical experiment"', *Journal of Educational Psychology* 58: 129–136.

Hunter, J. E. (1986) 'Cognitive ability, cognitive aptitude, job knowledge, and job performance', *Journal of Vocational Behavior* 29: 340–362.

Jackson, D. N. (1967) *Personality Research Form Manual*. Goshen, NY: Research Psychologists Press.

Jensen, A. R. (1998) *The G Factor: The Science of Mental Ability*. Westport, CT: Praeger.

Kanfer, R. (2003) Personal communication.

Kanfer, R., Ackerman, P. L., Murtha, T. and Goff, M. (1995) 'Personality and intelligence in industrial and organizational psychology', in D. H. Saklofske and M. Zeidner (eds) *International Handbook of Personality and Intelligence*, pp. 577–602. New York: Plenum Press.

Kanfer, R., Ackerman, P. L. and Heggestad, E. D. (1996) 'Motivational skills and self-regulation for learning: A trait perspective', *Learning and Individual Differences* 8: 185–209.

Kelly, T. L. (1927) *Interpretation of Educational Measurements*: Yonkers, NY: World Press.

Matthews, G. and Deary, I. J. (1998) *Personality Traits*. New York: Cambridge University Press.

Norman, W. T. (1963) 'Toward an adequate taxonomy of personality attributes: Replicated factor structure in peer nomination personality ratings', *Journal of Abnormal and Social Psychology* 66: 574–583.

Paulhus, D. L. and Martin, C. L. (1988) 'Functional flexibility: A new conception of interpersonal flexibility', *Journal of Personality and Social Psychology* 55: 88–101.

Prediger, D. J. (1982) 'Dimensions underlying Holland's hexagon: Missing link between interests and occupations', *Journal of Vocational Behavior* 21: 259–287.

Pressey, S. L. and Pressey, L. W. (1919) ' "Cross-out" tests, with suggestions as to a group scale of emotions', *Journal of Applied Psychology* 3: 138–150.

Randahl, G. J. (1991) 'A typological analysis of the relations between measured vocational interests and abilities', *Journal of Vocational Behavior* 38, 3: 333–350.

Rocklin, T. (1994) 'Relation between typical intellectual engagement and openness: Comment on Goff and Ackerman (1992)', *Journal of Educational Psychology* 86: 145–149.

Roe, A. (1956) *The Psychology of Occupations*. New York: Wiley.

Rosse, J. G., Stecher, M. D., Miller, J. L. and Levin, R. A. (1998) 'The impact of response distortion on preemployment personality testing and hiring decisions', *Journal of Applied Psychology* 83: 634–644.

Rounds, J., and Tracey, T. J. (1993) 'Prediger's dimensional representation of Holland's RIASEC circumplex', *Journal of Applied Psychology* 78, 6: 875–890.

Rushton, J. P., Brainerd, C. J. and Pressley, M. (1983) 'Behavioral development and construct validity: The principle of aggregation', *Psychological Bulletin* 94: 18–38.

Snow, R. E. (1963) 'Effects of learner characteristics in learning from instructional films', unpublished doctoral thesis. Purdue University. University Microfilms #6404928.

Spearman, C. (1904) ' "General intelligence," objectively determined and measured', *American Journal of Psychology* 15: 201–293.

Spearman, C. (1927) *The Nature of 'Intelligence' and the Principles of Cognition*. New York: Macmillan.

Spearman, C. (1930) 'Disturbers of tetrad differences: Scales', *Journal of Educational Psychology* 21: 559–573.

Strong, E. K. Jr. (1943) *Vocational Interests of Men and Women*. Palo Alto, CA: Stanford University Press.

Strong, E. K. Jr. (1952) 'Twenty year follow-up of medical interests', in L. L. Thurstone (ed.) *Applications of Psychology*. New York: Harper.

Tellegen, A. (1982) *Brief Manual for the Multidimensional Personality Questionnaire (MPQ)*. Minneapolis: A. Tellegen.

Terman, L. M. (1924) 'The mental test as a psychological method', *Psychological Review* 31: 93–117.

Thurstone, L. L. (1938) 'Primary mental abilities', *Psychometric Monographs* 1.

Thurstone, L. L. (ed.) (1952) *Applications of Psychology*. New York: Harper.

Thurstone, L. L. and Thurstone, T. G. (1941) 'Factorial studies of intelligence', *Psychometric Monograph* 2.

Thurstone, T. G. (1962) *Primary Mental Abilities*. Chicago: Science Research Associates.

Tupes, E. C. and Christal, R. E. (1961) *Recurrent Personality Factors Based on Trait Ratings (ASD-TR-61-97)*. Lackland Air Force Base, TX: Aeronautical Systems Division, Personnel Laboratory.

Willerman, L., Turner, R. G. and Peterson, M. (1976) 'A comparison of the predictive validity of typical and maximal personality measures', *Journal of Research in Personality* 10: 482–492.

Wittmann, W. W. and Süß, H.-M. (1999) 'Investigating the paths between working memory, intelligence, knowledge, and complex problem-solving performances via Brunswik Symmetry', in P. L. Ackerman, P. C. Kyllonen and R. D. Roberts (eds) *Learning and Individual Differences: Process, Trait, and Content Determinants*, pp. 77–108. Washington, DC: American Psychological Association.

Zeidner, M., Matthews, G. and Roberts, R. D. (2001) 'Slow down, you move too fast: Emotional intelligence remains an "elusive" intelligence', *Emotion* 1: 265–275.

Chapter 6

Phenotypes and genotypes of personality and intelligence

Similarities and differences

Nathan Brody

Personality traits and cognitive abilities may both be construed as heritable dispositions that influence the ways in which individuals respond to the social world. Using this very general starting point, I consider relationships between phenotypic and genotypic characteristics of personality and intelligence. The chapter is divided into five general sections. First, I consider differences in the measurement of these dispositions. Second, I contrast and compare behavioural genetic analyses in both domains. Third, I consider continuity and change in personality and intelligence. Fourth, I consider structural relationships between laboratory measures of basic processes and broader socially relevant outcomes. Fifth, the chapter concludes by sketching a very general model of isomorphic relationships between intelligence and personality that emphasizes the ways in which both may be construed within a common intellectual framework.

THE MEASUREMENT OF DISPOSITIONS

The data typically used to infer the values of personality and intellectual dispositions differ. Intelligence is measured behaviourally by sampling performance on a variety of tests that are measures of the ability to solve some type of cognitive problem. Self-reports and ratings are almost never used to assess intelligence. Personality is rarely assessed by sampling performance in situations that permit observations of trait-related behaviours. Self-reports and ratings are often used to measure personality and these are used as surrogates for direct observations of the behaviour of individuals. For example, the behaviour of being talkative is often used as a marker for Extraversion. Extraversion is typically assessed by self-reports or ratings of talkativeness rather than by the direct measure of the frequency of talking.

Measurement of intelligence

If a psychologist wished to measure the size of a person's vocabulary it would be possible to obtain a sampling of his or her ability to define a series of words. We do not obtain self-reports or ratings of a person's vocabulary. A more general index of verbal ability may also be readily obtained by aggregating performance in other verbal tasks, for example, solving verbal analogies. The verbal ability factor is clearly defined and the kinds of tasks that may be used to measure verbal ability are known. Measures of verbal ability obtained from different tasks are highly correlated. The Spearman-Brown prophecy formula implies that the hypothetical commonality that defines the latent trait is similar to the observed behaviourally defined aggregate index derived from performance on several different verbal ability measures. The rule of the indifference of the indicator applies implying that the precise choice of behavioural indices from the extraordinarily large set of potential indices is irrelevant.

Carroll (1993) re-analysed over 400 factor analytic investigations of cognitive abilities. His analyses led to a comprehensive taxonomy of intellectual abilities. Carroll's taxonomy contains three strata. There are eight second stratum ability factors that are rank ordered in terms of their loadings on a third stratum general factor – g. Carroll's analyses indicate the appropriate tests that may be used to measure factors at each stratum of his taxonomy. Thus g may be defined as the commonality among an appropriately sampled set of tests (measures) that load on each of several distinct second stratum factors. Since all of the tests that are to be sampled are positively correlated (they form a positive manifold) the g factors that are obtained from appropriate (i.e. diverse) sampling of the domain are similar. The principle of the indifference of the indicator applies supported by the Spearman-Brown prophecy formula. This analysis implies that it is possible to list an indefinitely large number of tests that may be used to construct an index of g. Since the tests listed are direct behavioural measures of performance on a task this implies that it is possible to develop a behaviourally defined index of each of several ability measures and g. The behaviourally defined measures of the hypothetical latent traits provide an index of the trait that is similar to the true score value of the trait.

Personality measurement

Personality traits such as Extraversion could be measured by observing a person in many different social situations. The behaviours that are indicative of Extraversion are specifiable. Funder and Sneed (1993) had undergraduates list behaviours that would be indicative of Extraversion in a social setting in which two strangers met to converse. They then videotaped the conversations and had the videotapes rated by another set of raters. They also obtained acquaintance ratings for extraverted behaviours for the subjects in their study. They found that acquaintance ratings of Extraversion were correlated with the ratings of behaviour that were indicative of Extraversion. Behaviour ratings of videotaped interactions of the 15 behaviours that were selected by lay raters as being most likely to be positively related to Extraversion were all positively correlated with acquaintance ratings of Extraversion. The nine behaviours that lay raters assumed were negatively related to Extraversion had negative correlations with the acquaintance ratings of Extraversion. These results indicate that lay people are aware of the behavioural manifestations of Extraversion. It should be possible to construct a behavioural description of Extraversion that would specify the situations in which an individual is likely to manifest behaviours that are indicative of this trait and to describe the kinds of behaviours that might be used to infer a person's level of Extraversion. In order to use such a hypothetical listing of behaviours to measure Extraversion, it would be necessary to observe a person in several different relevant situations and to aggregate indices of extraverted behaviour exhibited in each of several situations.

Funder and Sneed also found that acquaintance ratings of Neuroticism were not related to ratings of behaviours that were assumed to be indicative of Neuroticism in the situation in which two strangers conversed. They found that the correlations between acquaintance ratings of Neuroticism and behaviour ratings for the 13 behaviours selected by lay people as being indicative of Neuroticism ranged from −0.04 to 0.12. It is possible that this situation is not an appropriate setting in which to measure Neuroticism, or Neuroticism is not as directly manifested in a person's observable behaviour. Neuroticism as a socially undesirable trait may be concealed. In addition, traits that have an intrapersonal feeling component may be difficult to assess by behavioural observations.

It may be possible to measure personality traits behaviourally. But it has rarely been done (for a behavioural genetic analyses of traits incorporating behavioural observations see Spinath *et al.*, 2002; see also Funder, Furr and Colvin, 2000 for a discussion of Q-sort measurement of trait-related behaviours). There is no comprehensive listing of the appropriate behaviours that may be used to measure any personality trait. If we extrapolate from Funder and Sneed's findings with respect to Neuroticism, it is not even clear that such a behavioural index could be developed for some traits. Even where such a listing could be constructed it would be difficult to use in practice owing to the effort entailed in observing behaviours in several different social settings. Ratings and self-report methods of measurement are easy to use. They substitute for the practical and theoretical difficulty of behavioural measurement of personality traits.

Contrasts in the measurement of personality and intelligence

The measures of personality traits that are typically used in personality research are saturated with method-specific sources of variance, are usually not behavioural, and do not provide indices that are highly congruent with the true score value of the disposition. We measure intellectual dispositions and we infer the value of personality dispositions.

The measurement of intelligence is additionally advantaged. Indices of intellectual abilities for large and representative samples of several populations exist. For example, time series exist for measurements of the intelligence of the population of all male 18-year-olds in several European countries obtained as part of testing for universal military registration. Standard tests of intelligence such as the Wechsler tests are normed on representative samples of the population. Also, from time to time, intelligence tests have been administered to all students in various public schools. Thus it is possible to ascertain the distribution of intelligence in large and representative samples of the population of different countries. Comparable data sets do not exist for the measurement of personality dispositions.

Measurement and cohort and life-span changes

Differences in the adequacy of measurement of personality and intellectual dispositions lead to differences in the ability to address fundamental substantive issues in both domains. Consider cohort and life-span changes in both domains. Flynn (1998) documented cohort changes in intelligence (see also Neisser, 1998). Scores on various measures of intelligence have increased in all industrialized countries. This assertion is based on comprehensive analyses of tests given to representative samples of individuals or to entire populations (of males). Data exist for the same tests given at the same age to different cohorts. We do not have comparable data for personality. Are there secular changes in personality dispositions? We simply do not know with anything like the certainty with which we can infer the existence of secular changes in both g and in more narrowly defined intellectual abilities. Consider the claim that there are secular increases in depression. We do not have measurements of depression using the same instruments on representative samples of different cohorts assessed at the same age. Measurements of depression are not behavioural – they are typically based on self-reports of behaviours and feelings. Whether they are dependent on judgements by experts using rating scales or are based solely on self-report indices, the measures are ultimately derived from reports provided by subjects. Cohort effects in such indices may reflect changes in the disposition that they measure or secular changes in the way in which individuals describe their psychological states. It is difficult to know which of the two factors are at work. Comparable questions may be raised with respect to research on cohort effects on intelligence. Perhaps individuals have become more sophisticated test takers. While this is possible, the diversity of behavioural indices that may be used to measure either general or specific intellectual abilities renders such an interpretation somewhat more problematic in this domain than it does in the personality domain.

Similar issues exist with respect to the determination of changes in personality and intellectual dispositions over the life span. Intelligence declines over the life span. The declines, which begin to occur at an accelerated rate after the seventh decade of life, differ for different intellectual abilities. They are larger for measures of fluid ability than for measures of crystallized ability. Changes in intellectual abilities also influence the ability of people to perform many everyday tasks such as the ability to comprehend a newspaper article (see Willis and Schaie, 1986). Are there age-related changes in personality dispositions over the life span? There are studies indicating that there are changes in personality dispositions over the life span. Helson *et al.* (2002) report that Conscientiousness and Agreeableness exhibit increases of approximately one half a standard deviation over the adult life span and Neuroticism exhibits a comparable decline. Changes in fluid intelligence between age 25 and 81 in representative samples may exceed 1.5 standard deviation (see Brody, 1992, Chapter 8). These data indicate that changes in intelligence over the adult life span of individuals are larger than changes in personality. It is also the case that most of the evidence for changes in personality traits over the adult life span is based on self-report data. Changes in self-reports and ratings may simply reflect changes in the measures of personality that we use to infer dispositions rather than changes in the dispositions themselves. Even if we were to measure personality dispositions behaviourally we would be faced with the possibility that behavioural settings that are used to measure personality dispositions may not be invariant over the life span. The centrality of workplace settings declines for the elderly. The decline in independent residence for the aged creates a change in the behavioural settings in which individuals live their lives. If the settings in which behavioural observations are made change, then it is impossible to know whether or not observed changes reflect changes in the disposition that is being measured or changes in the measures that are used to infer the status of the disposition.

BEHAVIOURAL GENETICS

Both intelligence and personality dispositions are heritable. There may, however, be subtle differences in the structure of genetic and environmental influences on these dispositions

Magnitude

Standard estimates for the heritability of intelligence and personality traits indicate that adult intelligence has higher heritability than personality dispositions.

Intelligence

Several recent studies are compatible with heritability estimates for adult intelligence that are as high as 0.8. Consider, for example, the findings obtained in the Swedish study of older MZ and DZ twins reared together and apart (Pedersen *et al.*, 1992). Pedersen and her colleagues obtained correlations of 0.78 for MZ twins reared apart, 0.80 for MZ twins reared together, 0.32 for DZ twins reared apart and 0.22 for DZ twins reared together on measures of g for a systematically ascertained sample of older Swedish twins. The estimated heritability based on a model-fitting procedure for these data was 0.8.

Plomin *et al.* (1997) repeatedly administered intelligence tests to adopted children for the first 16 years of life in a longitudinal study. Their study also included a control sample of children reared in the same community by their natural parents. They obtained correlations between the IQs of the biological parents and the IQs of their adopted-away children at different ages. These correlations were compared to correlations between the IQs of the adoptive parents of these children and the IQs of their adopted children. In addition, correlations were obtained between the IQs of the biological parents in the control families who were rearing their natural children and the IQs of their children at comparable ages. The correlations between biological parents and children are quite similar for the biological parents who are rearing their children and for the biological parents whose children have been adopted-away and who have limited post-natal contact with their biological parents. Table 6.1 presents the terminal correlations between parents and children at age 16. Note that the terminal correlations reported at age 16 are marginally (but not statistically) higher for biological parents whose children have been adopted-away shortly after birth than the correlations for natural parents rearing their own children. The correlations between adopted parents and their adopted children are close to zero. Model fitting analysis for these data indicate that the heritability of intelligence is 0.56. These results indicate that the estimate of heritability derived from the Colorado Adoption Project study is lower than the estimate of heritability derived from the Swedish separated twin study. I focus on these two studies because they are, arguably,

Table 6.1 Parent–child correlations at age 16 (based on Plomin *et al.*, 1997)

Parent	r
Adoptive father to adopted child	0.11
Adoptive mother to adopted child	−0.05
Biological father to his adopted-away child	0.32
Biological mother to her adopted-away child	0.39
Control group father and his natural child	0.33
Control group mother and her natural child	0.28

the most informative contemporary studies of the heritability of intelligence. The Swedish study is informative because it includes data on separated MZ and DZ twins and is based on a systematically ascertained sample. The Colorado adoption study includes data on the intelligence of biological fathers and mothers, is longitudinal providing information about changes in relationships from childhood to late adolescence, and has a well-chosen control group.

The heritability estimates obtained in the Colorado Project may underestimate the heritability of g. The correlations between biological parents and their children who are adopted shortly after birth exhibit monotonic increases from age 1 to 16. The correlation of parent and child may not have reached its asymptotic value at age 16. If the correlation would continue to increase, then an estimate of heritability would be larger as the adopted children grow older. The obtained correlation is also influenced by restrictions in the range of talent of IQ among the biological parents. It is possible that the restriction in the range may attenuate the magnitude of the correlation between biological parents and their children who are reared in adopted families. If this analysis is correct, then the heritability values derived from the Colorado Project are too low.

My analysis of the outcomes of the Colorado and Swedish studies implies that the heritability of g is high – perhaps exceeding 0.5. More comprehensive analyses of the heritability of intelligence based on joint structural equation modelling of twin and family adoption data generally yield values closer to 0.5 (see Plomin and Spinath, 2003). These analyses include data from studies that are, for a variety of reasons, less informative than the data obtained from the Colorado and Swedish studies. While there is considerable uncertainty regarding the exact value of the heritability of adult intelligence in representative samples of individuals, it is clear that adult general intelligence is a heritable trait. Of course, heritability is not a property of the phenotype but is rather a property of the phenotype as measured in a particular population.

Personality

The heritability of personality traits is slightly lower than the heritability of intelligence. Loehlin (1992) summarized studies of the heritability of personality traits. His review is compatible with heritability estimates close to 0.4 or 0.5. MZ twins rarely correlate substantially above 0.5 on measures of personality and parents and children usually have correlations below 0.2, suggesting relatively moderate levels of heritability for personality traits. Estimates of the heritability of personality for adult samples are almost always based on self-reports and in a few instances on ratings. If such indices are imperfect measures of personality dispositions, then heritability estimates obtained from such data may not be accurate estimates of the heritability of personality dispositions. Studies of the heritability of personality traits that have used different methods of measurement of personality to obtain measures of personality dispositions less saturated with method specific variance have obtained heritability estimates that are closer to the values obtained for estimates of the heritability of intelligence. There are four studies that provide support for this assertion.

Heath *et al.* (1992) obtained co-twin ratings of Extraversion and Neuroticism as well as self-reports for these traits for a large sample of female twins. They formed a composite index of each of these traits based on both methods of measuring the traits. They obtained heritability estimates for Extraversion and Neuroticism for their composite indices of 0.73 and 0.63, respectively. These values are approximately 50 per cent higher than those obtained from the typical heritability estimates derived from twin studies based on analysis of self-report measures of these traits.

Riemann, Angleitner and Strelau (1997) obtained self-report ratings and ratings from two different peers for each of the Big Five traits. They obtained mean MZ correlations of 0.51 for the self-report measures of the traits and mean MZ correlations of 0.40 for single trait ratings. The disattenuated composite peer trait ratings yielded mean MZ correlations of 0.67. Comparable DZ mean correlations were less than half the value of the mean MZ twin correlations. The mean MZ correlation for the disattenuated peer rating measure is higher than that for a single peer rating and for the self-report measure. These results suggest that an estimate of heritability based either on self-reports or on single trait ratings is likely to be attenuated owing to the presence of error variance in the phenotypic measure of the trait. The mean MZ correlation of 0.67 is compatible with heritability estimates that are close to 0.7.

Kendler *et al.* (1993) used a longitudinal study to obtain two different measures of depression from a large sample of female twins. They obtained a self-report measure of depression and a measure of depression based on a psychiatric rating scale one year later. They obtained heritabilities close to 0.4 for each of their single method, single occasion measures of depression. The heritability of a composite index based on multi-method, multi-occasion measurement was 0.70. They noted that it is traditional to consider depression as a characteristic of persons that is moderately heritable and that is reliably assessed by single methods of measurement obtained on a single occasion. Their findings imply that depression is not reliably assessed by single methods of measurement obtained on a single occasion. More comprehensive indices based on multi-occasion, multi-method measurement imply that the disposition to experience depression is highly heritable.

Lykken *et al.* (1993) obtained measures of occupational and leisure interests in a sample of MZ twins reared together and apart and DZ twins. Their study was longitudinal and they obtained the same data three years later. They obtained correlations for different ways of aggregating these data including analyses for single items, for general factors, and for general factors corrected for attenuation using test-retest correlations as a basis for removing sources of variance attributable to instability. Table 6.2 presents the mean correlations obtained for these different levels of aggregation of their data. Note that for each of the three levels of aggregation mean correlations for MZ twins reared apart do not differ substantially from correlations for MZ twins reared together. Mean DZ twin correlations are approximately half the value of MZ correlations. Note also that the mean MZ correlations for the disattenuated factors are higher than the mean correlations for attenuated factors and items. These results imply that the heritabilities of single occasion measures are lower than the heritabilities of measures of enduring interests.

The four studies described above all point to a common conclusion. Heritability estimates for personality phenotypes are attenuated by method specific variance. Phenotypes that are based on multi-method, multi-occasion indices have higher heritability than mono-method single occasion measures. Although it may be premature to assert that the heritability of personality dispositions is as high as the heritability of g for adults, the available evidence suggests that the differences, if any, in the heritability of g and of personality dispositions are not large.

Additive and non-additive influences

The heritability of intelligence based on adoption studies of older children appears to be at least 0.5. This result implies that genetic influences on general intelligence are additive. If g were influenced by non-additive sources of variance, estimates of heritability for adoption studies would be lower than estimates of heritability derived from twin studies. Correlations for MZ twins reflect the influence of both additive and non-additive sources of genetic variance.

Behavioural genetic analyses of the heritability of personality traits have occasionally concluded that non-additive genetic influences are present. Loehlin's (1992) comprehensive review of behavioural genetic studies of the Big Five personality traits yielded a mean heritability estimate of 0.42. Additive genetic influences had a mean estimated value of 0.30 and non-additive influences had a value of 0.12 (see also Bouchard and Loehlin, 2001).

Cloninger *et al.* (1998) argued that there were discrepancies between

Table 6.2 Twin correlations for items, factors, and factors corrected for instability (based on Lykken *et al.*, 1993)

Twins	Items	Factors	Corrected factors
MZ reared together	0.32	0.49	0.66
MZ reared apart	0.34	0.42	0.58
DZ reared together	0.14	0.23	0.30

estimates of heritability based on twin studies and on adoption studies for the personality traits of harm avoidance, novelty seeking and persistence. Twin studies suggested heritability estimates between 0.4 and 0.6 for these traits and adoption studies suggested heritability values of 0.2 to 0.3 for these traits. They tested the hypothesis that these discrepancies were attributable to epistatic genetic influences. Cloninger *et al.* reported that as much as 38 per cent of the variance in harm avoidance was attributable to the influence of a genetic locus on chromosome 8. They found that a consideration of other genetic loci that did not have additive main effect influences on harm avoidance contributed additional predictive variance to harm avoidance trait measures. Loci on chromosomes 21q21–22.1, 18p and 20p added an additional 20 to 30 per cent of the explained variance on the trait measure. These results have not been replicated and should be viewed as suggestive rather than as a confirmed finding. The search for epistatic interactions is complicated by the exponential increase in possible false positive outcomes and the need to replicate results. What is interesting about the Cloninger study from the point of view of relationships between personality and intelligence is that it illustrates two respects in which there are discrepancies between research in these two domains. First, there is relatively little evidence for non-additive genetic influences for g. If this is correct, the search for epistatic influences on intelligence at the molecular level is not likely to be successful. Second, at the time of writing there are no replicated findings indicating that there are identifiable genes or genetic loci that are related to g (see Plomin, 2003). There is some evidence indicating that there are genetic loci related to personality traits (see Ebstein, Benjamin and Belmaker, 2003; Lesch, 2003) although there are many failures to replicate these findings. (For a summary of this area of research see Plomin *et al.*, 2003.)

Shared and non-shared environmental influences

Behavioural genetic analyses of personality and intelligence are in agreement with respect to the relative importance of shared and non-shared environmental influences after adolescence. Research in both domains suggests that shared environmental influences are vanishingly small. In early childhood shared environmental influences are important determinants of individual differences in intelligence (Spinath 2003). After adolescence, however, shared environmental influences are not important determinants of individual differences in intelligence. Differences in adult intelligence and personality between MZ (and in some rare instances DZ) twins reared together or apart are small. Differences in the degree of separation among MZ twins reared apart and differences in the relative social advantages associated with the family in which MZ twins were reared do not influence the magnitude of the correlations for intelligence obtained for MZ twins reared apart (see Pedersen *et al.*, 1992). DZ twin correlations rarely exceed half the value of

MZ correlations in both domains. Biologically unrelated older siblings reared in the same family show little or no similarity on measures of personality or intelligence (see Plomin and Daniels, 1987). These findings imply that most of the environmental influences that influence personality and adult intelligence are non-shared environmental influences that lead individuals reared in the same family to differ from one another.

Although behavioural genetic analyses of personality and intelligence indicate that non-shared environmental influences are larger than shared environmental influences, relatively little is known about such influences. Loehlin and Nichols (1976) studied differences in pairs of MZ twins. They were unable to relate personality differences among MZ twins to specific environmental events. While it is easy to document differences in the experiences of siblings reared in the same family, it has not been easy to discover systematic relationships between such differences and personality outcomes that are independent of genetic influences. Reiss et al. (2000) conducted a comprehensive investigation of siblings reared in the same family. They used a large and representative sample of siblings including various classes of siblings who differed in the degree to which they were biologically related and they obtained comprehensive measures of the differences in the environmental experiences of siblings. Although Reiss and his colleagues did find evidence indicating that differential parental negativity was associated with differences in adolescent antisocial behaviour, the effect was very small. They found that many non-shared environmental influences are heritable. One reason that individuals reared in the same family experience different environments is that they are genetically different. Those characteristics of the non-shared environment that are not heritable were, for the most part, unrelated to measures of personality. Genetic covariance analyses that consider the contribution of genetic and environmental components of variance to the relationship between measures indicate that genetic components of variance present in both personality measures and in non-shared environmental measures account for much of the phenotypic relationship between these two kinds of measures. Despite a massive research effort, Reiss and his colleagues were not able to ascertain the significant non-heritable sources of non-shared environmental variance that contribute to personality.

It has also been difficult to identify non-shared environmental sources of variance that contribute to intellectual development. Moffitt et al. (1993) studied changes in intelligence using a longitudinal design for a population of children between the ages of 7 and 13 in Dunedin, New Zealand. Changes in scores on tests of intelligence could be explained by random fluctuations in test scores. Approximately 10 per cent of the children in their study exhibited gains or losses in scores on tests of intelligence that appeared to be too large to be attributable to random fluctuations. Moffitt et al. collected data on 37 different environmental measures. Several of the measures could be construed as non-shared environmental events. Only three of the variables were related to systematic changes in intelligence – a number well within the range of the number of significant findings expected by chance. Moffitt *et al.* concluded that changes in intelligence were not systematically related to the environmental measures they investigated.

The available evidence indicates that the non-shared environmental events that influence the development of personality and intelligence are similarly opaque. I can think of two possible explanations for this state of affairs. In most behavioural genetic analyses non-shared environmental influences are treated as residuals and contain error variance as well as systematic sources of variance. If personality dispositions have heritabilities that are higher than has been previously thought, non-shared environmental influences that account for the largest portion of the remaining variance in the phenotype may be smaller than has been thought. Second, non-shared environmental influences may be idiographic. That is, they may be different for different individuals. They may consist of a large number of events that are likely to have small effects and perhaps different effects for different individuals. Even events that are assumed to have aversive effects such as divorce might have positive effects for some individuals. If this is correct, it will be difficult to develop law like relationships between particular non-shared environmental influences and individual differences in personality and intelligence.

Genetic X environmental interactions

Both personality and intelligence are subject to genetic X environmental interactions. Caspi *et al.* (2002) obtained an aggregate index of antisocial behaviour for young adults. They obtained a significant main effect for the relationship between measures of childhood abuse and antisocial behaviour. The main effect was modified by the presence of an interaction between the presence of a gene that regulates monoamine oxidase located on the X chromosome. The allele for this gene has been associated with violent behaviour. Individuals with the allele who had not experienced childhood abuse were no more likely to develop antisocial behaviour than individuals without this genotype. Individuals with the allele were more likely to develop antisocial behaviour if they were exposed to childhood abuse than individuals without this genotype who were exposed to childhood abuse. Thus the genotype may be viewed as a marker for a disposition to respond to particular environmental encounters with the development of antisocial behaviour. Alternatively, individuals without the allele may be described as having genotypes that render them less likely to develop antisocial behaviour in response to childhood abuse. It is interesting to note that the genotype is unrelated to the probability of encountering abusive environments in childhood. Thus the interaction obtained in this study cannot be attributed to genetic-environmental covariance in which individuals with a particular genotype are likely to elicit or encounter particular environments.

Rowe (2003) obtained evidence for a genetic X environmental interaction for intelligence using a genetically informative design based on comparisons between full and half sibling pairs, cousins reared together and MZ twins. He estimated the heritability of verbal intelligence as 0.74 for the subset of children reared in families whose parents had more than a high school education. For individuals reared in families with parents with less formal education, heritability of verbal intelligence was 0.24. In other analyses based on these data, Rowe, Jacobsen and Van den Oord (1999) reported near zero heritability for individuals reared in families by parents with less than an eighth grade education. Individuals with genotypes that might predispose them to develop high intelligence may be less likely to develop this phenotype if they are reared in educationally disadvantaged families.

The presence of genetic X environmental interactions indicates that the influence of genotypes on phenotypes is subject to modification by the environment.

Taxonomic structures

Explorations of correlation matrices using factor analysis led to the development of hierarchically arrayed taxonomies of personality and intelligence. Considerable support exists for a five-factor taxonomy in the domain of personality (see McCrae and Costa, 1990). Each of the Big Five has several facets consisting of more narrowly defined traits that are positively related to each other. The Big Five and their facets are hierarchically arrayed in a pyramidal structure going from narrow to more general traits. The taxonomic structure of intelligence developed by Carroll is also hierarchically arrayed.

Behavioural genetic analyses of relationships among diverse intellectual abilities and personality characteristics indicate that the taxonomic structures of personality and intelligence are isomorphic with the structure of genetic covariances. Genetic covariance analyses partition phenotypic relationships by a consideration of the extent to which they are attributable to genetic and environmental components of variance. These analyses attempt to ascertain the degree to which the relationship between two measures is attributable to genetic or environmental influences. If the correlation between two traits measured in different individuals varies as a function of the degree of genetic relationship of the individuals, it is possible to infer that the relationship between the traits is partially attributable to common genetic influences. Consider an example. There is a positive correlation between performance on tests of verbal ability and tests of spatial reasoning. A behavioural genetic analysis can be used to ascertain the extent to which genetic influences contribute to this relationship. Data from a twin study might be used to obtain cross-correlations between verbal and spatial ability test scores. In such an analysis, a score for an MZ twin on a spatial ability test would be correlated with his or her co-twins score on a verbal ability test. A cross-correlation is obtained for all of the MZ twin pairs. A comparable analysis is performed for all DZ twin pairs. If the cross-correlations between these measures were the same for MZ and DZ twin pairs, then it would be possible to infer that genes did not contribute to the relationship between these measures. If the cross-correlation for MZ twins is twice the value of the cross-correlation for DZ twins, this would imply that there are additive genetic influences that contribute to the relationship between verbal and spatial ability. If the cross-correlation between verbal and spatial ability for MZ twin pairs is less than twice the value of the comparable correlation for DZ twin pairs, this would imply that shared family influences might contribute to the relationship between verbal and spatial ability.

Petrill (2002) reviewed and re-analysed adoption and twin studies of the relationship between different ability measures. His analyses indicate that the cross-correlations between different intellectual abilities are related to the degree of genetic relationship among individuals. Cross-correlations between different intellectual ability measures are higher for MZ than for DZ twins. The general factor in the domain of intelligence is observable in an analysis of the genetic relationships among diverse intellectual abilities (see also Plomin and Spinath, 2002).

There is also evidence that genetic factors contribute to variations in narrower intellectual abilities. It is possible to statistically remove the variance attributable to g (the shared component of variance) in various measures of intelligence. Variance in measures of intellectual ability that is independent of g is heritable – although the level of heritability of these measures is lower than the heritability of g (see Cardon et al., 1992).

Genetic covariance analyses also indicate that phenotypic relationships among personality traits are isomorphic with genetic covariances among traits. Eaves, Eysenck and Martin (1989) analysed relationships among individual items in the Eysenck Personality inventory. They used a twin sample to analyse genetic covariances among all possible pairs of items. The genetic covariance matrix is analogous to a correlation matrix for personality test items. The values in the matrix are estimates of the degree to which genetic influences contribute to the correlation between items. High values occur for item pairs for which the correlation for MZ twins is higher than the correlation for DZ twins. Zero values occur in the matrix when the correlation between items is the same for MZ and DZ twins. They factor analysed the genetic covariance matrix and obtained factors of Neuroticism and Extraversion that were congruent with the factor structures for these traits derived from conventional factor analyses of the phenotypic relationships among the items. Items that were markers for the Extraversion and Neuroticism factors on the Eysenck test were markers for genetically derived Extraversion and Neuroticism factors.

McCrae et al. (2001) used a large sample of German and Canadian twins to obtain genetic covariance matrices for the five factors included in the NEO inventory. They obtained a genetic covariance matrix derived from correlations among pairs of trait components for MZ twin pairs. This method of estimating genetic covariances among trait components confounds genetic and shared environmental influences. The method was used after these researchers ascertained that the structure of shared environmental covariances among trait components was unrelated to the usual factor structure of trait components based on extensive investigations of the NEO. The congruence coefficients between factors derived from MZ correlations and the standard phenotypic factor structures varied from 0.95 to 0.98 for the five factors defining the Big Five traits. Non-shared environmental relationships among trait components exhibited low congruence with the structure of phenotypic relationships among traits. These results indicate that personality taxonomies arise in part because of the influence of genetic relationships among their components.

Jang *et al.* (1998) analysed facet scores on the NEO after removing variance associated with the Big Five factors. They found that the facet scores were heritable. These results indicate that genetic factors influence the patterning of narrower components of the taxonomy of personality.

Genetic covariance analyses in the domains of personality and intelligence yield similar results. Relationships among various components of taxonomies are related to the structure of genetic covariances among the components. Neither shared nor non-shared environmental influences appear to have a strong influence on the development of taxonomic relationships. In addition, in both domains, narrow factors occupying a lower order in the hierarchical structure are heritable.

CONTINUITY AND CHANGE

From child to adult

The heritability of general intelligence increases from the first year of life until adulthood. Longitudinal twin studies find that DZ twin correlations decrease over time and MZ twin correlations increase and approach an asymptote dictated by the test-retest reliability for the measures (see Wilson, 1983). The data from the Colorado Adoption Project provide clear evidence of an increase in heritability in intelligence over the first 16 years of life. (For an overview of the changing influences of different components of environmental and genetic variance on intelligence from infancy to adulthood see McGue *et al.*, 1993.) Comparable data do not exist for personality.

There are other differences in the outcomes of longitudinal research in personality and intelligence. Columbo (1993) reviewed longitudinal research in which measures of infant information-processing abilities are related to childhood IQ. Several different researchers measured fixation times in a habituation paradigm in which infants under age one and in some instances younger than one month are repeatedly presented with the same stimulus. Fixation time measures are predictive of performance on measures of IQ obtained in the first several years of life. Columbo estimates that the disattenuated relationship between infant information-processing measures and childhood IQ accounts for over 65 per cent of the variance in childhood IQ. Rose and Feldman (1995) obtained a correlation of 0.5 between a measure of information processing obtained prior to age one and a measure of general intelligence obtained at age 11. Given the relatively high continuity between measures of intelligence obtained at age 11 and adult intelligence it is plausible to assume that infant information-processing abilities are predictive of adult intelligence.

DiLalla et al. (1990) and Benson et al. (1993) used mid-parent, mid-twin regressions to assess continuity in intelligence between infant information-processing ability and adult intelligence. The method involves the analysis of the relationship between mean parental intelligence and the mean intelligence of their twin children. The mid-parent, mid-twin regression provides an estimate of longitudinal continuity for a trait. The mid-parent to adult child IQ correlation is close to 0.6 (Bennett, Fulker and DeFries, 1985). This value sets an upper bound for the correlation between infant measures and adult intelligence. If infant measures are perfect indexes of adult intelligence, then the correlation between an infant measure and the IQs of their parents would be the same as the correlation between the IQs of parents and their adult children. An estimated value of the correlation between an infant measure and adult IQ is obtained by doubling the obtained correlation between infant and adult IQ to reflect the 0.6 upper bound value. Benson et al. obtained correlations ranging from 0.18 to 0.32 for various indices of childhood auditory habituation and the intelligence of the children's parents. These correlations may be compared to the correlations for adult children and parents. The latter correlations are familial relationships that include additive genetic and shared family environmental sources of variance. Since the influence of the latter appears to be vanishingly small in adulthood, most of the phenotypic covariance between adult parents and children in intelligence is attributable to shared additive genetic influences. These analyses imply that a substantial portion of the hypothetical covariance between infant measures and measures of adult intelligence is attributable to common genetic influences on both measures (see Thompson, 1989).

The relationships between infant measures and personality traits measured in young adults are weak or non-existent. Caspi (2000) noted that the earliest age at which prediction of adult personality can be made is age 3 years. Adult personality dispositions may be unrelated to infant characteristics because of dispositional discontinuity or because of an inability to assess the appropriate infant characteristics that are predictively related to adult personality. Standard infant intelligence measures such as the Bayley test in contrast to infant information-processing measures have relatively weak relationships to later intelligence. Until the discovery of relationships between infant information-processing measures and childhood IQ it was believed that infant characteristics were not predictive of adult intelligence.

There are continuities in personality assessed at age 3 and in early adulthood. Caspi (2000) reported the results of a longitudinal study of personality starting with observations of behaviour at age 3 and continuing until young adulthood for a cohort of children born in Dunedin in New Zealand. Caspi classifies children as well adjusted, under-controlled or inhibited based on behavioural observations. Children rated as under-controlled at age 3 relative to children rated as well adjusted are more likely to be described by informants at age 18 as being low in culture ($r = -0.44$) and low in conscientiousness ($r = -0.24$). Under-controlled children were more likely to attempt suicide as young adults and were more likely to have criminal records than well-adjusted children. Although age 3 classifications are only weakly predictive of young adult characteristics, the relationships are attenuated by error variance associated with judgements based on observations of behaviour exhibited on a single occasion. Classifications of children based on multiple observations of behaviours in early childhood would undoubtedly lead to more accurate predictions.

There are similarities in the outcomes of longitudinal research relating childhood to adult characteristics in the domains of personality and intelligence. The continuities observed in both domains are heterotypic. That is, the manifestations of dispositions assessed at different ages are different in form. Three-years-olds do not have criminal records and do not attempt suicide. Infant information processing is not the same as the ability to solve a verbal analogy. The initial manifestations of the disposition assessed at earlier ages are either pre-verbal or pre-cognitive. Infant information processing may be assessed prior to the development of language. Temperamental personality structures assessed at age 3 use children who have acquired language skills but who surely do not have fully articulated cognitive representations of their personality. These findings suggest that the cognitive components of dispositions may be secondary and perhaps even of marginal significance. These results also call into question a model of change in dispositions based on an attempt to change self-perception and self-understanding.

There are also differences in the outcomes of research relating childhood to adult characteristics in personality and intelligence. The continuities in intelligence derive from the neo-natal period – those in the domain of personality begin with observations made at an older age. The analysis of temperament and young adult personality employs concepts that are at least metaphorically analogous (see Molfese and Molfese, 2000 for a collection of papers that explore the analogies between the language of infant and adult personality descriptions). The heterotypic continuities in the domain of intelligence clearly involve constructs and theoretically derived measurements that are not metaphorically analogous. The infant information-processing indices are embedded in theories of cognitive development that are linguistically and empirically remote from the assessments used to measure adult intelligence. Of course the attempt to explain the continuities may involve appeals to somewhat oversimplified and conceptually analogous linguistic frameworks employing such terms as the speed and fidelity of information processing. Such constructs are problematic when used to describe infant characteristics, but even if accepted as reasonably accurate first level construals of infant characteristics they are not adequate representations of g. At most, what is claimed is that the latter *derives* from the former – not that they are conceptually identical even at a metaphorical level.

The differences in continuities between early childhood indices of personality and intelligence and adult personality and intelligence are not necessarily indicative of fundamental differences in dispositional continuities in these domains. Research on the heritability of adult phenotypes provides evidence for continuities between a latent (genotypic) disposition present at conception and adult phenotypes. Recent progress in the identification of genes that influence such personality traits as Neuroticism also provide evidence for continuities of personality dispositions (see Ebstein *et al.*, 2003; Lesch, 2003).

Continuity after early childhood

Intelligence is a highly stable trait of individuals. The most dramatic evidence for the continuity of intellectual dispositions derives from the analyses of the cohort of Scottish children who took a group intelligence test (Moray House test) at age 11 and at age 77. Deary *et al.* (2000) obtained a test-retest correlation of 0.73 (corrected for restrictions in range of talent) for the Moray House test. They found that the time-lagged correlation between the Moray House test administered at age 11 and the Ravens test administered at age 77 was 0.48. This value may be compared to the concurrent correlation between the Ravens and Moray House test administered at age 77 of 0.57. The relatively small differences between concurrent and time-lagged correlations indicates that the latent disposition of general intelligence imperfectly assessed by both of these tests remains relatively invariant from age 11 to age 77.

There are no data indicating continuities in personality that are as dramatic as those obtained for the Scottish cohort by Deary and his colleagues. There is considerable evidence that personality traits are relatively stable over the adult life span of individuals (McCrae and Costa, 1990). Angleitner (2002) reported the results of a longitudinal analysis of adult personality for a large twin sample. He found that genetic influences contributed to the measure of stability of personality accounting for 50 to 70 per cent of the longitudinal continuity in personality traits over a five-year period.

Resilience

Evidence for the continuities of personality and intelligence imply that these dispositions are not highly responsive to many environmental variations that individuals are likely to encounter over their life spans. For example, there is evidence indicating that variations in educational exposures are not likely to have a large enduring influence on intelligence. I believe that research on preschool interventions, educational deprivation, and research on the intelligence of deaf individuals provides evidence for this assertion.

The Abecedarian Project randomly assigned children reared in extreme poverty to an experimental intervention in which they were provided with intensive early childhood education beginning shortly after birth and extending through the preschool period or a control group. Children assigned to the experimental group had higher scores on tests of intelligence than children in the control group. The effect sizes for the intervention on measures of intelligence declined from 0.38 at age 6.5, to 0.31 at age 12, to 0.19 at age 21 – the most recent follow-up data obtained 16 years after the end of the early childhood intervention (Campbell, 2001). Campbell reported the results for a regression analysis in which childhood verbal ability scores were entered as a variable prior to the entry of the dummy coded experimental variable. The effect sizes for intelligence in this analysis declined from 0.10 at age 6.5, to −0.21 at age 12, to −0.38 at age 21. The negative effect sizes for the experimental intervention may be interpreted by assuming that childhood verbal ability is influenced by two components of variance – a component indicative of a core intellectual disposition and a component reflecting the effects of early intervention. This latter component declines over the adult life span of an individual. Predictions of adult intelligence that include the latter component are likely to err by over-predicting adult performance. These results are compatible with the assertion that intensive early intervention has only marginal and declining influences on core intellectual dispositions.

DeGroot (1951) studied the intelligence of Dutch adolescents who had been deprived of one or more years of formal education owing to the German occupation of the Netherlands during World War II. DeGroot's study is often cited as providing evidence for the influence of education on intelligence. Less often noticed is that the oldest cohort in DeGroot's study who had experienced educational deprivations several years earlier did not exhibit declines in intelligence. DeGroot's analysis thus provides simultaneous evidence of the effects of educational deprivation on intelligence and the resilience of intelligence in response to educational deprivations. The effects of the educational deprivation were not long-lived.

Braden (1994) comprehensively reviewed the performance of deaf individuals on various tests of intelligence. Deaf individuals exhibit cumulative deficits on various measures of verbal ability and verbal achievement relative to hearing individuals over the course of their educational career. Despite the difficulties they exhibit in acquiring verbal skills, deaf individuals do not exhibit deficits on nonverbal measures of abstract reasoning ability that are markers for fluid intelligence. These results indicate that deaf individuals do not exhibit declines in g despite the apparent difficulties they have in benefitting from tuition requiring verbal skills.

There is evidence that personality traits are also resilient in response to variations in experiences that individuals commonly encounter. Angleitner (2002) studied the influence of a large number of life events that were assumed to have an impact on personality. Aggregated indices of the number of life events were not highly associated with changes in personality as assessed by self-report measures and peer reports. None of the correlations exceeded 0.2. Measures of life events that had an impact on personality assessed at time 2 were also related to measures of personality obtained at time 1 prior to the occurrence of the life events. These results indicate that personality characteristics were related to the probability of experiencing some life events that were alleged to change personality dispositions. Angleitner's results indicate that many events that are commonly encountered in adulthood may have only a marginal effect on personality traits.

FOUNDATIONS AND SOCIAL BEHAVIOUR

Bottom-up models

Complex intellectual abilities are related to relatively simple measures of information processing. There are many relatively simple tasks that correlate with intelligence (for a review of some of these relationships see Deary, 2000). For example, intelligence is related to performance in inspection time tasks. One version of this task presents subjects with two vertical lines that clearly differ in length followed by two wide black lines that occlude the original stimulus and serve as backward masks. The stimulus onset asynchrony is varied and a threshold is obtained for the judgement of differences in line lengths. The threshold is inversely related to intelligence (see Deary, 2000). Intelligence is also inversely related to performance in reaction time tasks in which individuals must decide which of two or more lights were flashed (Jensen, 1998, Chapter 8). It is possible to argue that elementary information processes are causally related to the development of complex intellectual abilities. There are three kinds of evidence that are relevant. First, composite indices of different laboratory measures form a latent trait that is congruent with g (Luo and Petrill, 1999) and that is strongly related to nonverbal intelligence (Deary, 1999). Second, Deary (1995) used a cross-lagged panel analysis to demonstrate that inspection time measures were causally related to changes in intelligence. He found no evidence that intelligence was related to changes in inspection time. Third, there is evidence suggesting that the relationship between elementary information-processing measures of inspection time and reaction time and intelligence is attributable to common genetic influences (Luciano *et al.*, 2003). Luo, Thompson and Detterman (2002) derived a broad information-processing factor by analysing several different measures of elementary information processing in a large sample of twins. The factor correlated with a psychometrically derived general factor and approximately two-thirds of this correlation was attributable to common genetic influences.

These data indicate that it is possible to infer the value of intellectual dispositions from a set of relatively simple information-processing measures that, on the surface, appear to be unrelated to the complex abilities and knowledge assessed by psychometric tests of intelligence. The elementary information-processing correlates of intelligence measure components of variance that are not captured by conventional psychometric measures. Luo *et al.* found that they were able to predict scores on tests of academic achievement more accurately by the use of measures of g that were based on both elementary processing performance and psychometric measures than by the use of measures of g based solely on psychometric measures.

In principle, it should be possible to construct measures of personality that are based on standard self-report and peer measures and genetically covariant physiological and behavioural measures. Measures of personality traits could be constructed that include a variety of physiological indices that are assumed to be related to a trait, behavioural responses to laboratory testing situations, as well as self-reports and peer ratings. Such broad multi-method indices of latent traits might have enhanced construct validity.

Social outcomes

Individual differences in intelligence are related to diverse social outcomes including social mobility and educational attainments (Brody, 1992). Rowe, Versterdahl and Rodgers (1998) studied genetic covariances between intelligence and educational attainments and incomes using differences between full and half siblings to obtain estimates of the heritability of their measures. They found that approximately two-thirds of the phenotypic relationship between intelligence and these socially relevant outcome variables was related to common genetic influences on intelligence and social outcome variables.

It is known that various social outcomes related to personality are heritable. For example, divorce (McGue and Lykken, 1992) and criminality (Mednick, Gabrielli and Hutchings, 1984; Raine, 1993) are heritable. Personality characteristics are related to these outcomes. Rowe (2003) obtained measures of the number of repeat units in the coding region of the D4 gene. Rowe found that women with the 7-repeat allele had a higher number of marriages than women without the allele. The 7-repeat allele is related to novelty seeking and attention deficit and hyperactivity (Faraone *et al.*, 2001; Thapar, 2003). Rowe interprets this result as evidence for a gene-environmental covariance. Women with the 7-repeat allele may evoke marital discord and may have difficulty in sustaining stable marital relationships. The increase in divorce for women with a particular genotype may thus be thought of as the result of a process in which genes influence the environmental encounters of an individual. Rowe's analysis implies that genes that influence personality traits may also influence socially relevant outcomes. On his analysis, novelty seeking and divorce are both influenced by the same genotypes.

SUMMARY AND CONCLUSION

In this chapter I have examined research in personality from the perspective of research in intelligence. The research in intelligence briefly reviewed in this chapter indicates that there are empirically established linkages leading to a theoretically coherent model of intelligence. Intelligence may be understood as a heritable characteristic of persons initially manifested in information-processing skills exhibited in the first year of life that influence the development of a complex structure of ability that influences diverse socially relevant outcomes such as educational attainment, social mobility and income. The disposition is relatively invariant over the life span and is resilient, that is resistant to change as a result of variations in environmental experiences which are likely to be encountered by most individuals in technologically advanced societies with universal exposure to formal education. Genetic co-variance analyses indicate that the nomological network of laws and relations that relate the diverse manifestations of intelligence are linked by common genetic influences. Personality dispositions exhibit an isomorphic similarity to intellectual dispositions. Personality dispositions also exhibit genetically covariant linkages between childhood temperament, complex adult representations and socially relevant outcomes.

Intelligence and personality are also isomorphic with respect to what is not known in both domains. We have relatively little knowledge about the intermediate processes in this broad analysis. We are not able to identify many of the specific genes that are related to the heritable characteristics which are observed in population genetic studies, although we can look forward to new discoveries in molecular genetics that will be relevant to this task. We do not know very much about the intermediate physiological pathways that relate genes to dispositions. Nor do we understand very much about the processes of interaction that link childhood to adult manifestations of dispositions. And we do not have a good understanding of possible interactions between heritable dispositions and social structures that influence social outcomes.

What is known and what is unknown about personality and intelligence suggest that they may be construed within a common isomorphic structure. The study of personality and of intelligence should be based on an analysis of heritable dispositions that influence the ways in which individuals respond to the social world they encounter. A science of personality bereft of such dispositional attributes is jejune.

REFERENCES

Angleitner, A. (2002) 'Personality in adulthood: Findings from the Bielefeld Longitudinal Study of Adult Twins (BILSAT)', keynote lecture, 11th European Conference on Personality, Jena, Germany.

Bennett, B., Fulker, D. W. and DeFries, J. C. (1985) 'Familial resemblance for general cognitive ability in the Hawaii Family Study of Cognition', *Behavior Genetics* 15: 401–406.

Benson, J. B., Cherny, S. S., Haith, M. M. and Fulker, D. W. (1993) 'Rapid assessment of infant predictors of adult IQ: Mid-twin mid-parent analyses', *Developmental Psychology* 29: 434–447.

Bouchard, T. J. Jr. and Loehlin, J. (2001) 'Genes, evolution, and personality', *Behavior Genetics* 31: 243–273.

Braden, J. A. (1994) *Deafness, Deprivation and IQ*. New York: Plenum.

Brody, N. (1992) *Intelligence*, 2nd edn. San Diego: Academic Press.

Campbell, F. A. (2001) 'Early childhood intervention', paper presented at the 2001 Spearman Conference, Sydney.

Cardon, L. R., Fulker, D. W., DeFries, J. C. and Plomin, R. (1992) 'Multivariate genetic analyses of specific cognitive abilities in the Colorado Adoption Project at age 7', *Intelligence* 16: 383–400.

Carroll, J. B. (1993) *Human Cognitive Abilities*. New York: Cambridge University Press.

Caspi, A. (2000) 'The child is father of the man: Personality continuities from childhood to adulthood', *Journal of Personality and Social Psychology* 78: 158–172.

Caspi, A., McClay, J., Moffitt, T. E., Mill, J., Martin, J., Craig, I. W., Taylor, A. and Poulton, R. (2002) 'Role of genotype in the cycle of violence in maltreated children', *Science* 297: 851–854.

Cloninger, C. R. *et al.* (1998) 'Anxiety proneness related to epistatic loci in genome scan of human personality traits', *American Journal of Medical Genetics* 81: 313–317.

Columbo, J. (1993) *Infant Cognition: Predicting Later Intellectual Functioning*. Newbury Park, CA: Sage.

Deary, I. J. (1995) 'Auditory inspection time and intelligence: What is the direction of causation?', *Developmental Psychology* 31: 237–250.

Deary, I. J. (1999) 'Intelligence and visual and auditory information processing', in P. L. Ackerman, P. C. Kyllonen and R. D. Roberts (eds) *Learning and Individual Differences: Process, Trait, and Content Determinants*. Washington, DC: American Psychological Association.

Deary, I. J. (2000) *Looking Down on Human Intelligence: From Psychometrics to the Brain*. New York: Oxford University Press.

Deary, I. J. (ed.) (2001) 'Inspection time'. *Intelligence* 29: 441–552.

Deary, I. J., Whalley, L. J., Lemmon, H., Crawford, J. R. and Starr, J. M. (2000) 'The stability of mental ability from childhood to old age: Follow-up of the 1932 Scottish Mental Survey', *Intelligence* 28: 49–55.

DeGroot, A. D. (1951) 'War and the intelligence of youth', *Journal of Abnormal and Social Psychology* 46: 596–597.

DiLalla, L. F., Thompson, L. A., Plomin, R., Phillips, K., Fagan, J. F., Haith, M. M., Cyphers, L. H. and Fulker, D. W. (1990) 'Infant predictors of preschool and adult IQ: A study of infant twins and their parents', *Developmental Psychology* 26: 759–769.

Eaves, L. J., Eysenck, H. J. and Martin, N. G. (1989) *Genes, Culture and Personality: An Empirical Approach*. London: Academic Press.

Ebstein, R. P., Benjamin, J. and Belmaker, R. H. (2003) 'Behavioral genetics, genomics, and personality', in R. Plomin, J. C. DeFries, I. W. Craig, and P. McGuffin (eds) *Behavioral Genetics in the Postgenomic Era*, pp. 365–388. Washington, DC: American Psychological Association.

Faraone, S. V., Doyle, A. E., Mick, E. and Bierderman, J. (2001) 'Meta-analysis of the association between the 7-repeat allele of the dopamine d4 gene and attention-deficit disorder', *American Journal of Psychiatry* 158: 1052–1057.

Flynn, J. R. (1998) 'IQ gains over time. Toward finding the causes', in U. Neisser (ed.) *The Rising Curve*, pp. 25–66. Washington, DC: American Psychological Association.

Funder, D. C. and Sneed, C. D. (1993) 'Behavioral manifestations of personality: An ecological approach to judgmental accuracy', *Journal of Personality and Social Psychology* 64: 479–490.

Funder, D. C., Furr, R. M. and Colvin, C. R. (2000) 'The Riverside Behavioral Q-sort: A tool for the description of social behavior', *Journal of Personality* 68: 451–490.

Heath, A. C., Neale, M. C., Kessler, R. C., Eaves, L. J. and Kendler, K. S. (1992) 'Evidence of genetic influences on personality from self-reports and informant ratings', *Journal of Personality and Social Psychology* 63: 85–96.

Helson, R., Kwan, V. S. Y., John, O. P. and Jones (2002) 'The growing evidence for personality change in adulthood: Findings from research with personality inventories', *Journal of Research in Personality* 36: 287–306.

Jang, K. L., McCrae, R. R., Angleitner, A., Riemann, R. and Livesley, W. J. (1998) 'Heritability of facet-level traits in a cross-cultural twin study: Support for a hierarchical model of personality', *Journal of Personality and Social Psychology* 74: 1556–1565.

Jensen, A. R. (1998) *The G Factor*. Westport, CT: Praeger.

Kendler, K. S., Neale, M. C., Kessler, R. C., Heath, A. C. and Eaves, L. J. (1993) 'A longitudinal twin study of 1-year prevalence of major depression in women', *Archives of General Psychiatry* 50: 843–852.

Lesch, K. P. (2003) 'Neuroticism and serotonin: A developmental genetic perspective', in R. Plomin, J. C. DeFries, I. W. Craig and P. McGuffin (eds) *Behavioral Genetics in the Postgenomic Era*, pp. 389–423. Washington, DC: American Psychological Association.

Loehlin, J. C. (1992) *Genes and Environment in Personality Development*. Newbury Park, CA: Sage.

Loehlin, J. C. and Nichols, R. C. (1976) *Heredity, Environment and Personality*. Austin: University of Texas Press.

Luciano, M., Wright, M. J., Smith, G. A., Geffen, G. M., Geffen, L. B. and Martin, N. G. (2003) 'Genetic covariance between processing speed and IQ', in R. Plomin,

J. C. DeFries, I. W. Craig and P. McGuffin (eds) *Behavioural Genetics in the Post-genomic Era*, pp. 163–181. Washington, DC: American Psychological Association.

Luo, D. and Petrill, S. A. (1999) 'Elementary cognitive tasks and their roles in g estimates', *Intelligence* 27: 157–174.

Luo, D., Thompson, L. A. and Detterman, D. K. (2002) 'Aggregation of basic cognitive processes: The common denominator for complex intellectual abilities', submitted.

Lykken, D. T., Bouchard, T. J., McGue, M. and Tellegen, A. (1993) 'Heritability of interests: A twin study', *Journal of Applied Psychology* 78: 649–661.

McCrae, R. R. and Costa, P. T. (1990) *Personality in Adulthood*. New York: Guilford Press.

McCrae, R. R., Jang, K. L., Livesley, W. J., Riemann, R. and Angleitner, A. (2001) 'Sources of structure: Genetic, environmental, and artifactual influences on the covariance of personality traits', *Journal of Personality* 69: 511–535.

McGue, M. and Lykken, D. T. (1992) 'Genetic influences on risk of divorce', *Psychological Science* 3: 368–373.

McGue, M., Bouchard, T. J. Jr., Iacono, W. G. and Lykken, D. T. (1993) 'Behavioural genetics of cognitive ability: A life-span perspective', in R. Plomin and G. E. McLearn (eds) *Nature, Nurture, and Psychology*, pp. 59–76. Washington, DC: American Psychological Association.

Mednick, S. A., Gabrielli, W. F. and Hutchings, B. (1984) 'Genetic factors in criminal behaviour: Evidence from an adoption cohort', *Science* 224: 891–893.

Moffitt, T. E., Caspi, A., Harkness, A. R. and Silva, P. A. (1993) 'The natural history of change in intellectual performance: Who changes? How much? Is it meaningful?', *Journal of Child Psychology and Psychiatry* 14: 455–506.

Molfese, V. J. and Molfese, D. L. (eds) (2000) *Temperament and Personality Development across the Life Span*. Mahwah, NJ: Lawrence Erlbaum Associates Inc.

Neisser, U. (ed.) (1998) *The Rising Curve*. Washington, DC: American Psychological Association.

Pedersen, N. L., Plomin, R., Nesselroade, J. R. and McClearn, G. E. (1992) 'A quantitative genetic analysis of cognitive abilities during the second half of the life-span', *Psychological Science* 3: 346–352.

Petrill, S. A. (2002) 'The case for general intelligence: A behavioural genetic perspective', in R. Sternberg and E. Grigorenko (eds) *The General Factor of Intelligence: How General Is It?*, pp. 281–298. Mahwah, NJ: Lawrence Erlbaum Associates Inc.

Plomin, R. (2003) 'General cognitive ability', in R. Plomin, J. C. DeFries, I. W. Craig and P. McGuffin (eds) *Behavioural Genetics in the Postgenomic Era*, pp. 183–201. Washington, DC: American Psychological Association.

Plomin, R. and Daniels, D. (1987) 'Why are children in the same family so different from each other?', *Behavioural and Brain Sciences* 10: 1–16.

Plomin, R. and Spinath, F. M. (2002) 'Genetics and general cognitive ability (g)', *Trends in Cognitive Science* 6: 169–176.

Plomin, R. and Spinath, F. M. (2003) 'Intelligence: Genetics, genes and genomics', *Journal of Personality and Social Psychology* 86: 112–129.

Plomin, R., Fulker, D. W., Corley, R. and DeFries, J. C. (1997) 'Nature, nurture, and cognitive development from 1 to 16 years: A parent–offspring adoption study', *Psychological Science* 8: 442–447.

Plomin, R., DeFries, J. C., Craig, I. W. and McGuffin, P. (2003) *Behavioural Genetics in the Postgenomic Era*. Washington, DC: American Psychological Association.

Raine, A. (1993) *The Psychopathology of Crime: Criminal Behaviour as a Clinical Disorder*. San Diego: Academic Press.

Reiss, D., Neiderhiser, J. M., Hetherington, E. M. and Plomin, R. (2000) *The Relationship Code: Deciphering Genetic and Social Patterns in Adolescent Development*. Cambridge, MA: Harvard University Press.

Riemann, R., Angleitner, A. and Strelau, J. (1997) 'Genetic and environmental influences on personality: A study of twins reared together using the self- and peer report NEO-FFI Scales', *Journal of Personality* 65: 449–475.

Rose, S. and Feldman, J. (1995) 'Prediction of IQ and specific cognitive abilities at age 11 from infancy measures', *Developmental Psychology* 31: 685–696.

Rowe, D. C. (2003) 'Assessing genotype-environment interactions and correlations in the postgenomic era', in R. Plomin, J. C. DeFries, I. W. Craig and P. McGuffin (eds) *Behavioral Genetics in the Postgenomic Era*, pp. 71–86. Washington, DC: American Psychological Association.

Rowe, D. C., Jacobsen, K. C. and Van den Oord, E. J. C. G. (1999) 'Genetic and environmental influences on vocabulary IQ: Parental educational level as moderator', *Child Development* 70: 1151–1162.

Rowe, D. C., Vesterdahl, W. J. and Rodgers, J. L. (1998) 'Herrnstein's syllogism: Genetic and shared environmental influences on IQ, education, and income', *Intelligence* 26: 405–423.

Spinath, F.M., Riemann, R., Hempel, S., Schlangen, B., Weiss, R., Borkenau, P. and Angleitner, A. (1999) 'A day in the life: Description of the German Observational Study of Adult Twins (GOSAT) assessing twin similarity in controlled laboratory settings', in I. Merivelde, I. Deary, F. DeFruyt and F. Ostendorf (eds) *Personality Psychology in Europe*, vol. 7, pp. 311–328. Tilburg: Tilburg University Press.

Spinath, F. M., Angleitner, A., Borkenau, P., Riemann, R. and Wolf, H. (2002) 'German Observational Study of Adult Twins: A multimodal investigation of personality, temperament and cognitive ability', *Twin Research* 5: 372–375.

Spinath, F. M., Ronald, A., Harlaar, N., Price, T. and Plomin, R. (2003) 'Phenotypic "g" early in life: On the etiology of early cognitive ability in a large sample of twin children aged 2 to 4 years', *Intelligence* 31: 195–210.

Thapar, A. (2003) 'Attention deficit hyperactivity disorder: New genetic findings, new directions', in R. Plomin, J. C. DeFries, I. W. Craig and P. McGuffin (eds) *Behavioural Genetics in the Postgenomic Era*, pp. 445–462. Washington, DC: American Psychological Association.

Thompson, L. A. (1989) 'Developmental behavior genetic research on infant information processing: Detection of continuity and change', in S. Doxiades and S. Stewart (eds) *Early Influences Shaping the Individual*. New York: Plenum.

Willis, S. L. and Schaie, K. W. (1986) 'Practical intelligence in later adulthood', in R. J. Sternberg and R. K. Wagner (eds) *Practical Intelligence: Nature and Origins of Competence in the Everyday World*, pp. 236–268. Cambridge: Cambridge University Press.

Wilson, R. S. (1983) 'The Louisville Twin Study: Developmental synchronies in behaviour', *Child Development* 54: 298–316.

Chapter 7

Personality structure across cultures

Indigenous and cross-cultural perspectives

A. Timothy Church and Marcia S. Katigbak

Alternative perspectives – cross-cultural, evolutionary, indigenous, and cultural – and typical methods and levels of analysis in the study of personality structure across cultures are first introduced. Cross-cultural research on personality structure, using both imported and indigenous approaches, is then reviewed. Results suggest that the five-factor or Big Five model may provide an adequate and fairly comprehensive representation of personality structure in most cultures. However, recent research on alternative models and indigenous dimensions also suggests that alternative structures may provide more optimal representations of personality structure in some cultural contexts. Research on personality structure in the Philippines, using both imported measures of the five-factor model and indigenous lexical and inventory approaches, is consistent with these conclusions. Several recent controversies, including the need for dimensions 'beyond' the Big Five and the nature of Positive and Negative Valence dimensions, are addressed in the context of structural studies in the Philippines.

INTRODUCTION

Researchers who study personality structure investigate the organization or pattern of covariation among personality attributes. Their goal is to determine the nature and number of categories or dimensions of personality that are needed to describe individual differences. A well-defined taxonomy or structure of personality can provide a systematic account of the individual differences that are significant in particular cultural groups, guide theory and research on personality determinants and processes, and provide a framework for organizing personality constructs, scales, and research findings (John, Angleitner and Ostendorf, 1988; Saucier and Goldberg, 2003). When personality taxonomies and dimensions are compared across cultures the universality versus cultural uniqueness of personality language, person perception categories and individual–differences dimensions is addressed. Cross-cultural studies are thus relevant to the question of whether personality dimensions are primarily biologically based or mediated or 'constituted' by culture (McCrae and Costa, 1997; Markus and Kitayama, 1998). From an applied perspective, structural studies reveal which dimensions should be included in a comprehensive assessment of personality and the extent to which existing personality inventories encompass constructs that are relevant in diverse cultures. Indeed, cross-cultural generalizability is an important criterion in evaluating alternative personality models or structures.

Presently, the investigation of personality structure across cultures is of particular importance and interest. In the past decade, there has been a rapid expansion of research on the cross-cultural generalizability of personality dimensions, using both translated inventories and more indigenous approaches. Proponents of the five-factor model – comprised of Extraversion, Agreeableness, Conscientiousness, Emotional Stability (versus Neuroticism), and Intellect or Openness to Experience – have made an ever stronger case for the universality of the model (McCrae and Allik, 2002) and a plethora of instruments have emerged to assess these Big Five dimensions (de Raad and Perugini, 2002). Concurrently, however, researchers using indigenous lexical and inventory approaches have increasingly argued the need to consider alternative personality models and dimensions (e.g. Ashton and Lee, 2001; Cheung *et al.*, 2001; Saucier and Goldberg, 2001; Yang and Wang, 2002). Furthermore, some researchers have now begun to move beyond comparisons of personality structures to cross-cultural comparisons of mean profiles. Such comparisons are not meaningful in the absence of structural and other forms of conceptual and measurement equivalence. Therefore, the extent to which personality structures are equivalent across cultures has become a more important question than ever.

Chapter overview

In this chapter: (a) we introduce alternative perspectives on the study of personality structure across cultures, including cross-cultural, evolutionary, indigenous and cultural; (b) we describe typical methods and levels of analysis in cross-cultural studies of personality structure, including issues of conceptual and measurement equivalence; (c) review and critique the results of imported (imposed-etic) and indigenous (emic) lexical and inventory approaches in the investigation of personality structure; (d) review our own research on personality structure in the Philippines, using both indigenous and cross-cultural approaches; (e) draw conclusions about the structure of personality across cultures; (f) suggest some areas of needed research.

Overall, we conclude that there is a considerable degree of cross-cultural comparability of personality dimensions across cultures and that the five-factor or Big Five model may provide an adequate and fairly comprehensive representation of personality structure in most cultures. However, recent research suggests that alternative dimensions or structural models may provide more optimal representations of personality structure in some cultural contexts.

SUMMARY AND CRITIQUE OF RECENT LITERATURE

Alternative theoretical perspectives on personality structure across cultures

Researchers have approached the study of personality across cultures from diverse perspectives including cross-cultural, evolutionary, indigenous and cultural (Church, 2001a; Triandis, 2000). Cross-cultural approaches typically involve comparisons of multiple cultures, with some optimism about discovering cultural universals or culture specifics amidst universals (e.g. Barrett et al., 1998; McCrae, 2001). Cross-cultural trait psychologists tend to treat culture as an independent variable 'outside' the individual that can impact the level, expression and correlates of personality dimensions, but not the underlying personality structure.

Evolutionary perspectives, which try to explain individual differences in terms of evolved psychological mechanisms (Buss, 2001), are generally compatible with cross-cultural trait perspectives in their expectation of cultural universals in personality structure. Indeed, evolutionary perspectives have been used to explain the emergence across cultures of the Big Five (Buss, 1996; MacDonald, 1998) or Big Six (Ashton and Lee, 2002) dimensions that have been identified using trait approaches. Evolutionary psychologists have also focused on the identification of individual–differences dimensions in the sexuality domain and have considered whether these dimensions add to the Big Five (Schmitt and Buss, 2000).

Proponents of indigenous perspectives tend to be sceptical about the transportability of personality dimensions across cultures. Instead, the focus is on identifying indigenous constructs that may or may not be generalizable outside the local context (Church and Katigbak, 2002a). Some indigenous psychologists have provided rich elaborations of single concepts (e.g. Choi, Kim and Choi, 1993; Doi, 1978; Enriquez, 1992; Yang and Ho, 1988). Others have sought to identify near-comprehensive sets of indigenous dimensions (Guanzon-Lapeña et al., 1998; La Rosa and Díaz-Loving, 1991; Yang and Wang, 2002) or have combined indigenous (emic) and imported (imposed-etic) dimensions to obtain a comprehensive assessment of personality (Cheung et al., 1996). More portentous for cross-cultural research on personality structure is the view of some indigenous psychologists in Asia. They note the relational nature of personality and suggest that the unit of analysis should be the person-in-relations – that is, the person in different relational contexts – rather than the individual person in isolation (Ho, 1998). This raises the question of whether inventory items written to reflect the person-in-relations would exhibit different structures than traditional personality items.

Finally, cultural psychologists, who emphasize the mutually constitutive nature of culture and personality, may be most likely to question the significance of finding comparable personality dimensions across cultures. For example, Markus and Kitayama (1998, p. 7) questioned whether comparable factor structures imply that 'personality' in the western sense of an 'internal package of attributes' is a cultural universal. In any case, personality trait structures would probably be deemed less crucial to identify in the cultural psychology perspective, because traits are viewed as less central aspects of self-concept and less important in the explanation and prediction of behaviour (Church, 2000; Heine, 2001; Markus and Kitayama, 1998). In sum, while most cross-cultural psychologists are inclined to view the preponderance of cross-cultural evidence in support of comparable personality dimensions as 'incompatible with the idea that the pie of personality would be made up of largely different ingredients cross-culturally' (Poortinga, van de Vijver and van Hemert, 2002), the significance of finding universal factors or dimensions is doubted by some cultural psychologists.

Methods and levels of analysis

Van de Vijver and Leung (1997) described three types of cross-cultural equivalence, all of which are relevant in the investigation of personality struc-ture across cultures. For personality dimensions to be considered universal or 'etic' (Berry, 1969; Church and Katigbak, 1988) they would need to exhibit a significant degree of *construct equivalence* across cultures, that is, equivalence of construct definitions and behavioural exemplars. Cross-cultural compari-sons of the nomological networks (e.g. behavioural correlates) of personality dimensions would be best achieved in the presence of *measurement unit equivalence* (i.e. the instrument has the same unit of measurement across cultures, although perhaps not the same origin). Cross-cultural comparisons of mean scores also require scalar equivalence or full score comparability, that is, equivalence of both measurement unit and scale origin. The presence of item bias, or differential item functioning (DIF) across cultures, would make full score comparability questionable and might also imply construct inequivalence.

Cross-cultural studies of personality structure address the *structural equivalence* of personality measures, as determined by such methods as exploratory, targetted (e.g. Procrustes), and confirmatory factor analysis (CFA). Structural equivalence is particularly relevant to construct equiva-lence – that is, the cross-cultural comparability of the nature and number of dimensions assessed. When conducted at the item level, structural analyses also address whether the items refer to situational behaviours that are equally good exemplars of the trait dimensions across cultures.

Exploratory factor analysis (EFA), often followed by Procrustes rotations, continues to be applied most frequently in structural studies. Some researchers dismiss EFA as nonconfirmatory, but the method can provide persuasive 'confirmation' of an hypothesized structure if the dimensions are replicated across cultures. Procrustes rotations have the advantage of eliminating cultural differences in somewhat arbitrary factor orientations, but might also obscure real cultural differences in personality structure (Konstabel, Realo and Kallasmaa, 2002; Rolland, 2002).

Simultaneous components analysis (SCA; Kiers, 1990) has been applied much less frequently but is pleasing conceptually because it treats each culture equally. Weights are derived that define identical components optimally and simultaneously in all cultures, rather than targetting or favouring the factor structure of a particular culture. Caprara et al. (2000) applied the method and found that EFA, SCA and confirmatory factor analysis (CFA) led to similar conclusions about structural equivalence in a facet-level analyses of the Big Five Questionnaire (BFQ).

Several researchers have questioned the efficacy of confirmatory factor analysis (CFA) for investigating the structural equivalence of personality inventories (Katigbak, Church and Akamine, 1996; McCrae et al., 1996). Most inventories exhibit limited simple structure and even trivial sources of covariation (e.g. modest secondary loadings, shared uniquenesses between items or scales) can lead to inadequate model fit. Researchers are unable to specify these sources of covariation a priori based on theoretical or conceptual considerations. As a result, researchers who have applied CFA with reasonable success have tended to fix secondary loadings or correlated uniquenesses a priori based on the results of exploratory factor analyses (e.g. Caprara et al., 2000; Church and Burke, 1994; Katigbak et al., 1996).

To compare indigenous and imported dimensions, a combined emic-etic approach is often used. Measures of both sets of dimensions are administered to the same cultural sample(s) and joint factor analyses or multiple regression analyses are used to determine whether the indigenous and imported scales load on the same factors or share substantial overlapping variance (e.g. Cheung et al., 2001; Katigbak et al., 2002).

As researchers accumulate personality profiles in many cultures, multilevel structural analyses become important. These analyses determine whether the structure of personality attributes is the same at the level of cultures and individuals. In culture-level factor analyses, cultural mean scores for each scale, rather than individual respondent scores, are the input for the factor analysis and the sample size is the number of cultures rather than individuals. Multilevel structural equivalence indicates that the trait dimensions have the same meaning in comparisons of cultures and individuals. Methods for multilevel confirmatory factor analysis (CFA) have been developed (Muthén, 1994) and van de Vijver and Poortinga (2002) described a multilevel procedure based on exploratory factor analyses. McCrae (2001, 2002) found good congruence between cultural and individual level factor structures with the Revised NEO Personality Inventory (NEO-PI-R). In contrast, in a multilevel analysis of the Eysenck Personality Questionnaire, van Hemert et al. (2002) found good multilevel equivalence for the Extraversion and Neuroticism dimensions but not the Psychoticism and Lie dimensions.

Mean and covariance structure analyses (MACS; Sörbom, 1974) have been applied to determine the cross-cultural equivalence of mean 'structures' (Little, 1997). If regression weights (loadings) and intercepts relating observed indicators to latent constructs can be considered equivalent across cultural samples, direct cross-cultural comparisons of mean scores become reasonable (e.g. Reise, Smith and Furr, 2001). The method has also been applied in the detection of uniform and non-uniform differential item functioning (DIF) (Chan, 2000).

DIF analyses address the equivalence of personality structure at the level of specific behavioural exemplars of traits. Even if factor dimensions are replicable across cultures, some behavioural exemplars (items) of the dimensions may be less relevant in some cultures. In psychometric terms, DIF is present when respondents with the same level of the trait, but from different cultural groups, do not have the same probability of endorsing an item used to measure the trait. Investigations of DIF, using classical test theory and item response theory (IRT) indices, have yielded inconsistent results. In cross-cultural studies, some researchers have reported small proportions of DIF items (i.e. 15 per cent or less; Butcher, 1996; Ellis, Becker and Kimmel, 1993; van Leest, 1997) while others have reported large percentages (e.g. 20–60 per cent; Huang, Church and Katigbak, 1997; Taylor and Boeyens, 1991; van Leest, 1997). DIF methods that control for trait level are preferred and several cross-cultural studies have now employed IRT-based methods (Ellis *et al.*, 1993; Huang *et al.*, 1997) or MACS (Chan, 2000), both of which control for trait level.

McCrae (2001) has suggested that DIF might average or cancel out across items within a scale, making full score equivalence at the scale level possible even in the presence of DIF items. A few studies suggest that McCrae might be correct, at least in some cases. Reise *et al.* (2001) and Smith and Reise (1999) found gender DIF for items in NEO-PI-R facet scales, but the effects cancelled out at the facet-scale level. Also, in an analysis of culture DIF and Differential Trait Functioning (DTF; i.e. measurement inequivalence at the scale or trait level) in the Global Personality Inventory, Schmit, Kihm and Robie (2002) found DIF in a large number of items, but few items needed to be deleted to prevent DTF. Schmit *et al.* (2002, p. 207) concluded: 'The presence of several items displaying DIF, which can cancel each other, may not be indicative of serious measurement bias at the scale level.' Poortinga *et al.* (2002), however, warned that the NEO-PI-R facet scales may contain too few items to make such averaging or cancelling out of DIF effective. Additional doubt about the accuracy of cultural mean profiles is raised by recent studies that have found negligible relationships between judges' or authors' a priori expectations regarding cultural mean profiles and actual NEO-PI-R profiles (Church and Katigbak, 2002b; Hřebíčková *et al.*, 2002; McCrae, 2001). In any case, major questions remain about the conceptual and measurement equivalence of trait dimensions at the behavioural (item) level.

Imported (imposed-etic) approaches

There is now extensive evidence for the cross-cultural replicability of personality dimensions assessed by western inventories such as the NEO-PI-R and the Eysenck personality questionnaires (Barrett *et al.*, 1998; McCrae, 2001). A recent volume contains reports on many of the studies with the NEO-PI-R (McCrae and Allik, 2002). The Big Five dimensions have also been identified across cultures with several other measures developed specifically to measure the five-factor model (Benet-Martínez and John, 1998; Caprara *et al.*, 1993; Hendriks, Hofstee and de Raad, 2002; Leininger, 2002; Schmit *et al.*, 2002). Cross-cultural replication of the five-factor model with the Five-Factor Nonverbal Personality Inventory, a nonverbal measure that uses line drawings to depict behaviours associated with the Big Five traits, suggests that the generalizability of the model is not an artifact of universal linguistic structures (Paunonen and Ashton, 2002). The Big Five dimensions have also been replicated using various Big Five marker scales (Benet-Martínez and John, 2000; Kashiwagi, 2002; Perugini and Di Blas, 2002; Yang and Bond, 1990; Yik and Bond, 1993), although in some cultural samples replication has been less successful (Guthrie and Bennett, 1971; Heaven, Connors and Stones, 1994; Rodriguez de Díaz and Díaz-Guerrero, 1997). More impressive is replication of the Big Five dimensions using transported inventories that were not originally developed to measure the five-factor model, such as Jackson's Personality Research Form and the Nonverbal Personality Questionnaire (Paunonen and Ashton, 1998).

A number of issues remain, however, that may reduce the significance of these findings and the definitiveness of conclusions about the universality of personality structure. First, in findings with the NEO-PI-R, replication may be poorer in less industrialized, agrarian samples (Piedmont *et al.*, 2002). Second, in some cultures, the NEO-PI-R Extraversion and Agreeableness facets have reoriented along Love/Affiliation and Dominance/Surgency dimensions in varimax-rotated factor solutions (Katigbak *et al.*, 1996; Lodhi, Deo and Belhekar, 2002; Piedmont and Chae, 1997; see Rolland, 2002 for a review). Konstabel *et al.* (2002) provided evidence that this may be more likely in collectivistic cultures, consistent with cultural influences on the manifestation of traits.

Third, the lower reliability of Openness to Experience domain scores and facet scales is a widespread phenomenon (Church and Katigbak, 2002b; Heuchert *et al.*, 2000; Hřebíčková *et al.*, 2002; Leininger, 2002; Lodhi *et al.*, 2002; Martin *et al.*, 2002; Piedmont *et al.*, 2002; Piedmont and Chae, 1997), perhaps because of the more abstract ideas represented by this domain (Piedmont *et al.*, 2002). Reminiscent of the concerns of cultural psychologists, other researchers have warned that the limited contextualization of items used to assess the Big Five dimensions may frustrate respondents from some (e.g. collectivistic) cultures (Gülgöz, 2002) or inhibit more culture-relevant assessment (Leininger, 2002).

Fourth, the finding that researchers have been equally successful in replicating alternative structural models across cultures indicates that transported measures do facilitate emergence of their embedded structure in new cultural contexts (Church, 2000; Paunonen and Ashton, 1998). Fifth, there remains debate about whether there are important dimensions that are 'beyond' or relatively independent of the Big Five dimensions, such as Religiosity or Spirituality, Honesty, Positive and Negative Valence, and Sexuality/Sensuality, among others (Ashton and Lee, 2001; Benet-Martínez and Waller, 1997; MacDonald, 2000; Paunonen and Jackson, 2000; Saucier, 2002; Saucier and Goldberg, 1998; Schmitt and Buss, 2000). This debate should be extended to a greater range of cultures.

Sixth, there is little consensus on the structure of more specific traits or facets that define the Big Five within and across cultures. For example, among Big Five measures, there are 30 facets in the NEO-PI-R, 10 in the Big Five Questionnaire, 45 in the Global Personality Inventory, and 15 in a Japanese adjective measure (Kashiwagi, 2002). Item-level factor analyses would help to resolve this issue. Cultural differences in personality structure may be greater at the facet level than at the more global level of the Big Five. Although Saucier and Ostendorf (1999) found that 18 subcomponents of the Big Five dimensions replicated well across the English and German languages in a lexical study, less generalizability may be found across less similar cultures or languages.

Finally, cross-cultural comparisons of the behavioural exemplars of traits have rarely been made (Huang *et al.*, 1997). The content of DIF items may provide clues to cultural differences in the behavioural manifestation of traits. Of course, the practice of avoiding items with culture-specific situational or behavioural referents greatly reduces the likelihood of identifying such differences (e.g. Schmit *et al.*, 2002).

Indigenous approaches

Lexical studies

Assuming that salient individual differences in personality will be encoded in the natural language (Saucier and Goldberg, 1996b), many researchers have examined the structure of comprehensive collections of indigenous trait terms. Major advantages of the lexical approach include its indigenous (emic) nature – dimensions can emerge independently of dimensions external to the culture – and the finite universe of trait attributes from which representative or near-comprehensive samples of terms can be drawn (Saucier and Goldberg,

2001). Disadvantages include

- the possibility that not all important individual differences will be sufficiently encoded in the natural language
- the absence of behavioural or contextual specification in abstract trait terms
- the ambiguity or multidimensionality of some terms
- the greater difficulty of translating single terms than phrases
- some disagreement about which terms should be considered part of the personality domain.

Comprehensive lexical taxonomies or structures have now been derived in Czech (Hřebíčková, Ostendorf and Angleitner, 1995), Dutch (de Raad, Hendriks and Hofstee, 1992), English (e.g. Saucier and Goldberg, 1996a), French (Boies et al., 2001), Filipino (Church, Katigbak and Reyes, 1998), German (Ostendorf, 1990), Hungarian (Szirmák and de Raad, 1994), Italian (Caprara and Perugini, 1994; Di Blas and Forzi, 1998), Korean (Hahn, Lee and Ashton, 1999), Polish (Szarota, 1996), and Turkish (Somer and Goldberg, 1999). Structural studies based on fairly representative collections of trait terms have also been conducted in Hebrew (Almagor, Tellegen and Waller, 1995), Russian (Shmelyov and Pokhil'ko, 1993), Spanish (Benet-Martínez and Waller, 1997), Japanese (Isaka, 1990), and Chinese (Yang and Bond, 1990; Yang and Wang, 2002; Yik and Bond, 1993). The major projects have been reviewed in several excellent sources (Ashton and Lee, 2001; de Raad, 2000; de Raad et al., 1998; Saucier and Goldberg, 2001, 2003; Saucier, Hampson and Goldberg, 2000), so here we primarily note some remaining debates or issues.

One key issue involves the number of lexically based dimensions that can be viewed as universal. Support for the generalizability of the Big Five has been good, with the Intellect dimension exhibiting the most cultural variation (Ashton and Lee, 2001; de Raad et al., 1998). In some languages it has been necessary to extract more than five factors to obtain an Intellect dimension (e.g. in Hungarian: de Raad and Szirmak, 1996; in Italian: Di Blas and Forzi, 1998). The composition of this dimension has also varied, resulting in factors in some cultures that might be better labelled Rebelliousness, Conventionality or Creativity (e.g. in Italian: Caprara and Perugini, 1994; in Dutch: de Raad et al., 1992; in French: Boies et al., 2001). Some cultural differences may reflect differences in taxonomic procedures (de Raad et al., 1998).

With increasing evidence that the Big Five dimensions might not all replicate in closely comparable form, researchers have shown an increasing willingness to consider alternative models or numbers of factors. In the direction of *fewer* factors, some researchers have argued that three-factor solutions, comprised of Extraversion, Agreeableness and Conscientiousness, or four-factor solutions, adding Emotional Stability, are the most generalizable across cultures (Boies et al., 2001; de Raad et al., 1998; Peabody and de Raad, 2002; Saucier and Goldberg, 2003). There are exceptions, however (e.g. in French:

Boies *et al.*, 2001). Some researchers have noted that one-factor solutions, alternatively interpreted as General Evaluation, Social Desirability, Competence or Coping (e.g. see Hofstee, 2001), and two-factor solutions, interpretable as Agency/Dynamism and Socialization/Social Propriety, are widely replicable (Digman, 1997; Saucier and Goldberg, 2003). However, Ashton and Lee (2001, footnote 5) observed that these high order 'superfactors' may be less useful because of the considerable loss in variance accounted for in going from five or six factors to smaller numbers of factors and because such superfactors are more heavily saturated with response style variance.

In the direction of *more* dimensions, structural models of six and seven factors have been advocated. Ashton and Lee (2001) have made a persuasive case for the addition of an Honesty dimension to variants of the Big Five, noting that it appears often enough (in 70 per cent of the languages studied so far) to warrant inclusion in a comprehensive model. This proposal has stimulated debate about whether Honesty content is better viewed as an aspect of Agreeableness, or perhaps as the positive pole of a Negative Valence (NV) dimension defined by very negative, infrequently endorsed descriptors (Ashton and Lee, 2001, 2002; Saucier, 2002).

Saucier (2001; Saucier and Goldberg, 2003) has proposed a seven-dimensional model, the Multi-Language 7 (ML7). Saucier observed resemblances between the seven-factor solutions reported in two very different languages – Hebrew (Almagor *et al.*, 1995) and Filipino (Church *et al.*, 1998) – and largely adopted the factor labels used by the Filipino team: Gregariousness, Self-Assurance, Even Temper (versus Temperamentalness), Concern for Others (versus Egotism), Conscientiousness, Intellect and Negative Valence (NV). Saucier (2001; Saucier and Goldberg, 2003) also noted that similar factors emerged in one of the Italian lexical studies (Di Blas and Forzi, 1998) and that the ML7 dimensions can be reproduced in US samples by selecting appropriate markers.

A different seven-factor model, referred to as the Big Seven, has been proposed by researchers who have culled from dictionaries representative samples of terms, rather than all trait terms, using page sampling methods. They have also included state terms and evaluative terms (Almagor *et al.*, 1995; Benet-Martínez and Waller, 1997, 2002; Tellegen, 1993). These researchers have found fairly good support for the generalizability across the English, Hebrew and Spanish languages of Big Five-like dimensions, plus Positive Valence (PV) and Negative Valence (NV) dimensions defined by more purely evaluative terms (Almagor *et al.*, 1995; Benet-Martínez and Waller, 1997; Tellegen, 1993). Sample PV terms include *remarkable, extraordinary*, and *exceptional*. Sample NV terms include *stupid, slow-witted, bad, useless, beastly* and *shameless*.

Considerable controversy about the importance and interpretation of the PV and NV dimensions remains. Proponents have argued that PV and NV reflect important components of self-evaluation, referring to self-perceptions of status and prominence (PV) and virtue versus social deviance (NV) (Benet-Martínez and Waller, 2002; Saucier, 2002). Opponents have variously argued that (a) PV and NV terms should be excluded because they do not refer to substantive traits; (b) PV and NV may represent 'difficulty factors' caused by skewed response distributions; (c) the content of NV is too heterogeneous to cohere on a single dimension were it not for the shared skewed distributions; (d) the NV dimension may reflect low base-rate attributes or an Infrequency scale reflecting careless responding or other response biases; (e) PV and NV are adequately subsumed by the Big Five; (f) the PV dimension in some studies blends with Big Five Intellect; and (g) inclusion of NV terms might distort lexical structures by pulling other terms with skewed distributions away from their substantive factors (Ashton and Lee, 2002; Church *et al.*, 1998; McCrae and Costa, 1995; Saucier, 1997, 2002; Saucier and Goldberg, 1998). Benet-Martínez and Waller (2002) demonstrated that conceptual and self-report structures of highly evaluative English terms converge on five meaningful factors (Distinction, Stupidity, Worthlessness, Unconventionality and Depravity). This suggests that these terms do have substantive meaning and refer to multiple aspects of self-evaluation.

Less well known is a Chinese seven-factor model proposed by Yang (in press; Yang and Wang, 2002). The Chinese team started from a pool of more than 4000 personality adjectives collected in Taiwan and mainland China from dictionaries, novels and newspapers, and from personality descriptions provided by students and adults. Ratings of meaningfulness, familiarity, social desirability and modernity were obtained for 1520 of these descriptors and 410 descriptors were selected for self-rating studies. Six factors that replicated well across Taiwan and mainland Chinese samples were labelled Competence, Industriousness, Agreeableness, Other-Orientedness (versus Self-Centredness), Extraversion and Large-Mindedness versus Small-Mindedness. Sample-specific factors were Contentedness versus Boastfulness in mainland China and Optimism versus Pessimism in Taiwan. Based on correlations with adjective markers of the Big Five, the NEO-FFI, and other measures, the authors concluded that the Chinese Industriousness, Agreeableness, Extraversion and Optimism dimensions are similar to Big Five Conscientiousness, Agreeableness, Extraversion and Emotional Stability, respectively, but that the Competence, Large-Mindedness and Other-Orientedness dimensions were beyond the coverage of the US models.

It would be useful to conduct further emic-etic comparisons with these Chinese lexical dimensions, using alternative markers of the Big Five (e.g. the NEO-PI-R) and other dimensions. The Competence dimension contains descriptors that seem to assess Big Five Intellect or Culture (e.g. clever, brainy, shrewd, superior, smart, capable vs. foolish, dull, mediocre, unrefined, inexperienced and uninformed). The Other-Orientedness (vs. Self-Centredness) dimension shows a striking resemblance to the Filipino

Concern for Others (vs. Egotism) dimension and the Large-Mindedness dimension shares some descriptors with the Filipino Self-Assurance dimension (e.g. vigorous, domineering, straightforward, bold, with heroic spirit, upright and outspoken).

A few lexical researchers have constructed circumplex representations of personality structure, which may better reflect the multidimensional or inter-stitial nature of many specific traits. Trait circumplexes based on combinations of two (Wiggins, 1979), three (Di Blas and Forzi, 1999; Peabody and Goldberg, 1989), and all five of the Big Five dimensions (Hofstee, de Raad and Goldberg, 1992; Saucier, 1992) have been developed. Circumplex studies suggest that some blends or combinations of Big Five dimensions may be more densely represented than others (i.e. contain more trait terms) in a number of languages. They also help to explain the likelihood of obtaining rotational variants of the Big Five dimensions across different studies and languages (e.g. Hofstee et al., 1992; Johnson and Ostendorf, 1993).

Several areas of needed lexical research can be mentioned. Most researchers have not followed up on Saucier and Goldberg's (1996b) suggestion that the density of terms in different sectors of the personality space might provide clues to cultural values or preoccupations in person perception. Additional peer-rating studies are needed because lexical structures may be less refined in peer ratings than in self ratings (Peabody and Goldberg, 1989). Studies of personality-relevant nouns and verbs are rare. Some have suggested that dimensions beyond those obtained with adjectives might not emerge (de Raad, 1992; de Raad and Hoskens, 1990; de Raad et al., 1988). However, Saucier (2003), in a study of English type nouns, concluded that taxonomies based solely on adjectives are probably not comprehensive because type nouns produce dimensions with different content emphases. The structure of attributes in other person-descriptive categories (e.g. social roles) have not been extended beyond initial studies in English (Saucier, 1997, 2000). More studies that address the cross-cultural comparability of lower order facets are also needed (e.g. Saucier and Ostendorf, 1999).

Indigenous inventories

A promising, yet relatively untapped, source of information on the universality versus uniqueness of personality structure is indigenous inventory projects, which identify items and dimensions that are particularly salient, if not unique, in particular cultures. Unfortunately, as Church (2001b) observed: 'Many of the personality inventories developed around the world . . . do not feel very culture-specific, despite their local origins, because they assess constructs that are familiar to western psychologists' (p. 988). This may reflect legitimate cross-national convergence in the constructs considered important to assess, but also some shared reliance on the western literature on personality constructs.

Some inventories that appear to be indigenous at first glance turn out to be rather imposed-etic in nature. For example, the authors of the NPI in Japan (Yanai, Kashiwagi and Kokusho, 1987) and the South African Personality Questionnaire (see Taylor and Boeyens, 1991) developed items locally but drew on American inventories and construct definitions to select and define the inventory constructs. Similarly, there is a recent trend to develop inventories that assess the (imported) Big Five constructs with indigenous items (e.g. Benet-Martínez and John, 2000; Hendricks et al., 2002; Kashiwagi, 2002; Schmit et al., 2002; Tsaousis, 2002). Of particular interest is the development of the Global Personality Inventory (Schmit et al., 2002). Items were contributed by psychologists in 14 countries and an attempt was made to balance the number of items contributed from each country in the final inventory. However, items thought to be culture specific were eliminated. Although these inventories may contain items that are somewhat culturally decentred, this approach is unlikely to reveal culture-specific dimensions.

More indigenous are some multidimensional inventories developed for Filipinos (Guanzon-Lapeña et al., 1998), Mexicans (e.g. La Rosa and Díaz-Loving, 1991) and Chinese (Cheung et al., 1996). The Filipino inventories are discussed in the second half of this chapter. The Mexican inventory developed by La Rosa and Díaz-Loving (1991) has been described as a self-concept measure. However, like many Big Five scales, the items are trait adjectives. The measure contains several factor analytically derived dimensions that appear to correspond with the Big Five dimensions as follows: (a) Affiliative Sociability (e.g. courteous, amiable) and Inter-Individual Feelings (e.g. tender, loving) resemble Big Five Agreeableness; (b) Expressive Sociability (e.g. friendly, communicative) and Initiative (e.g. dynamic, quick, dominant) resemble Extraversion; (c) Emotional States (e.g. happy, jovial) and Emotional Health (e.g. calm, serene) resemble Emotional Stability; (d) the Occupational dimension (e.g. reliable, studious, capable, responsible) resembles Conscientiousness; (e) the Ethical dimension (e.g. loyal, honest, sincere, upright) resembles Ashton and Lee's (2001) Honesty dimension. These indigenous factors may carve up the personality space somewhat differently, but they do not appear to be highly culture specific.

Combined emic-etic studies have been conducted with the Chinese Personality Assessment Inventory, which measures a number of indigenous constructs (Cheung et al., 1996, 2001). Of special interest is the Interpersonal Relatedness factor (formerly referred to as Chinese Tradition). This is one of four higher order factors found among the 22 scales in the original CPAI and the 28 scales in the revised CPAI-2 (Cheung, 2002). Although the scales loading on the Interpersonal Relatedness factor shift somewhat across samples and versions of the instrument, joint factor analyses with the NEO-PI-R have suggested that the Interpersonal Relatedness dimension may be independent of the Big Five. In addition, Zhang and Bond (1998) showed that Interpersonal Relatedness provides incremental prediction of a measure of filial piety beyond that provided by the Big Five.

Recent research suggests, however, that the Interpersonal Relatedness dimension is not unique to Chinese populations, although it may be more salient for those who identify with Chinese culture (Lin and Church, 2004). For example, the dimension has recently been replicated in European American and Chinese American samples (Cheung *et al.*, 2003; Lin and Church, 2004). It is also not entirely clear how to interpret the dimension. For example, not all of the associated scales measure interpersonal relations. In addition, in an American sample, Lin and Church (2004) showed that the dimension is unrelated to relational self-construal and only modestly related to collective self-construal. It would also make sense to examine the convergence of the CPAI-2 dimensions with the Chinese dimensions derived by Yang and Wang (2002) using a lexical approach.

INDIGENOUS AND CROSS-CULTURAL RESEARCH ON FILIPINO PERSONALITY STRUCTURE

Much of our own research on personality structure has been conducted in the Philippines and has involved both indigenous and cross-cultural perspectives. In the following overview, we organize our findings around a number of questions that are the primary foci of most cross-cultural studies of personality traits. We also use our Philippine results to address some of the controversies referred to in the first half of this chapter.

Are personality traits used to describe or understand persons in all cultures?

Some cultural psychologists have argued that people in collectivistic cultures such as the Philippines will be less inclined to make use of trait concepts in describing persons and their behaviour (e.g. Kanagawa, Cross and Markus, 2001). Psychological and anthropological research suggest that persons in collectivistic cultures may indeed be more attuned to contextual factors than persons in individualistic cultures, but that the use of trait concepts may be a cultural universal (Choi, Nisbett and Norenzayan, 1999; Church, 2000). In any case, it is clear that Filipinos make ready use of trait concepts, so that efforts to determine the structure of personality traits are meaningful in this cultural context.

For example, we have asked Filipino college students in interview and questionnaire studies to describe the characteristics of Filipinos with healthy or unhealthy personalities. In their responses, these respondents often made use of abstract trait terms (Church and Katigbak, 1989). Our lexical studies of Filipino trait attributes show that Filipinos have a large and refined lexicon for describing personality traits, indeed approximately 1300 adjectives and 1000 nouns (Church, Katigbak and Reyes, 1996).

Recently, we have begun to investigate the extent to which individuals in different cultures *believe* in the 'traitedness' versus contextual nature of behaviour (Church *et al.*, 2003). To do so, we developed a measure of implicit trait beliefs, encompassing five belief components: (a) belief in the longitudinal stability of traits; (b) belief in the cross-situational consistency of trait-relevant behaviour; (c) belief in the ability to predict behaviour from traits; (d) belief in the ability to infer traits from relatively few behavioural instances; (e) belief in the importance of traits in understanding persons and their behaviour. We found that such beliefs can be reliably measured and that the component belief structure is comparable across cultures. Significantly, implicit trait beliefs were fairly strongly endorsed in both an individualistic culture (the United States) and a collectivistic culture (Mexico). This suggested that trait beliefs may be widely, if not universally, held.

Do the trait terms in different cultures refer to similar personality characteristics?

In our Philippine studies we have addressed this question by comparing (a) the size of the Filipino (Tagalog) trait lexicon to the size of the trait lexicons in other cultures and (b) the specific content coverage of the Filipino and English trait lexicons. We first culled from a comprehensive Filipino dictionary 6900 adjectives that can be used to describe aspects of persons (Church *et al.*, 1996). This number of person-descriptive adjectives is roughly comparable in size to that reported for the German, Dutch, Italian, Spanish, Hungarian, Czech and Polish languages, but substantially smaller than the English person-descriptive lexicon. On the other hand, whereas more than 80 per cent of Filipino trait adjectives were rated as moderately to very familiar by college-educated Filipinos, about three-quarters of English trait terms are obscure, ambiguous, vague, slangy or quaint (Norman, 1967). Thus, the number of English terms that are useful for personality description may not be significantly larger than the number of useable terms in Filipino or the other languages studied thus far. Indeed, in both Filipino and English, the most definitive studies of personality dimensions based on the lexical approach have been based on about 500 trait adjectives (Church *et al.*, 1998; Saucier and Goldberg, 1996a).

Using trained judges to classify these person-descriptive terms into categories (e.g. personality traits, mental abilities, experiential states, social roles and effects, etc., Angleitner, Ostendorf and John, 1990) and the trait prototypicality judgements of Filipino college students, we identified 1297 Filipino terms referring to personality traits or mental abilities. We then had judges classify these terms, plus a representative list of 1431 English trait terms compiled by Norman (1967), into a 133-category taxonomy based on the Big

Five dimensions (Goldberg, 1990). We found that Filipino terms could be identified for each of the 133 categories and that the relative sizes of the Big Five domains were quite similar across the two languages. The Agreeableness domain was by far the largest, Extraversion and Conscientiousness were the next largest, and Emotional Stability and Intellect were the smallest. We concluded that (a) the Filipino and English languages make comparable trait distinctions; (b) the Filipino trait lexicon is well subsumed by the Big Five domains; (c) the relative size of the Big Five domains may indicate their relative importance, or at least degree of refinement, in person perception and trait attribution in most if not all cultures (Church *et al.*, 1996).

How well do trait dimensions assessed by imported inventories replicate across cultures?

In a large US sample, we found that Tellegen's (1985) hierarchical model of 11 primary dimensions and three or four higher order dimensions was superior to Costa and McCrae's (1985) NEO five-factor model in its structural integrity at the item and primary scale level, but that the NEO five-factor model was superior in terms of the number of higher order dimensions specified (Church and Burke, 1994). Many NEO facets were not well differentiated in item-level factor analyses, within or across the Big Five domains, which is noteworthy in light of the varying number of lower order facets contained in alternative Big Five measures. In an important methodological finding, subsequently confirmed by other researchers (Katigbak *et al.*, 1996; McCrae *et al.*, 1998), we noted several limitations of confirmatory factor analysis (CFA) for testing personality structure models, some of which were noted in the first half of this chapter.

In the Philippines, two of our studies (Katigbak *et al.*, 1996, 2002), plus a third study reported by McCrae *et al.* (1998), obtained very similar results regarding the replicability of the NEO-PI-R five-factor model. Varimax-rotated solutions have produced Neuroticism, Openness to Experience, and Conscientiousness factors, but the Agreeableness and Extraversion facet scales have realigned into factors that we labelled Affiliation and Surgency and others have labelled Love and Dominance (see Rolland, 2002). In all three samples Procrustes solutions targetting the US normative solution produced the intended alignment of facets for all five factors, however. The reliabilities of the facet scales were usually lower than in the US normative sample, suggesting that some behaviour exemplars of the traits may be less relevant or cohere less well in the Philippine context.

Can cultural differences in average trait levels be inferred from comparisons of scores on personality inventories?

The issue is one of full-score comparability. A review of inventory comparisons involving Filipinos has suggested that mean score comparisons sometimes do reveal cultural differences that conform to expectations regarding Filipino culture and personality (Church and Katigbak, 2000). Also, in a 36-culture study that included the Philippines, McCrae (2002) found sensible correlations between cultural means on the NEO-PI-R domain scales and various cultural dimensions (e.g. cultural means on Extraversion correlated highly with individualism).

We have conducted three lines of research, however, that raise questions about such mean comparisons. First, in two studies, we have found evidence of response style differences between Americans and Filipinos, which could bias mean comparisons (Church and Katigbak, 1992; Grimm and Church, 1999). Second, in a DIF analysis of NEO-PI items we found that about 40 per cent of the items exhibited DIF in a comparison of American and Filipino samples. When DIF items were eliminated there were fewer significant cultural mean differences on the NEO-PI traits.

Third, we investigated whether mean profile levels of Filipinos, as compared to American norms, could be predicted from the literature on Filipino personality and the ratings of 43 bicultural judges regarding whether Filipinos or Americans would tend to average higher, or would average the same, on the 30 traits of the NEO-PI-R (Church and Katigbak, 2002b). We found rather good agreement between hypotheses derived from the literature and the judgements of the bicultural raters. However, the resulting predictions received only limited or partial support in the actual Filipino mean profiles. We considered a number of reasons for this, including the possibility that the NEO-PI-R items, which are rather context free, do not sufficiently take into account the ingroup–outgroup distinction that may be more important in collectivistic cultures.

Do indigenous lexical studies suggest culture-specific or alternative personality structures?

In a series of studies we obtained self-ratings of Filipino college and high school students on large and representative sets of trait adjectives from the taxonomic study described earlier. In factor analyses, seven dimensions have emerged and provide a rather comprehensive and replicable representation of Filipino personality structure as derived using the lexical approach: Concerned for Others versus Egotism, Gregariousness, Temperamentalness, Self-Assurance, Conscientiousness, Intellect, and Negative Valence (NV) (Church et al., 1996, 1997, 1998; Katigbak et al., 2002). Table 7.1 shows sample

Table 7.1 Sample terms for the Philippine dimensions

English (Filipino)	English (Filipino)
I Concern for Others versus Egotism	**V Self-Assurance**
other-oriented (makakapwa)	strong-willed (malakas ang loob)
understanding (maunawain)	brave (matapang)
helpful (matulungin)	steadfast (matatag)
humble (mapagpakumbaba)	strong (matibay)
disparaging (mapanlait)	alert (alisto)
opportunistic (mapanlamang)	cowardly (duwag)
cheater (madaya)	fearful (matatakutin)
selfish (makasarili)	weak (mahina)
II Negative Valence (NV)	**VI Intellect**
troublesome (basag-ulero)	intelligent (matalino)
beastly (ugaling-hayop)	able (magaling)
useless (walang-kuwenta)	competent (mahusay)
impudent (tarantado)	talented (may-talino)
uneducated (walang-pinag-aralan)	brainy (may-utak)
drunkard (lasenggo)	learned (marunong)
slow-witted (bobo)	mentally keen (matalas ang isip)
stupid (tanga)	sensible (may-isip)
III Conscientiousness	**VII Temperamentalness**
disciplined (disiplinado)	sulky (tampuhin)
industrious (masipag)	hot-headed (mainitin ang ulo)
diligent (matiyaga)	ill-tempered (masungit)
thrifty (matipid)	moody (sumpungin)
orderly (masinop)	irritable (mainisin)
pious (madasalin)	easily angered (magagalitin)
lazy (tamad)	calm (kalmado)
wasteful (maaksaya)	restrained (mapaghunos-dili)
IV Gregariousness	**VIII Positive Valence (PV)**
noisy (maingay)	outstanding (bukod-tangi)
cheerful (masayahin)	extraordinary (ekstraordinaryo)
talkative (madaldal)	special (espesyal)
humorous (mapagpatawa)	admirable (kahanga-hanga)
quiet (tahimik)	unique (kakaiba)
passive, silent (walang-kibo)	praiseworthy (kapuri-puri)
serious (seryoso)	exceptional (katangi-tangi)
melancholic (malungkutin)	important (mahalaga)

Filipino markers and English translations for these seven dimensions, plus sample Positive Valence (PV) terms. Table 7.2 shows the correlations between these lexical dimensions and various measures of the Big Five across several samples. We have found good one-to-one correspondences between Philippine Concerned for Others and Agreeableness, Philippine Conscientiousness and Big Five Conscientiousness, Philippine Gregariousness and Extraversion, and to a lesser extent, Philippine Intellect and Big Five Intellect or Openness to Experience. The Philippine Temperamentalness and Self-Assurance dimensions, although generally most related to Neuroticism, have tended to be multidimensional in Big Five terms. In sum, lexical studies in the Philippines do not reveal any clearly culture-specific dimensions. However, they do suggest that more than five dimensions, albeit resembling the Big Five, are needed for an adequate structural representation.

Do Philippine lexical dimensions correspond to the Multi-Language 7 model?

Saucier (2001) noted a resemblance between the seven Filipino factors and factors reported in the Hebrew language (Almagor *et al.*, 1995). He proposed a Multi-Language 7 model and showed that scales comprised of English markers of the ML7 showed good one-to-one correspondence with a seven-factor solution in the US obtained with a large set of English trait adjectives. A key test, however, of whether his marker scales assess universal dimensions is whether they correspond in a one-to-one manner in Philippine samples with the Philippine dimensions that partly inspired them. We would expect this to be the case because some of Saucier's ML7 markers are English translations of markers from the original Filipino and Hebrew factors. However, he also included additional English markers that correlated well in a US sample with the original markers. We can ask whether Filipino terms corresponding to Saucier's 60 ML7 markers define ML7 factors in Philippine samples? If so, do ML7 scales correspond in a one-to-one manner with the original Philippine lexical dimensions?

To investigate this, we identified the most equivalent Filipino term for the ML7 markers from 502 terms we had administered to a large Philippine sample of college students ($N = 740$). For 52 of the 60 ML7 markers we could identify acceptable Filipino translations in our 502-word set. Using these 52 terms, we conducted a principal components analysis with varimax rotations and extracted seven factors. We identified factors corresponding to each of the ML7 dimensions except Intellect. Saucier's nine ML7 markers for the Intellect dimension include four terms for which we could not identify good translations in our 502-term set (imaginative, philosophical, average and unreflective). Three of the remaining Intellect markers (artistic, analytical, sophisticated) have never been strong or replicable markers of the Philippine Intellect dimension in our studies. One or more ML7 markers of the

Table 7.2 Correlations between seven Philippine dimensions and measures of the Big Five

Big Five measures	Philippine dimensions						
	Gregariousness	Concern for Others versus Egotism	Conscientiousness	Temperamentalness	Self-assurance	Intellect[a]	Negative Valence (NV)
Extraversion scales							
Adjective scales: Sample 1	**0.69****	−0.14**	−0.31**	−0.06	0.42**	0.15**	−0.18**
Adjective scales: Sample 2	**0.66****	−0.03	−0.35**	0.22**	0.31**	0.05	−0.24**
NEO-FFI: Sample 2	**0.44****	0.18**	−0.16**	−0.09	0.25**	0.08	−0.21**
NEO-PI-R: Sample 3	**0.61****	−0.09*	−0.14*	−0.09*	0.23**	0.13**	−0.08
Agreeableness scales							
Adjective scales: Sample 1	−0.08*	**0.87****	0.55**	−0.37**	0.24**	0.24**	−0.24**
Adjective scales: Sample 2	−0.13**	**0.81****	0.59**	−0.45**	0.13**	0.30**	−0.42**
NEO-FFI: Sample 2	0.08	**0.54****	0.24**	−0.19**	−0.11	0.13*	−0.18**
NEO-PI-R: Sample 3	−0.17**	**0.55****	0.35**	−0.34**	0.08	0.03	0.17**
Conscientiousness scales							
Adjective scales: Sample 1	−0.20**	0.52**	**0.72****	−0.36**	0.52**	0.33**	−0.15**
Adjective scales: Sample 2	−0.37**	0.56**	**0.77****	−0.54**	0.24**	0.32**	−0.09**
NEO-FFI: Sample 2	−0.02	0.36**	**0.33****	0.01	0.29**	0.32**	−0.21**
NEO-PI-R: Sample 3	−0.18**	0.38**	**0.58****	−0.23**	0.43**	0.20**	0.12**

Neuroticism scales

Adjective scales: Sample 1	−0.11**	−0.06	**0.55****	−0.12**	−0.49**	−0.25**	−0.15**
Adjective scales: Sample 2	0.03	−0.17**	0.40**	−0.20**	**−0.58****	−0.26**	−0.10**
NEO-FFI: Sample 2	−0.16*	−0.21**	0.22**	−0.14*	**−0.33****	−0.21**	0.01
NEO-PI-R: Sample 3	−0.04	0.30**	**0.55****	−0.28**	−0.52**	−0.33**	−0.25**

Intellect or Openness to Experience scales

Adjective scales: Sample 1	0.11**	0.10**	−0.10**	−0.05	0.48**	**0.52****	−0.43**
Adjective scales: Sample 2	0.10**	0.10**	−0.11**	−0.01	0.36**	**0.56****	−0.32**
NEO-FFI: Sample 2	0.04	0.12	0.01	0.02	0.02	**0.34****	−0.17**
NEO-PI-R: Sample 3	0.18**	−0.03	−0.04	−0.09*	0.18**	**0.22****	−0.02

Note

The highest correlation in each row is shown in bold. NEO-FFI = NEO Five Factor Inventory; NEO-PI-R = Revised NEO Personality Inventory; Sample 1 correlations are from 'Further exploration of Filipino personality structure using the lexical approach: Do the Big-Five or Big-Seven dimensions emerge?' by A. T. Church, M. S. Katigbak and J. A. S. Reyes, 1998, *European Journal of Personality* 12: 261. © 1998 by John Wiley and Sons, Ltd. Sample 2 correlations are from 'Filipino personality structure and the Big Five model: A lexical approach', by A. T. Church, J. A. S. Reyes, M. S. Katigbak and S. D. Grimm, 1997, *Journal of Personality* 65: 498. © 1997 by Duke University Press. Sample 3 correlations are from 'Are indigenous personality dimensions culture specific? Philippine inventories and the Five-Factor model', by M. S. Katigbak, A. T. Church, M. A. Guanzon-Lapeña, A. J. Carlota and G. H. del Pilar, 2002, *Journal of Personality and Social Psychology* 82: 96. © 2002 by the American Psychological Association, Inc. *p < 0.05. **p < 0.01.

[a] In Sample 1 the Philippine Intellect scale is a blend of Intellect and Positive Valence (PV) terms.

Conscientiousness, Negative Valence, Concerned for Others and Self-Assurance dimensions also failed to have good loadings on their respective factors in our Philippine sample.

Nonetheless, when we correlated ML7 scale scores based on the 52 markers with the scale scores for the original Philippine dimensions, we found good one-to-one correspondences, although less so for the Intellect dimension. The convergent correlations for the seven dimensions were as follows: Concerned for Others versus Egotism (0.74), Negative Valence (0.71), Conscientiousness (0.68), Gregariousness (0.89), Self-Assurance (0.78), Temperamentalness (0.91), and Intellect (0.52). The largest off-diagonal or discriminant correlation was 0.43, which was the correlation between ML7 Concerned for Others and Philippine Conscientiousness. These results indicate that, overall, Saucier's ML7 marker scales match up well with the Philippine dimensions. However, some of the terms chosen by Saucier to define the ML7 dimensions in a US sample are not good markers of the ML7 or Philippine dimensions in the Philippines. Thus, even if the ML7 dimensions turn out to be cultural universals, some of the markers of these dimensions probably will not be. In particular, the Philippine Intellect dimension is more narrow in content than Saucier's English ML7 markers for the dimension. Indeed, given its variable content across cultures, the universality of the ML7 Intellect dimension may be the most difficult to demonstrate (e.g. see Ashton and Lee, 2001, Table 1).

Do the Philippine lexical dimensions include honesty?

Ashton and Lee (2001, pp. 334–335) acknowledged that the Filipino results do not provide clear support for their preferred six-factor taxonomy of Big Five variants plus Honesty. However, they opined that the Filipino results do produce 'recognizable variants' of each of the six factors. We applaud Ashton and Lee's (2001) identification of an Honesty dimension in a number of languages (see also Ashton et al., 2004). However, we think that the *absence* of an Honesty variant in the Filipino data is more definitive than Ashton and Lee's (2001) conclusion would suggest.

In two of our data sets we searched for Filipino equivalents of Honesty terms as defined by Ashton, Lee and colleagues (e.g. see Table 1 in Boies et al., 2002). In these data sets we had factor analysed 280 and 502 trait adjectives respectively (Church et al., 1997, Study 2; Church et al., 1998). In both data sets, the majority of Filipino Honesty terms loaded on the Concerned for Others versus Egotism dimension. Honesty terms referring to sincerity, loyalty, honesty and trustworthiness were greatly outnumbered by (dis)Honesty terms referring to arrogance and conceit, hypocrisy, pretentiousness, boastfulness, condescension, lying, cheating and secretiveness. Most of the remaining (dis)Honesty terms loaded on the Negative Valence (NV) factor, probably because they refer to the most extreme or negative forms of arrogance, hypocrisy, treachery, and so forth, and have very low endorsement rates.

In short, in our Philippine data sets, Honesty markers are just one aspect of a much broader Concern for Others versus Egotism dimension, which in Big Five terms is strongly related to Agreeableness (Church *et al.*, 1998). In some of our factor solutions the Egotism terms split off and define their own factor, but in these cases, the positive Honesty terms remain associated with the Concern for Others factor. Furthermore, Egotism seems to be a more appropriate label than Honesty for this factor when it does split off, because many more terms refer to arrogance, boastfulness and conceit than to lying and secretiveness.

Recently, Ashton *et al.* (2004) have adopted the somewhat broader label of Honesty-Humility for this dimension. This new label does a better job of encompassing the breadth of content subsumed by their dimension, which includes not only the core honesty content, but also humility terms such as *modest, greedy, arrogant, conceited* and *boastful*. When Egotism appears as a separate Philippine factor, the (low) Humility label would be reasonably appropriate, but the Honesty terms would still remain as a subset of the Concerned for Others dimension. Thus, even the broader Honesty-Humility label is too narrow to encompass the breadth of content in the Philippine Concerned for Others versus Egotism dimension.

Are there additional dimensions beyond the Big Five or Philippine dimensions?

Interestingly, the best candidates for additional Philippine dimensions are among those cited by Paunonen and Jackson (2000) in an analysis of dimensions that might be beyond the Big Five in US samples.

Egotism

Paunonen and Jackson (2000) and Barelds and Luteijn (2002) suggested that Egotism might be beyond the Big Five. We frequently obtain a distinct Egotism dimension depending on the number of factors extracted. However, we have also seen that Egotism content can parsimoniously define the negative pole of the Concerned for Others dimension.

Honesty

Like Ashton and Lee (2001), Paunonen and Jackson (2000) suggested that content referring to being honest, ethical and moral versus sly, deceptive and manipulative might be independent of the Big Five. As discussed above, however, we find that Honesty content is well subsumed by the Concerned for Others versus Egotism dimension.

Religiosity

Both Saucier and Goldberg (1998) and Paunonen and Jackson (2000) mentioned Religiosity as a candidate dimension beyond the Big Five. In our Philippine studies, Religious terms have most frequently loaded highly on the Conscientiousness dimension, although in one study they loaded more highly on the Concerned for Others dimension (Church *et al.*, 1997). Indeed, religious terms typically have dual loadings on these two Philippine dimensions, and we can often identify a separate Religiosity factor if we extract enough factors (Church *et al.*, 1997, Studies 1 and 2; Church *et al.*, 1998; Katigbak *et al.*, 2002). Furthermore, the Religiosity scale that we sometimes score separately correlates moderately with both NEO-PI-R Agreeableness and Conscientiousness (Katigbak *et al.*, 2002, Table 3). Taken together, these results strongly suggest that religious terms lie between the Concerned for Others (Agreeableness) and Conscientiousness dimensions. Using Paunonen and Jackson's (2000) cut-off for distinctiveness – a squared multiple correlation of less than 0.20 with the Big Five dimensions – our Religiosity scale would be considered 'beyond the Big Five' as measured by the NEO-PI-R (Katigbak *et al.*, 2002, Table 3). In short, there might be advantages in treating Religiosity as a distinct dimension in our Philippine data, particularly given the salience of religious life in Philippine culture. Of course, some psychologists might view Religiosity as a dimension of belief or worldview, rather than a personality dimension.

Sexy/sensual and thrifty versus extravagant

Paunonen and Jackson (2000) suggested that sexy, sensual and erotic content and thrifty, frugal and miserly content might define dimensions beyond the Big Five. Indeed, in an early factor analysis of 39 terms that had not loaded highly on our primary Philippine dimensions, we identified three interpretable factors, which we labelled Seductiveness (11 terms), Extravagance (9 terms) and Frugality (4 terms) (Church *et al.*, 1997, Study 1). In subsequent studies, however, we have excluded Seductiveness terms because several of them are lewd and gender specific. In a few samples we have identified a small Extravagance or Flamboyance factor when larger numbers of factors have been extracted. However, terms referring to extravagance and frugality have also proven to be good positive and negative markers, respectively, of the Philippine Conscientiousness dimension (e.g. see Church *et al.*, 1997, Study 2).

Other categories

Paunonen and Jackson (2000) also suggested that terms referring to being (a) humorous, (b) conservative and traditional and (c) masculine versus feminine might define dimensions beyond the Big Five. In our Philippine studies, humorous and witty characteristics have been strong and consistent markers of the Gregariousness dimension. Filipino terms referring to conservativism, traditionality or modernity have tended to have moderate loadings on the Conscientiousness dimension, and there do not seem to be enough Filipino terms in this category to identify a distinct factor. There are no terms for masculinity or femininity in our Filipino trait lists. In sum, of the content categories most often mentioned as beyond the Big Five, Religiosity shows the most potential as a separate dimension in our Filipino lexical studies.

What is the nature of the Positive and Negative Valence dimensions in the Philippines?

Negative Valence

Like most trait taxonomers we initially excluded terms classified by judges as pure evaluation terms (Church et al., 1996). Nonetheless, when we factor analysed presumably substantive trait terms we obtained a Negative Valence (NV) factor. In later studies we intentionally added pure positive or negative evaluation terms, and the NV dimension has proven to be robust across studies (Church et al., 1997, Studies 1 and 2; Church et al., 1998). The terms that initially defined the NV dimension were classified by Filipino judges as trait terms, not pure evaluation terms, which suggests that they do have some substantive meaning. However, their extremely low endorsement rates and low social desirability ratings (Church et al., 1997) seem to make them susceptible to response style variance as well.

Table 7.2 shows the correlations of our NV scales with several Big Five measures in our previous studies. The majority of our NV terms refer to extremely negative characteristics in the Agreeableness domain (e.g. treacherous, sadistic, extremely rude), and secondarily to the Intellect domain (e.g. feeble-minded, stupid, ignorant). Thus, if the NV scores have substantive meaning, we would expect NV to correlate most with Big Five Agreeableness and Intellect/Openness scales. There is modest support for this in Table 7.2, but more so for the Intellect scales and primarily when trait adjective scales were used. In contrast, when NV scores were correlated with inventory measures of the Big Five (i.e. the NEO-FFI and NEO-PI-R) there was no clear tendency for NV scores to correlate more highly with any particular Big Five dimension. Indeed, if respondents' ratings of the NV terms have strong substantive meaning, one would probably expect the negative correlations with NEO Agreeableness scores to be significantly more negative than they are.

For this chapter, we conducted an additional analysis that is relevant to the interpretation of the Positive and Negative Valence dimensions. Inspired by Benet-Martínez and Waller's (2002) factor analyses of highly evaluative terms in the English language, we factor analysed 60 PV and NV terms in one of our previous samples (N = 740; Church *et al.*, 1998). If the PV and NV terms have substantive meaning in self-rating data, then we should identify interpretable factors defined by terms with similar meanings. A five-factor solution was most interpretable. Although simple structure was limited (i.e. there were many secondary loadings), the highest loading terms for each factor were similar in meaning. The first factor could be labelled Poor Mental Functioning and is slightly broader in content than Benet-Martínez and Waller's (2002) Stupidity factor. The highest loading terms refer to (a) stupidity, lack of education or illiteracy (e.g. *bobo* [slow-witted], *tanga* [stupid], *mangmang* [ignorant, illiterate]); (b) insanity (e.g. *kulang-kulang* [feeble-minded, somewhat crazy], *may-sira ang ulo* [insane]; or (c) general uselessness or worthlessness (e.g. *walang-kuwenta* [useless], *walang-halaga* [worthless]). The second factor resembled Benet-Martínez and Waller's Distinction factor (e.g. *katangi-tangi* [exceptional], *kahanga-hanga* [admirable], *napakahusay* [excellent]). The third factor resembled Benet-Martínez and Waller's Depravity factor (e.g. *walang-kaluluwa* [lacking soul, cruel], *makademonyo* [wicked], *walang-konsiyensiya* [without conscience]). The two remaining factors, which we labelled Delinquent Behaviours (e.g. *lasenggo* [drunkard], *sugarol* [given to gambling]) and Mistreatment of Others (e.g. *mapang-alipusta* [contemptuous], *mapang-api* [oppressive], *walang-puso* [heartless]) did not correspond well with Benet-Martínez and Waller's Worthlessness and Unconventionality factors.

All in all, we are inclined to agree with the multifaceted perspective on Negative Valence (NV) put forth by Ashton and Lee (2002). We are open to the possibility that NV is due, in part, to substantively meaningful personality variance. Our factor analysis of PV and NV terms is consistent with this view. However, we also believe that the NV factor is strongly influenced by individual differences in (a) the tendency to endorse very negative self-evaluations and (b) tendencies 'to endorse low base-rate terms regardless of meaning (i.e. infrequent responding), which may be due either to careless responding or to "faking bad", or both' (Ashton and Lee, 2002, p. 66). From our experience with several large Philippine data sets, we are also inclined to agree with Ashton and Lee (2002, p. 69) that the inclusion of NV terms can sometimes cause terms that would otherwise load on more clearly substantive factors to 'pull away' to the NV factor because of shared low endorsement rates.

Positive Valence and Intellect

Ironically, inclusion of Positive Valence (PV) terms in our more recent studies has raised questions about the meaning of the Philippine Intellect dimension. The Intellect dimension has shown moderate to strong convergence with measures of Big Five Intellect or Openness to Experience in some of our studies, particularly when Big Five adjective scales were used (see Table 7.2).

However, Intellect terms have also shown a strong tendency to blend with PV terms to define a single factor (Church *et al.*, 1998; Katigbak *et al.*, 2002). In addition, PV and Intellect scales showed a very similar pattern of correlations with NEO-PI-R domain scores in a recent study, correlating most highly (in the negative direction) with Neuroticism. This result provides some support for interpreting PV as high self-confidence or positive self-evaluation, but it also implies that the Intellect dimension should be interpreted similarly, at least in a student sample. Katigbak *et al.* (2002, p. 98) noted that 'Filipinos value modesty, so for Filipino students to describe themselves as intelligent, brainy, talented, learned, competent, and wise may require them to respond in a very, if not overly, positive or self-confident manner.' This blending of PV and Intellect terms is not unique to the Philippines and warrants further study (e.g. Almagor *et al.*, 1995; Saucier, 1997). This finding also adds to questions about the meaning and make-up of the Intellect dimension in different lexical studies (e.g. see Ashton and Lee, 2001, Table 1).

Do indigenous inventories reveal culture-specific or alternative personality structures?

We have also investigated the structure of Filipino personality using indigenous inventories. Perhaps the most persuasive support for the relevance of the Big Five model in the Philippines comes from our factor analysis of the scales of the indigenous *Panukat ng Pagkataong Pilipino* (PPP; Carlota, 1985). In this inventory, Carlota (1985) included 16 traits that were most frequently mentioned by respondents when asked to describe traits and behaviours of Filipinos, and three traits of particular interest to the test developer. Our principal components analysis (with varimax rotations) of these scales ($N = 387$) favoured a four-factor solution (Katigbak *et al.*, 2002). Interpretation of the factors and correlations between the factor scores and NEO-PI-R domain scores strongly suggested that the four dimensions could be interpreted in Big Five terms as follows: Factor 1, a blend of Agreeableness ($r = 0.53$ with NEO-PI-R Agreeableness) and (inverse) Neuroticism ($r = -0.57$ with Neuroticism); Factor 2, Conscientiousness ($r = 0.57$ with Conscientiousness); Factor 3, Extraversion ($r = 0.71$ with Extraversion); and Factor 4, Openness to Experience ($r = 0.45$ with Openness to Experience). The failure to obtain a distinct Neuroticism factor was probably due to the inclusion of only two scales relevant to this Big Five domain (i.e. Emotional Stability, Sensitiveness).

Indeed, when we factor analysed the PPP jointly with the NEO-PI-R facet scales and scales measuring the Philippine lexical dimensions, the Big Five dimensions clearly emerged in the five-factor solution, and the PPP scales aligned with factors representing all Big Five dimensions. The PPP Emotional Stability and Sensitiveness scales now loaded highly on the Neuroticism factor instead of blending with the Agreeableness scales. In multiple regression analyses relating the indigenous PPP and lexical scales to the Big

Five domain scores, we found that most of the Philippine dimensions overlapped considerably with the Big Five. A few Philippine scales (Social Curiosity, Risk Taking and Religiosity) were less well accounted for by the Big Five dimensions and may be particularly salient or comprised somewhat differently in the Philippines, although the constructs are not unknown in western cultures.

Another way to determine whether indigenous dimensions add anything to imported dimensions is to examine their incremental validity in predicting societal criteria. We compared the ability of the Philippine dimensions and the domain and facet scores of the Filipino NEO-PI-R to predict self-reported smoking, drinking, gambling, praying, accident proneness, tolerance of homosexuality, and tolerance toward extramarital and premarital sexual relations. The indigenous scales did not outperform the NEO-PI-R scales, but did add modest incremental validity (Katigbak *et al.*, 2002).

Our item-level factor analysis of a second Philippine inventory, the *Panukat ng Ugali at Pagkatao* (PUP; Enriquez and Guanzon, 1985) favoured six dimensions, four of which were clear Philippine analogs of Big Five Agreeableness, Conscientiousness, Neuroticism and Extraversion (*r*s of 0.53 to 0.60 with the corresponding NEO-PI-R domain scores). A fifth factor represented a communality or validity scale and was comprised of items with extremely high respondent agreement (high positive loadings) or disagreement (high negative loadings). A sixth dimension, which we labelled Self-Directedness, was most related with inverse Agreeableness ($r = -0.36$) and, in particular, with the NEO-PI-R Compliance facet ($r = -0.40$). No dimension resembled Intellect or Openness to Experience, but four of the Big Five dimensions were identified.

We have also constructed an indigenous inventory to measure Filipino college students' conceptions of healthy and unhealthy personality. Content coverage was based on a content analysis of personality descriptions provided in interviews and questionnaires, and items were derived from situational behavioural exemplars of the relevant traits provided by the students (Church and Katigbak, 1988, 1989). Factor analyses of self-ratings on these items resulted in six dimensions, which we labelled Responsibility, Social Potency, Emotional Control, Concern for Others, Broad-Mindedness and Affective Well-Being (Katigbak *et al.*, 1996). Although developed using a different method, these dimensions showed fairly good conceptual overlap with the lexical dimensions based on Filipino trait adjectives. Furthermore, in both Philippine and US samples, we found moderate to strong associations between the Philippine inventory dimensions and dimensions of the NEO-PI-R Big Five and Tellegen models. Although none of the Philippine dimensions were largely culture specific, the Broad-Mindedness and Concerned for Others dimensions showed weaker relationships with the western dimensions because of cultural differences in the behavioural exemplars of these dimensions (Katigbak *et al.*, 1996).

CONCLUSIONS

Using both cross-cultural and indigenous approaches, researchers have made significant strides in clarifying the structure of personality across cultures. Nevertheless, questions remain. Overall, cross-cultural results, and our results in the Philippines, reveal a considerable degree of cross-cultural comparability of personality dimensions, consistent with the expectations of many cross-cultural and evolutionary psychologists. Whether these dimensions play a comparable role in self-concepts and in the understanding and prediction of behaviour in all cultures is a central question from a cultural psychology perspective. However, research to date, including our own studies in the Philippines, suggests that traits are used in person description and predict societally relevant criteria in most, if not all, cultures. Our Philippine results are consistent with the following conclusions:

1 Filipinos make ready use of trait concepts and Filipino trait dimensions do predict societally relevant criteria. This supports the applicability of the trait approach in the Philippines.
2 The Filipino (Tagalog) and English languages make comparable trait distinctions.
3 The five-factor model as measured by the NEO-PI-R replicates well in the Philippines. However, as in some other cultures, the reorientation of Extraversion and Agreeableness facets into Affiliation and Surgency dimensions is a replicable finding.
4 Seven lexical dimensions – Gregariousness, Concerned for Others versus Egotism, Conscientiousness, Temperamentalness, Self-Assurance, Intellect and Negative Valence – are replicable across Philippine samples and show sensible correspondences with the Big Five dimensions. Although these dimensions carve up the personality space somewhat differently, they are not highly culture specific.
5 The Philippine lexical dimensions correspond to Saucier's (2001) Multi-Language 7 model, but some English markers of these dimensions are less relevant in the Philippines.
6 The Honesty-Humility dimension advocated by Ashton and Lee (2001; see also Ashton et al., 2004) does not emerge as a distinct dimension in Philippine lexical studies based on trait adjectives.
7 It might be appropriate to treat Religiosity as a separate Philippine dimension, although it can also be subsumed by the other lexical dimensions, especially Conscientiousness.
8 The Negative Valence (NV) dimension in the Philippines probably blends substantive and response style variance, but more research is needed on its possible substantive correlates.
9 Indigenous inventories in the Philippines overlap considerably with the

five-factor model; at best, only a few narrow dimensions are somewhat independent of the Big Five.

10   It is risky to compare Philippine mean profiles with personality profiles or norms in other cultures in hopes of drawing conclusions about personality differences.

It is clear from both our Philippine findings and cross-cultural research internationally that the personality structures embedded in existing inventories can be replicated well across cultures. Much of this evidence supports the generalizability of the five-factor or Big Five model. However, the dimensions in other inventories, some of which carve up the personality domain somewhat differently, also replicate well across cultures, calling into question the definitiveness or exclusivity of the five-factor model.

Interestingly, results from indigenous lexical and inventory approaches provide some of the best support for the universality of Big Five-like dimensions, because these indigenous dimensions have emerged from native languages or indigenous literatures and informants, independent of dimensions in other cultures. At the same time, however, dimensions derived using indigenous approaches have sometimes carved up the personality space somewhat differently than the five-factor or Big Five model (Cheung *et al.*, 1996, 2001; Church *et al.*, 1998; Katigbak *et al.*, 1996; Yang and Bond, 1990; Yang and Wang, 2002). This has been the case even in languages and cultures in which the Big Five dimensions replicate well when more imported approaches such as Big Five marker scales or the NEO-PI-R have been used (e.g. Hahn *et al.*, 1999; Boies *et al.*, 2001; Perugini and Di Blas, 2002). These findings highlight the imposed-etic nature of efforts that involve transporting existing inventories across cultures.

In sum, while the five-factor model may provide an adequate and fairly comprehensive representation of personality structure in most cultures, this does not mean it provides the optimal representation in these cultures. Perugini and Di Blas (2002) endorsed a similar view. They noted that the Big Five are important personality categories that *can* be used to organize personality attributes, but that 'they are not necessarily the universal coordinates of personality unless we so decide' (p. 301). In addition, some indigenous psychologists claim to have identified culture-specific dimensions that are independent of the Big Five (e.g. Cheung *et al.*, 2001; La Rosa and Díaz-Loving, 1991; Yang, in press; Yang and Wang, 2002), and it is conceivable that additional culture-specific dimensions will be identified because many cultures have not yet been studied using indigenous lexical or inventory approaches. Finally, we do not yet know whether comparable personality dimensions will be identified in less literate or educated samples. In such samples, alternative methods of data collection may be necessary (Poortinga *et al.*, 2002).

Significant gaps in cross-cultural research on personality structure include the sparse amount of research on the structure of personality at the level of more specific traits or facets and at the level of behavioural exemplars of traits. Cultural differences may be greatest at these levels of analysis, particularly if culturally salient situational or behavioural referents of traits are retained. Other areas of needed research include (a) more refined qualitative analyses of cultural differences in the composition of similar dimensions across cultures (e.g. see Peabody and de Raad, 2002); (b) further comparisons of culture-level and individual-level structures of personality using different inventories; (c) comparisons of the nomological networks (e.g. behavioural correlates) of comparable dimensions across cultures, including the controversial Positive and Negative Valence (NV) dimensions; (d) further emic-etic studies that relate indigenous and universal dimensions, or emic-emic studies that relate indigenous dimensions across cultures, to further test claims of culture-specificity; (e) lexical studies of personality nouns and other categories of person description, such as social roles, which may be important in collectivistic cultures; and (f) studies that examine the meaning and accuracy of cultural mean profiles by relating them to the personality judgements of cultural/bicultural informants, indigenous personality literatures, and subpopulations varying in acculturation level. Due to space considerations, we chose not to address the cross-cultural generalizability of personality types, but this is also a promising area of research on personality structure across cultures (Asendorpf, Caspi and Hofstee, 2002).

In summary, recent questioning of the five-factor or Big Five model may temporarily delay psychologists from attaining the advantages of a consensus taxonomy or structural model. However, the recent emergence of competing models, within and across cultures (e.g. the Big Six, Multi-Language 7, Chinese Seven, Chinese Interpersonal Relatedness dimension), can be viewed as positive developments in preventing premature foreclosure on what might not be the optimal structural model, at least in some cultural contexts. These efforts need to be extended to include an increasing variety of languages and cultures.

AUTHORS' NOTE

The Philippine research summarized in this chapter was supported by National Institute of Mental Health Grants R29-MH47343 and R01-MH59941.

Correspondence concerning this chapter should be addressed to A. Timothy Church or Marcia S. Katigbak, Department of Educational Leadership and Counseling Psychology, Cleveland Hall, Washington State University, Pullman, WA, 99164-2136. Email: church@mail.wsu.edu.

REFERENCES

Almagor, M., Tellegen, A. and Waller, N. (1995) 'The Big Seven model: A cross-cultural replication and further exploration of the basic dimensions of natural language of trait descriptions', *Journal of Personality and Social Psychology* 69: 300–307.

Angleitner, A., Ostendorf, F. and John, O. P. (1990) 'Towards a taxonomy of personality descriptors in German: A psycho-lexical study', *European Journal of Personality* 4: 89–118.

Asendorpf, J. B., Caspi, A. and Hofstee, W. K. B. (eds) (2002) 'The puzzle of personality types' (special issue), *European Journal of Personality* 16.

Ashton, M. C. and Lee, K. (2001) 'A theoretical basis for the major dimensions of personality', *European Journal of Personality* 15: 327–353.

Ashton, M. C. and Lee, K. (2002) 'Six independent factors of personality variation: A response to Saucier', *European Journal of Personality* 16: 63–75.

Ashton, M. C., Lee, K., Perugini, M., Szarota, P., de Vries, R. E., De Blas, L., Boies, K. and De Raad, B. (2004) 'A six-factor structure of personality-descriptive adjectives: Solutions from psycholexical studies in seven languages', *Journal of Personality and Social Psychology* 86: 356–366.

Barelds, D. P. H. and Luteijn, F. (2002) 'Measuring personality: A comparison of three personality questionnaires in the Netherlands', *Personality and Individual Differences* 33: 499–510.

Barrett, P. T., Petrides, K. V., Eysenck, S. B. G. and Eysenck, H. J. (1998) 'The Eysenck Personality Questionnaire: An examination of the factorial similarity of P, E, N, and L across 34 countries', *Personality and Individual Differences* 25: 805–819.

Benet-Martínez, V. and John, O. P. (1998) '*Los Cinco Grandes* across cultures and ethnic groups: Multitrait-multimethod analyses of the Big Five in Spanish and English', *Journal of Personality and Social Psychology* 75: 729–750.

Benet-Martínez, V. and John, O. P. (2000) 'Toward the development of quasi-indigenous personality constructs: Measuring *Los Cinco Grandes* in Spain with indigenous Castilian markers', *American Behavioural Scientist* 44: 141–157.

Benet-Martínez, V. and Waller, N. G. (1997) 'Further evidence for the cross-cultural generality of the "Big Seven" model: Imported and indigenous Spanish personality constructs', *Journal of Personality* 65: 567–598.

Benet-Martínez, V. and Waller, N. G. (2002) 'From *adorable* to *worthless*: Implicit and self-report structure of highly evaluative personality descriptors', *European Journal of Personality* 16: 1–41.

Berry, J. W. (1969) 'On cross-cultural comparability', *International Journal of Psychology* 4: 119–128.

Boies, K., Lee, K., Ashton, M. C., Pascal, S. and Nicol, A. A. M. (2001) 'The structure of the French personality lexicon', *European Journal of Personality* 15: 277–295.

Buss, D. M. (1996) 'Social adaptation and five major factors of personality', in J. S. Wiggins (ed.) *The Five-Factor Model of Personality: Theoretical Perspectives*, pp. 180–207. New York: Guilford Press.

Buss, D. M. (2001) 'Human nature and culture: An evolutionary psychological perspective', *Journal of Personality* 69: 955–978.

Butcher, J. N. (ed.) (1996) *International Adaptations of the MMPI-2*. Minneapolis: University of Minnesota Press.

Caprara, G. V. and Perugini, M. (1994) 'Personality described by adjectives: The generalizability of the Big Five to the Italian lexical context', *European Journal of Personality* 8: 357–369.

Caprara, G. V., Barbaranelli, C., Borgogni, L. and Perugini, M. (1993) 'The Big Five Questionnaire: A new questionnaire for the measurement of the five factor model', *Personality and Individual Differences* 15: 281–288.

Caprara, G. V., Barbaranelli, C., Bermudez, J., Maslach, C. and Ruch, W. (2000) 'Multivariate methods for the comparison of factor structures in cross-cultural research: An illustration with the Big Five Questionnaire', *Journal of Cross-Cultural Psychology* 31: 301–328.

Carlota, A. J. (1985) 'The development of the Panukat ng Pagkataong Pilipino (PPP)', *Philippine Journal of Educational Measurement* 4: 55–68.

Chan, D. (2000) 'Detection of differential item functioning on the Kirton Adaption-Innovation Inventory using multiple-group mean and covariance structure analyses', *Multivariate Behavioural Research* 35: 169–199.

Cheung, F. M. (2002) 'Significance of indigenous constructs in the study of personality', in A. T. Church (Chair) *Indigenous and Cross-Cultural Analysis of Personality*. Symposium conducted at the meeting of the 25th International Congress of Applied Psychology, Singapore July.

Cheung, F. M., Leung, K., Fan, R. M., Song, W. Z., Zhang, J. X. and Zhang, J. P. (1996) 'Development of the Chinese Personality Assessment Inventory', *Journal of Cross-Cultural Psychology* 27: 181–199.

Cheung, F. M., Leung, K., Zhang, J. X., Sun, H. F., Gan, Y. Q., Song, W. Z. *et al.* (2001) 'Indigenous Chinese personality construct: Is the five-factor model complete?', *Journal of Cross-Cultural Psychology* 32: 407–433.

Cheung, F. M., Cheung, S. F., Leung, K., Ward, C. and Leong, F. (2003) 'The English version of the Chinese Personality Assessment Inventory', *Journal of Cross-Cultural Psychology* 34: 433–452.

Choi, I., Nisbett, R. E. and Norenzayan, A. (1999) 'Causal attribution across cultures: Variation and universality', *Psychological Bulletin* 125: 47–63.

Choi, S-C., Kim, U. and Choi, S-H. (1993) 'Indigenous analysis of collective representations: A Korean perspective', in U. Kim and J. W. Berry (eds) *Indigenous Psychologies: Research and Experience in Cultural Context*, pp. 193–210. Newbury Park, CA: Sage.

Church, A. T. (2000) 'Culture and personality: Towards an integrated cultural trait psychology', *Journal of Personality* 68: 651–703.

Church, A. T. (2001a) 'Introduction', *Journal of Personality* 69: 787–801.

Church, A. T. (2001b) 'Personality measurement in cross-cultural perspective', *Journal of Personality* 69: 979–1006.

Church, A. T. and Burke, P. J. (1994) 'Exploratory and confirmatory tests of the Big Five and Tellegen's three- and four-dimensional models', *Journal of Personality and Social Psychology* 66: 93–114.

Church, A. T. and Katigbak, M. S. (1988) 'The emic strategy in the identification and assessment of personality dimensions in a non-Western culture: Rationale, steps, and a Philippine illustration', *Journal of Cross-Cultural Psychology* 19: 140–163.

Church, A. T. and Katigbak, M. S. (1989) 'Internal, external, and self-report structure of personality in a non-Western culture: An investigation of cross-language and cross-cultural generalizability', *Journal of Personality and Social Psychology* 57: 857–872.

Church, A. T. and Katigbak, M. S. (1992) 'The cultural context of academic motives: A comparison of American and Filipino college students', *Journal of Cross-Cultural Psychology* 23: 40–58.

Church, A. T. and Katigbak, M. S. (2000) 'Trait psychology in the Philippines', *American Behavioural Scientist* 44: 73–94.

Church, A. T. and Katigbak, M. S. (2002a) 'Indigenization of psychology in the Philippines', *International Journal of Psychology* 37: 129–148.

Church, A. T. and Katigbak, M. S. (2002b) 'The five-factor model in the Philippines: Investigating trait structure and levels across cultures', in R. R. McCrae and J. Allik (eds) *The Five-Factor Model across Cultures*, pp. 129–154. New York: Kluwer/Plenum.

Church, A. T., Katigbak, M. S. and Reyes, J. A. S. (1996) 'Toward a taxonomy of trait adjectives in Filipino: Comparing personality lexicons across cultures', *European Journal of Personality* 10: 3–24.

Church, A. T., Reyes, J. A. S., Katigbak, M. S. and Grimm, S. D. (1997) 'Filipino personality structure and the Big Five model: A lexical approach', *Journal of Personality* 65: 477–528.

Church, A. T., Katigbak, M. S. and Reyes, J. A. S. (1998) 'Further exploration of Filipino personality structure using the lexical approach: Do the big-five or big-seven dimensions emerge?', *European Journal of Personality* 12: 249–269.

Church, A. T., Ortiz, F. A., Katigbak, M. S., Avdeyeva, T. V., Emerson, A. M., Vargas Flores, J. D. and Ibáñez Reyes, J. (2003) 'Measuring individual and cultural differences in implicit trait theories', *Journal of Personality and Social Psychology* 85: 332–347.

Costa, P. T. Jr. and McCrae, R. R. (1985) *The NEO Personality Inventory Manual Form S and Form R*. Odessa, FL: Psychological Assessment Resources.

De Raad, B. (1992) 'The replicability of the Big Five personality dimensions in three word-classes of the Dutch language', *European Journal of Personality* 6: 15–29.

De Raad, B. (2000) *The Big Five Personality Factors: The Psycholexical Approach to Personality*. Göttingen: Hogrefe and Huber.

De Raad, B. and Hoskens, M. (1990) 'Personality-descriptive nouns', *European Journal of Personality* 4: 131–146.

De Raad, B. and Perugini, M. (eds) (2002) *Big Five Assessment*. Seattle, WA: Hogrefe and Huber.

De Raad, B. and Szirmák, Z. (1996) 'The search for the "Big Five" in a non-Indo-European language: The Hungarian trait structure and its relationship to the EPQ and the PTS', *European Review of Applied Psychology* 44: 17–24.

De Raad, B., Mulder, E., Kloosterman, K. and Hofstee, W. K. B. (1988) 'Personality-descriptive verbs', *European Journal of Personality* 2: 81–96.

De Raad, B., Hendriks, A. A. J. and Hofstee, W. K. B. (1992) 'Towards a refined structure of personality traits', *European Journal of Personality* 6: 301–319.

De Raad, B., Perugini, M., Hřebíčková, M. and Szarota, P. (1998) 'Lingua franca of personality: Taxonomies and structures based on the psycholexical approach', *Journal of Cross-Cultural Psychology* 29: 212–232.

Di Blas, L. and Forzi, M. (1998) 'An alternative taxonomic study of personality descriptors in the Italian language', *European Journal of Personality* 12: 75–101.

Di Blas, L. and Forzi, M. (1999) 'Refining a descriptive structure of personality attributes in the Italian language: The abridged Big Three circumplex structure', *Journal of Personality and Social Psychology* 76: 451–481.

Digman, J. M. (1997) 'Higher order factors of the Big Five', *Journal of Personality and Social Psychology* 73: 1246–1256.

Doi, L. T. (1978) 'Amae: A key concept for understanding Japanese personality structure', in R. J. Corsini (ed.) *Readings in Current Personality Theories*, pp. 213–219. Ithaca: Peacock.

Ellis, B. B., Becker, P. and Kimmel, H. D. (1993) 'An item response theory evaluation of an English version of the Trier Personality Inventory (TPI)', *Journal of Cross-Cultural Psychology* 24: 133–148.

Enriquez, V. G. (1992) *From Colonial to Liberation Psychology: The Philippine Experience.* Quezon City: University of the Philippines Press.

Enriquez, V. G. and Guanzon, M. A. (1985) 'Toward the assessment of personality and culture: The Panukat ng Ugali at Pagkatao', *Philippine Journal of Educational Measurement* 4: 15–54.

Goldberg, L. R. (1990) 'An alternative "description of personality": The big-five factor structure', *Journal of Personality and Social Psychology* 59: 1216–1229.

Grimm, S. D. and Church, A. T. (1999) 'A cross-cultural study of response biases in personality measures', *Journal of Research in Personality* 33: 415–441.

Guanzon-Lapeña, M. A., Church, A. T., Carlota, A. J. and Katigbak, M. S. (1998) 'Indigenous personality measures: Philippine examples', *Journal of Cross-Cultural Psychology* 29: 249–270.

Gülgöz, S. (2002) 'Five-factor model and NEO-PI-R in Turkey', in R. R. McCrae and J. Allik (eds) *The Five-Factor Model across Cultures*, pp. 175–196. New York: Kluwer Academic/Plenum.

Guthrie, G. M. and Bennett, A. B. Jr. (1971) 'Cultural differences in implicit personality theory', *International Journal of Psychology* 6: 305–312.

Hahn, D. W., Lee, K. and Ashton, M. C. (1999) 'A factor analysis of the most frequently used Korean personality trait adjectives', *European Journal of Personality* 13: 261–282.

Heaven, P. C. L., Connors, J. and Stones, C. R. (1994) 'Three or five personality dimensions? An analysis of natural language terms in two cultures', *Personality and Individual Differences* 17: 181–190.

Heine, S. J. (2001) 'Self as cultural product: An examination of East Asian and North American selves', *Journal of Personality* 69: 881–906.

Hendriks, A. A. J., Hofstee, W. K. B. and de Raad, B. (2002) 'The five-factor personality inventory: Assessing the Big Five by means of brief and concrete statements', in B. de Raad and M. Perugini (eds) *Big Five Assessment*, pp. 79–108. Seattle, WA: Hogrefe and Huber.

Heuchert, J. W. P., Parker, W. D., Stumpf, H. and Myburgh, C. P. H. (2000) 'The five-factor model of personality in South African college students', *American Behavioural Scientist* 44: 112–125.

Ho, D. Y. F. (1998) 'Indigenous psychologies: Asian perspectives', *Journal of Cross-Cultural Psychology* 29: 88–103.

Hofstee, W. K. B. (2001) 'Intelligence and personality: Do they mix?', in J. M. Collins and S. Messick (eds) *Intelligence and Personality: Bridging the Gap in Theory and Measurement*, pp. 43–60. Mahwah, NJ: Lawrence Erlbaum Associates Inc.

Hofstee, W. K. B., de Raad, B. and Goldberg, L. R. (1992) 'Integration of the Big Five and circumplex approaches to trait structure', *Journal of Personality and Social Psychology* 63: 146–163.

Hřebíčková, M., Ostendorf, F. and Angleitner, A. (1995) 'Basic dimensions of personality description in the Czech language', poster session presented at the 7th meeting of the International Society for the Study of Individual Differences, Warsaw, Poland, July.

Hřebíčková, M., Urbánek, T., Čermák, I., Szarota, P., Ficková, E. and Orlická, L. (2002) 'The NEO five-factor inventory in Czech, Polish, and Slovak contexts', in R. R. McCrae and J. Allik (eds) *The Five-Factor Model across Cultures*, pp. 53–78. New York: Kluwer/Plenum.

Huang, C. D., Church, A. T. and Katigbak, M. S. (1997) 'Identifying cultural differences in items and traits: Differential item functioning in the NEO Personality Inventory', *Journal of Cross-Cultural Psychology* 28: 192–218.

Isaka, H. (1990) 'Factor analysis of trait terms in everyday Japanese languages', *Personality and Individual Differences* 11: 115–124.

John, O. P., Angleitner, A. and Ostendorf, F. (1988) 'The lexical approach to personality: A historical review of trait taxonomic research', *European Journal of Personality* 2: 171–203.

Johnson, J. A. and Ostendorf, F. (1993) 'Clarification of the five-factor model with the abridged Big Five dimensional circumplex', *Journal of Personality and Social Psychology* 65: 563–576.

Kanagawa, C., Cross, S. E. and Markus, H. R. (2001) ' "Who am I?": The cultural psychology of the conceptual self', *Personality and Social Psychology Bulletin* 27: 90–103.

Kashiwagi, S. (2002) 'Japanese adjective list for the Big Five', in B. de Raad and M. Perugini (eds) *Big Five Assessment*, pp. 305–326. Seattle, WA: Hogrefe and Huber.

Katigbak, M. S., Church, A. T. and Akamine, T. X. (1996) 'Cross-cultural generalizability of personality dimensions: Relating indigenous and imported dimensions in two cultures', *Journal of Personality and Social Psychology* 70: 99–114.

Kaigbak, M. S., Church, A. T., Guanzon-Lapeña, M. A., Carlota, A. J. and del Pilar, G. H. (2002) 'Are indigenous personality dimensions culture specific? Philippine inventories and the five-factor model', *Journal of Personality and Social Psychology* 82: 89–101.

Kiers, H. A. L. (1990) *SCA: A Program for Simultaneous Components Analysis* Groningen: IEC ProGamma.

Konstabel, K., Realo, A. and Kallasmaa, T. (2002) 'Exploring the sources of variations in the structure of personality traits across cultures', in R. R. McCrae and J. Allik (eds) *The Five-Factor Model across Cultures*, pp. 29–52. New York: Kluwer/Plenum.

La Rosa, J. and Díaz-Loving, R. (1991) 'Evaluación del autoconcepto: Una escala multidimensional' [Evaluation of the self-concept: A multidimensional inventory], *Revista Latinoamericana de Psicología* 23: 15–33.

Leininger, A. (2002) 'Vietnamese-American personality and acculturation: An exploration of relations between personality traits and cultural goals', in R. R. McCrae and J. Allik (eds) *The Five-Factor Model across Cultures*, pp. 197–225. New York: Kluwer/Plenum.

Lin, E. J.-L. and Church, A. T. (2004) 'Are indigenous Chinese personality dimensions culture-specific? An investigation of the Chinese Personality Assessment Inventory in Chinese American and European American samples', *Journal of Cross-Cultural Psychology*, 35: 586–605.

Little, T. D. (1997) 'Mean and covariance structures (MACS) analyses of cross-cultural data: Practical and theoretical issues', *Multivariate Behavioural Research* 32: 53–76.

Lodhi, P. H., Deo, S. and Belhekar, V. M. (2002) 'The five-factor model of personality: Measurement and correlates in the Indian context', in R. R. McCrae and J. Allik (eds) *The Five-Factor Model across Cultures*, pp. 227–248. New York: Kluwer/Plenum.

McCrae, R. R. (2001) 'Trait psychology and culture: Exploring intercultural comparisons', *Journal of Personality* 69: 819–846.

McCrae, R. R. (2002) 'NEO-PI-R data from 36 cultures: Further intercultural comparisons', in R. R. McCrae and J. Allik (eds) *The Five-Factor Model across Cultures*, pp.105–125. New York: Kluwer/Plenum.

McCrae, R. R. and Allik, J. (eds) (2002) *The Five-Factor Model Across cultures*. New York: Kluwer/Plenum.

McCrae, R. R. and Costa, P. T. Jr. (1995) 'Positive and negative valence within the five-factor model', *Journal of Research in Personality* 29: 443–460.

McCrae, R. R. and Costa, P. T. Jr. (1997) 'Personality trait structure as a human universal', *American Psychologist* 52: 509–516.

McCrae, R. R., Zonderman, A. B., Costa, P. T. Jr., Bond, M. H. and Paunonen, S. V. (1996) 'Evaluating replicability of factors in the Revised NEO Personality Inventory: Confirmatory factor analysis versus Procrustes rotation', *Journal of Personality and Social Psychology* 70: 552–566.

McCrae, R. R., Costa, P. T. Jr., del Pilar, G. Y., Rolland, J.-P. and Parker, W. D. (1998) 'Cross-cultural assessment of the five-factor model: The Revised NEO Personality Inventory', *Journal of Cross-Cultural Psychology* 29: 171–188.

MacDonald, D. A. (2000) 'Spirituality: Description, measurement, and relation to the five-factor model of personality', *Journal of Personality* 68: 153–197.

MacDonald, K. (1998) 'Evolution, culture, and the five-factor model', *Journal of Cross-Cultural Psychology* 29: 119–149.

Markus, H. R. and Kitayama, S. (1998) 'The cultural psychology of personality', *Journal of Cross-Cultural Psychology* 29: 63–87.

Martin, T. A., Costa, P. T. Jr., Oryol, V. E., Rukavishnikov, A. A. and Senin, I. G. (2002) 'Applications of the Russian NEO-PI-R', in R. R. McCrae and J. Allik (eds) *The Five-Factor Model across Cultures*, pp. 261–277. New York: Kluwer/Plenum.

Muthén, B. O. (1994) 'Multilevel covariance structure analysis', *Sociological Methods and Research* 22: 376–398.

Norman, W. T. (1967) '2800 personality trait descriptors: Normative operating characteristics for a university population', unpublished manuscript, University of Michigan, Ann Arbor.

Ostendorf, F. (1990) *Sprache und persönlichkeitsstruktur: Zur validität des fünf-faktoren-modells der persönlichkeit* [Language and personality structure: Toward the validation of the five-factor model of personality]. Regensburg: S. Roderer.

Paunonen, S. V. and Ashton, M. C. (1998) 'The structured assessment of personality across cultures', *Journal of Cross-Cultural Psychology* 29: 150–170.

Paunonen, S. V. and Ashton, M. C. (2002) 'The nonverbal assessment of personality: The NPQ and the FF-NPQ', in B. de Raad and M. Perugini (eds) *Big Five Assessment*, pp. 171–194. Seattle, WA: Hogrefe and Huber.

Paunonen, S. V. and Jackson, D. N. (2000) 'What is beyond the Big Five? Plenty!', *Journal of Personality* 68: 821–835.

Peabody, D. and de Raad, B. (2002) 'The substantive nature of psycholexical personality factors: A comparison across languages', *Journal of Personality and Social Psychology* 83: 983–997.

Perugini, M. and Di Blas, L. (2002) 'The Big Five Marker Scales (BFMS) and the Italian AB5C taxonomy: Analyses from an etic-emic perspective', in B. de Raad and M. Perugini (eds) *Big Five Assessment*, pp. 281–304. Seattle, WA: Hogrefe and Huber.

Peabody, D. and Goldberg, L. R. (1989) 'Some determinants of factor structures from personality-trait descriptors', *Journal of Personality and Social Psychology* 57: 552–567.

Piedmont, R. L. and Chae, J. H. (1997) 'Cross-cultural generalizability of the five-factor model of personality: Development and validation of the NEO-PI-R for Koreans', *Journal of Cross-Cultural Psychology* 28: 131–155.

Piedmont, R. L., Bain, E., McCrae, R. R. and Costa, P. T. Jr. (2002) 'The applicability of the five-factor model in a sub-Saharan culture: The NEO-PI-R in Shona', in R. R. McCrae and J. Allik (eds) *The Five-Factor Model across Cultures*, pp. 155–173. New York: Kluwer/Plenum.

Poortinga, Y. H., van de Vijver, F. J. R. and van Hemert, D. A. (2002) 'Cross-cultural equivalence of the Big Five', in R. R. McCrae and J. Allik (eds) *The Five-Factor Model across Cultures*, pp. 281–302. New York: Kluwer/Plenum.

Reise, S. P., Smith, L. and Furr, R. M. (2001) 'Invariance on the NEO PI-R Neuroticism Scale', *Multivariate Behavioural Research* 36: 83–110.

Rodriguez de Díaz, M. L. and Díaz-Guerrero, R. (1997) '¿Son universales los rasgos de la personalidad?' [Are personality traits universal?], *Revista Latinoamericana de Psicologia* 29: 35–48.

Rolland, J. P. (2002) 'Cross-cultural generalizability of the five-factor model of personality', In R. R. McCrae and J. Allik (eds) *The Five-Factor Model across Cultures*, pp. 7–28. New York: Kluwer/Plenum.

Saucier, G. (1992) 'Benchmarks: Integrating affective and interpersonal circles with the Big-Five personality factors', *Journal of Personality and Social Psychology* 62: 1025–1035.

Saucier, G. (1997) 'Effects of variable selection on the factor structure of person descriptors', *Journal of Personality and Social Psychology* 73: 1296–1312.

Saucier, G. (2000) 'Isms and the structure of social attitudes', *Journal of Personality and Social Psychology* 78: 366–385.

Saucier, G. (2001) 'Going beyond the Big Five', paper presented at the meeting of the 109th Annual Convention of the American Psychological Association, San Francisco, August.

Saucier, G. (2002) 'Gone too far – or not far enough? Comments on the article by Ashton and Lee (2001)', *European Journal of Personality* 16: 55–62.

Saucier, G. (2003) 'Factor structure of English-language personality type-nouns', *Journal of Personality and Social Psychology* 85: 695–708.

Saucier, G. and Goldberg, L. R. (1996a) 'Evidence for the Big Five in analyses of familiar English personality adjectives', *European Journal of Personality* 10: 61–77.

Saucier, G. and Goldberg, L. R. (1996b) 'The language of personality: Lexical perspectives on the five-factor model', in J. S. Wiggins (ed.) *The Five-Factor Model of Personality: Perspectives*, pp. 21–50. New York: Guilford Press.

Saucier, G. and Goldberg, L. R. (1998) 'What is beyond the Big Five?', *Journal of Personality* 66: 495–524.

Saucier, G. and Goldberg, L. R. (2001) 'Lexical studies of indigenous personality factors: Premises, products, and prospects', *Journal of Personality* 69: 847–879.

Saucier, G. and Goldberg, L. R. (2003) 'The structure of personality attributes', in M. R. Barrick and A. M. Ryan (eds) *Personality and Work: Reconsidering the Role of Personality in Organizations*, pp. 1–29. San Francisco, CA: New York: Jossey-Bass.

Saucier, G. and Ostendorf, F. (1999) 'Hierarchical subcomponents of the Big Five personality factors: A cross-language replication', *Journal of Personality and Social Psychology* 76: 613–627.

Saucier, G., Hampson, S. E. and Goldberg, L. R. (2000) 'Cross-language studies of lexical personality factors', in S. E. Hampson (ed.) *Advances in Personality Psychology*, vol. 1, pp. 1–36. Philadelphia: Psychology Press.

Schmit, M. J., Kihm, J. A. and Robie, C. (2002) 'The Global Personality Inventory (GPI)', in B. de Raad and M. Perugini (eds) *Big Five Assessment*, pp. 195–236. Seattle, WA: Hogrefe and Huber.

Schmitt, D. P. and Buss, D. M. (2000) 'Sexual dimensions of person description: Beyond or subsumed by the Big Five?', *Journal of Research in Personality* 34: 141–177.

Shmelyov, A. G. and Pokhil'ko, V. I. (1993) 'A taxonomy-oriented study of Russian personality-trait names', *European Journal of Personality* 7: 1–17.

Smith, L. L. and Reise, S. P. (1999) 'Gender differences on negative affectivity: An IRT study of differential item functioning on the Multidimensional Personality Questionnaire Stress Reaction Scale', *Journal of Personality and Social Psychology* 75: 1350–1362.

Somer, O. and Goldberg, L. R. (1999) 'The structure of Turkish trait-descriptive adjectives', *Journal of Personality and Social Psychology* 76: 431–450.

Sörbom, D. (1974) 'A general method for studying differences in factor means and factor structure between groups', *British Journal of Mathematical and Statistical Psychology* 27: 229–239.

Szarota, P. (1996) 'Taxonomy of the Polish personality-descriptive adjectives of the highest frequency of use', *Polish Psychological Bulletin* 27: 343–351.

Szirmák, Z. and de Raad, B. (1994) 'Taxonomy and structure of Hungarian personality traits', *European Journal of Personality* 8: 95–118.

Taylor, T. R. and Boeyens, J. C. (1991) 'The comparability of the scores of blacks and whites on the South African Personality Questionnaire: An exploratory study', *South African Journal of Psychology* 21: 1–11.

Tellegen, A. (1985) 'Structures of mood and personality and their relevance to assessing anxiety with an emphasis on self-report', in A. H. Tuma and J. D. Maser (eds) *Anxiety and the Anxiety Disorders*, pp. 681–706. Hillsdale, NJ: Lawrence Erlbaum Associates Inc.

Tellegen, A. (1993) 'Folk concepts and psychological concepts of personality and personality disorder', *Psychological Inquiry* 4: 122–130.

Triandis, H. C. (2000) 'Dialectics between cultural and cross-cultural psychology', *Asian Journal of Social Psychology* 3: 185–195.

Tsaousis, I. (2002) 'The Traits Personality Questionnaire (TPQue)', in B. de Raad and M. Perugini (eds) *Big Five Assessment*, pp. 237–260. Seattle, WA: Hogrefe and Huber.

van de Vijver, F. and Leung, K. (1997) *Methods and Data Analysis for Cross-cultural Research*. Thousand Oaks, CA: Sage.

van de Vijver, F. J. R. and Poortinga, Y. H. (2002) 'Structural equivalence in multicultural research', *Journal of Cross-Cultural Psychology* 33: 141–156.

van Hemert, D. A., van de Vijver, F. J. R., Poortinga, Y. H. and Georgas, J. (2002) 'Structural and functional equivalence of the Eysenck Personality Questionnaire within and between countries', *Personality and Individual Differences* 33: 1229–1249.

van Leest, P. F. (1997) 'Bias and equivalence research in the Netherlands', *European Review of Applied Psychology* 47: 319–329.

Wiggins, J. S. (1979) 'A psychological taxonomy of trait-descriptive terms: The interpersonal domain', *Journal of Personality and Social Psychology* 37: 395–412.

Yanai, Y. H., Kashiwagi, S. and Kokusho, R. (1987) 'Construction of a new personality inventory by means of factor analysis based on Promax rotation', *Japanese Journal of Psychology* 58: 158–165.

Yang, K. S. (in press) 'Indigenous personality research: The Chinese case', in U. Kim, K. S. Yang and K. K. Hwang (eds) *Scientific Advances in Indigenous Psychologies: Philosophical, Cultural, and Empirical Contributions*.

Yang, K. S. and Bond, M. H. (1990) 'Exploring implicit personality theories with indigenous or imported constructs: The Chinese case', *Journal of Personality and Social Psychology* 58: 1087–1095.

Yang, K. S. and Ho, Y. F. (1988) 'The role of yuan in Chinese social life: A conceptual and empirical analysis', in A. C. Paranjpe, D. H. F. Ho and R. W. Rieber (eds) *Asian Contributions to Psychology*, pp. 263–281. New York: Praeger.

Yang, K. S. and Wang, D. F. (2002) 'Are corresponding indigenous and imported basic personality dimensions similarly related to motivation, attitude, and behaviour? The Chinese case', in A. T. Church (Chair) *Indigenous and Cross-cultural Analysis of Personality*. Symposium conducted at the meeting of the 25th International Congress of Applied Psychology, Singapore, July.

Yik, M. S. M. and Bond, M. H. (1993) 'Exploring the dimensions of Chinese person perception with indigenous and imported constructs: Creating a culturally balanced scale', *International Journal of Psychology* 28: 75–95.

Zhang, J. X. and Bond, M. H. (1998) 'Personality and filial piety among college students in two Chinese societies: The added value of indigenous constructs', *Journal of Cross-Cultural Psychology* 29: 402–417.

Chapter 8

Situations that matter
to personality

Boele De Raad

Personality psychologists operationalize personality conceptions in inventories and questionnaires by using trait terms or behavioural expressions of trait terms with or without situational specifications. For the situation part, there is no accepted system of personality relevant situational descriptions that may be relied on for coverage in questionnaire items. This chapter aims to provide a first step to fill this gap. Axiomatically put, personality is about traits, traits are expressed through behaviour in situations, and the communication about traits takes place through language. For the construction of personality-descriptive items, one main issue is which wordings should be used for an optimal communication. In this chapter the central statement that is supported by the data, is that behaviour and situations form specifications of traits. In accordance with this perspective different procedures were followed to arrive at an economic description of the full situational domain. The final tentative result is in the form of a 'Situational Four', which is proposed as a hypothetical model to describe the domain of situations from an individual differences viewpoint. The relationship between traits and situations is also discussed.

INTRODUCTION

Situations have been considered to be of crucial importance for the understanding of behaviour (see Argyle, Furnham and Graham, 1981). Although conceptualizations of situations are countless, they can be framed under certain perspectives (see e.g. Magnusson, 1981). A continuing problem is that relatively little has been done to describe situations fully and to classify them (cf. Caprara and Cervone, 2000). Quite a few situation taxonomies have been developed (see e.g. Ten Berge and De Raad, 1999, for a review), but with the exception of the situation taxonomy of Van Heck (1989), they are restricted domain taxonomies (e.g. Krause, 1970; Magnusson, 1971; Moos, 1973), each covering different parts of the situational field. Moreover, they vary in level of description and lack a common perspective.

Various perspectives for situation taxonomic description have been provided in the past. An 'objective' approach has, for example, been distinguished from a 'subjective' approach (e.g. Endler and Magnusson, 1976;

Magnusson, 1981). Another example is a perspective in terms of the facilitating or obstructing effects that a situation exerts on the person, or the 'press' in the environment (Murray, 1938; see also, Forgas and Van Heck, 1992; Van de Sande, 1996). Personality perspectives on situations are available as well. Magnusson (1981), for example, considered it important to study how people construe and evaluate situations in their cognitive processes. He and others (see Forgas and Van Heck, 1992) also emphasized the role of personality factors in people's preferences for situations. However, individual differences have not typically been incorporated into situation taxonomies. Barker's (1968) early work on behaviour settings, such as places or activities like piano lessons, religious service, football playing and a bank, explicitly did not take individual differences into consideration. Characteristic of those settings was the exchangeability of individuals; the function of a religious service, for example, does not change when different people attend or when the priest is replaced. To a considerable extent Barker's (1968) work defined subsequent situation research. In the same year, Mischel (1968) published his influential book fuelling the idea that personality traits failed to live up to their expectations as major variables in the prediction of behaviour. In the years to follow situations and person–situation interactions attracted significant attention (e.g. Endler, 1993), but this work did not result in a comprehensive description of situations. Personality questionnaire development, for example, flourishes as never before (see De Raad and Perugini, 2002), but a systematic representation of situational characteristics in questionnaires is not possible to find.

At least three issues have been central in the discussion of situations and their definition, namely their geographical understanding, their presumed independence from traits, and their scope and delineation. Situations are generally assumed to have geographical properties. The usual connotation with the term situation corresponds to its etymology, which is indeed geographical: the Latin *situs* belongs to the geographical domain to which also belong position, location and condition. A person may find him or herself in a specific condition or state, as in an economic situation, a psychological situation, an interpersonal situation, a difficult situation, a conflict situation, an emergency situation, or an emotional situation: the adjective indicates the type of situation. In those cases, to the person the situation is the *external* context. The geographical understanding probably corresponds best with this external context. Sometimes, however, 'situation' is used to refer to the state or condition of a person, such as in 'a state of emergency' or 'emotional state'; the adjective indicates a characteristic of the person. In the latter cases the situation is *internal* to the person. So, a person can be in an emotional situation, which is possibly a situation with other people in which emotions of those involved determine the atmosphere. This is not the same as saying that a person is in an emotional state. In general, the involvement of situational information in the understanding of behaviour entails that contextual details are specified. Similarly, adding situational information in the under-standing of personality means that abstract traits are provided with con-textual details.

One issue in the person–situation debate is the fact that persons and situ-ations have been treated as separate realms and sometimes as competing forces in the determination of behaviour. The question whether persons or situations determine behaviour has been identified as a pseudo-issue (Alker, 1972; Endler and Edwards, 1978). With respect to the partition of persons and situations, Magnusson (1981), for example, emphasized their relative independence in saying that the study of situations can be made 'without paying special attention to the role of situations in the continuously ongoing person–situation interaction process' (p. 13). The underlying model is depicted in Figure 8.1.

The model emphasizes the non-reducibility of the person as an individual and the existence of the situation as independent from the individual. Although distinctions have been made between actual environment and per-ceived environment (Magnusson, 1981, p. 4), the latter presumes the former. It is this perspective, in which situations and persons are seen as independent entities, that has gradually acquired the status of an acknowledged reference model for much of the thinking and research about interactionism and situ-ation taxonomies. This perspective is often substantiated by providing examples of situations in which individual differences are of low importance such as situations of the geographical type: a classroom, a study group, or an appointment with a professor. Additional complications arise when persons and situations have to be defined in terms of their behaviour determining characteristics. Persons, as ostensible agents or objects, are defined in terms of their characteristic traits. Although the geographic viewpoint may suggest a similarly apparent referent for situations, the extensive literature on defining situations (e.g. Magnusson and Endler, 1977; Magnusson, 1981) clearly points out the relatively elusive nature of situations. The delineation of character-istic features of situations may therefore be rather equivocal, as is exemplified in the diverse lists of situation characteristics provided by Magnusson (1981, pp. 19–20) and Van Heck (1984, pp. 155–156).

As regards the definition of situations – their scope and delineation – the

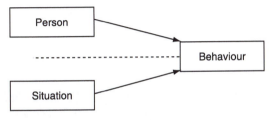

Figure 8.1 Person versus situation model.

history of trait psychology is not of much help. Though most definitions of personality from Freud, Adler, Horney, Allport, Sheldon, Theophrastus, Cattell, Eysenck, and many, many more, show awareness of or point to the relevance of situations, none of them provides us with insights on how to systematically use situational information in trait psychology. More recent views are exemplified by Endler (1993), who concluded that the differential psychology of situations was still in the dark ages, and by Hogan and Roberts (2000), who argued the person–situation debate to be futile because, among other things, the term 'situation' as used in the debate is still undefined.

The person–situation debate

How has the history of situationism and interactionism dealt with situations? Within the arena of the so-called person–situation debate, traits have been defined mainly in terms of *cross-situational consistencies*, which has been at the very core of the so-called dispute. Interactionists, including Mischel, have been persistent in conveying this view, although Mischel himself in 1973, as also pointed out by Johnson (1999), stated that 'the fact that behaviour varies across different situations is not questioned by anyone, including classical trait theorists'. Indeed it would be a caricature of personality psychology to assume that a person who is, for example, high on aggressiveness and there-fore should be more aggressive than most people when his or her toes are stepped on, should also be aggressive when given a present. The leading distinctive characteristic in personality thinking has been *temporal stability*; that is replicable behaviour in the same type of situation (see also Johnson, 1999). When being stepped on, or yelled at, or pushed, some people show more aggressive behaviour than others. The person–situation debate – and the interactionist view – have fared well on rather elusive and implicit ideas about how to conceptualize situations. Admittedly, there was no shortage of ideas for developing situation taxonomies, but these ideas did not incorporate individual differences.

Trait perspective on situations

In order to define situations, the relevance of traits for the prediction of behaviour is assumed to be axiomatic. Given traits, and thus assuming the differential trait position, information about situations is of value only if it sustains this differential position.

Which traits are given? Nowadays, many personality psychologists agree that the structure of personality traits can be approximately captured in a five-dimensional space, called the Big Five model. Peabody and Goldberg (1989) suggested that situational domains roughly corresponded to the Big Five personality trait domains. Extraversion was linked to contexts where expressions of power and energy are considered relevant; Agreeableness was linked to contexts where expressions of love are considered relevant; Conscientiousness was linked to work and task contexts; Emotional Stability was linked to affect or control; and Intellectual autonomy was linked to problem solving and creativity. Peabody and Goldberg's (1989) characterization emphasizes the significance of the Big Five factors on the one hand, while on the other they suggest a one-to-one relationship of the factors with broad and abstract contexts of application. Although such a one-to-one relationship is highly questionable, for certain traits, trait factors, or combinations of traits or trait-factor contexts are specifiable to a certain extent.

On the empirical side, for example, part of the Big Five domain, delineated especially by the factors Extraversion and Agreeableness, seems to involve a specialized personality lexicon; namely a lexicon that describes individual differences in interpersonal contexts (e.g. McCrae and Costa, 1989; Trapnell and Wiggins, 1990; De Raad, 1995). Typical non-interpersonal traits are to be found in the trait space made up by the factors Conscientiousness and Emotional Stability (De Raad, 1995). For the context of learning and education, another selection of traits from the Big Five domain is considered relevant. De Raad (1996) constructed a so-called educational trait circumplex that embodied especially traits from the domains Extraversion, Conscientiousness and Intellect. Conscientiousness has been found to be consistently related to school performance (e.g. Wolfe and Johnson, 1995) and job performance (e.g. Salgado, 1997). Emotional Stability or Neuroticism has been found relevant especially in clinical contexts (e.g. Larsen, 1992; Schroeder, Wormworth and Livesley, 1992).

So, from the empirical literature it may be concluded that the first suggestion of a one-to-one correspondence between broad traits and broad contexts should be abandoned in favour of a more differential picture. In such a more differential picture, some broad traits of the Big Five type seem to imply specific contexts and other traits may imply a variety of situational contexts. It is this implicative relationship between traits and situations that may be used as a general principle by which one might arrive at such a differential picture of situational specifications of the full trait domain. The model is simple and straightforward, and corresponds perfectly with the classical trait conception. It may be conceived of as the trait-specification model. The model states and confirms that a trait refers to behaviour in a situation. The model is presented in Figure 8.2.

In this trait-specification model, both behaviour and situations form interrelated specifications of the trait concept; the trait implies a certain behaviour or class of behaviours in a certain situation or class of situations. Typically, this is how the meaning of a trait is specified. For example, a person who frequently shows compliance (behaviour) upon reasonable requests (situation), can rightly be considered *cooperative* (trait). The trait cooperative is thus depicted as representing consistency in contextualized behaviour: that is, the *trait* stands for, is an abstraction of, *behaviour-in-a-situation*. As

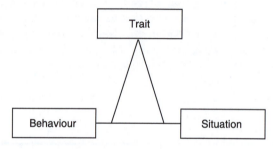

Figure 8.2 The trait-specification model.

formulated by Johnson (1999): 'Both behaviour and context are tacitly built into the socially shared meaning of the trait word.'

In accordance with the model, the trait *impudent,* for example, refers to *unwarranted behaviour* towards *superiors;* a role relationship is implicit in the definition of this trait. Similarly, *sociable* refers to *behaviour with other people. Aggressive* refers to behaviour in *situations of confrontation. Friendly* refers to behaviour with *positive interaction. Shy* refers to behaviour in certain *social situations, especially with strangers.* Each trait is thus to be considered as implying situational information. For the purposes of acquiring a comprehensive listing of situations or situational features, the task ahead is to specify the meaning of traits in terms of behaviours in situations. As a consequence of the trait-specification model, situations are defined in terms of an elaboration and refinement of the definition of traits.

The outcome of such an enterprise is not necessarily a match in terms of scope and dimensionality of behavioural specifications and situational specifications of traits. For some traits it may turn out that many behaviours can be specified in a small range of situations, and for other traits it may be the other way around. The more stylistic traits, for example, may be less defined by particular types of situations (Johnson, 1999). Alston (1975) offers *methodical* and *energetic* as examples of stylistic traits: 'It would seem that one may proceed in a methodical or energetic manner in any situation in which one is doing *anything*' (p. 21). The term 'style' is often used to stress the formal aspects of behaviour, because the question 'how' may be asked for any kind of behaviour, whatever its contents or direction (Strelau, 1987).

A key item on the agenda of personality psychology has long been to capture the *differentiating qualities* of individuals in a variety of *situational contexts.* Regarding differentiating qualities of individuals, that is traits, a fairly advanced psychology of individual differences as represented in the Big Five model is now available. Regarding situations, the psychology has been rather inchoate, particularly because existing situation taxonomies have not been developed to serve the psychology of individual differences.

Language of traits and situations

To put it simply and axiomatically, personality is about traits; traits are expressed through behaviour in situations, and communication about traits takes place through language. Traits are here defined such that they include dispositions, attitudes, interests and other more or less stable psychological characteristics. Trait-taxonomic work necessarily draws heavily on the lexicon of personality. Since situations are to be seen as specifications of traits, situation taxonomies may have to focus on language as well.

Although traits are the subject matter of personality psychology, they remain abstractions in the form of conceptualizations expressed in language. These conceptualizations can be abstract and complex constructions or simple everyday wordings. The psycholexical approach has, with good reason, favoured everyday language conceptualizations. Of these, *adjectival* expressions form the natural focus because such expressions describe characteristics of entities and concepts (e.g. persons). Furthermore, adjectival expressions are typically abstract expressions in which recurrent patterns of behaviours in situations are epitomized in trait terms. Such adjectival expressions are not equivalent with expressions that contain a trait adjective. Within language there is a division of labour related to linguistic categories, which seems to be lacking with respect to personality language. In a linguistic context, adjectives, nouns, adverbs and verbs follow different rules of use. In the psychological context, however, they are all considered relevant for personality description if they serve an adjectival function. Whereas adjectives may be the prototypical repositories of sedimentation of important individual differences, as has been argued by Saucier and Goldberg (1996), other word forms may function in an adjectival way and may contain trait meaning that is not contained in adjectives. So, to the extent that words have an adjectival function, they are referred to as adjectival expressions.

While traits may be assumed to be comprehensively catalogued in a tangible lexicon such as a dictionary, behavioural and situational specifications of traits, particularly in conjunction, may not find their way into a dictionary as systematically. An alternative resource for finding such information is the lexicon as it exists in the collective minds of the members of a language community. A problem may be that this collective lexicon is loaded with affective connotations and implicit suppositions.

People form a major topic of interest in everyday communication. Their doings and achievements are talked over and evaluated, and motives and explanations are provided. This person-talk is not simply a summing up of a number of characteristics. People express something with their words or use words to produce a certain effect. Words, particularly personality relevant ones, are not merely descriptive in nature. Correspondingly, language is not just a medium for the transfer of information; it is imbued with affective or pragmatic references. Particularly personality language is affective. Trait words inevitably carry more or less of a sense of approval or disapproval in their semantic make-up, which means that words used to describe a person's traits also function to evoke emotions in the users. The strongest emotions are possibly evoked by words that are loaded with *evaluative* meaning. Thus language is also a weapon and trait words, especially from the class of nouns, can be used to harm people.

Maybe even more than affective connotations, we should be aware of implicit suppositions in certain linguistic categories. There is, for example, a host of studies on the implicit *causality* of verbs (see, e.g. Mannetti and De Grada, 1991). Semin and Fiedler (1988) have shown that different types of words may convey different kinds of implicit suppositions, and that they maintain a different relationship with contexts. The more abstract wordings such as adjectives fulfil functions of cognitive economy, but they allow less disconfirmation than more concrete wordings.

In the context of person-talk, pragmatic information is important because of its corrective function. Single traits or single behaviours are often ambiguous when considered out of context. In general, nonverbal language and contextual information function to disambiguate verbal language and to correct possible misunderstandings with respect to verbal communication. In the context of the construction of personality descriptive items, the addition of contextual information may be useful because of its corrective capacity. It may enhance communicational accuracy, which is one more reason to focus on situations.

Does the lexical hypothesis apply to situations?

The lexical hypothesis states that important everyday phenomena will be represented in people's lexicons. Saucier and Goldberg (1996) have argued, for example, that the lexical perspective is particularly germane to the context of personality. Physics, chemistry and physiology, for example, would not be served well by restricting their constructs to those found in ordinary language. The science of personality, however, has as its subject the study of socially meaningful behaviour patterns; those behaviour patterns are abundantly represented in language. Saucier and Goldberg (1996) rightly restrict the lexical approach to scientific disciplines that are self-referential in nature.

The lexical approach as applied to traits mostly used the dictionary as the tangible repository of a lexicon. In accordance with the lexical approach, it is similarly assumed that the 'systematic confrontation with accumulated knowledge available in a particular culture will lead to consensually defined and consensually constructed situations' (Van Heck, 1982, p. 153). It is questionable, however, whether situations, as socially meaningful phenomena, have similarly found their way to the dictionary in the form of single word descriptors. If 'situations' had clear referents – like 'persons' have in Martin, Mary or Jessica – in the form of objects such as house, car, tree, or spider, their characteristics might possibly be described by trait terms such as *threatening* (car, spider), *sheltering* (house, car, tree), *natural* (tree, spider), or *passive* (house, tree). These could then be the terms by which those objects are distinguished or grouped together. Without an agreed upon definition of situation, however, it is not clear how to discern situations that are relevant to personality amidst the myriad forms which situations may take. It is for this reason that Ten Berge and De Raad (2001) deemed it wiser to follow an alternative approach to represent the lexicon, namely by tapping into the repository of situations as they are sedimented in the heads of language users. Those sedimented experiences need not be encoded in the form of single words. They may well come in sentences. Therefore, we may ask people to generate expressions from their memory that refer to the topic in question. The implicit conceptions that people have of situations are thus made explicit. The consequence of the decision to take this alternative lexical route is an empirical definition of the situation.

Trait-relevant and situation-taxonomic results

Different procedures were followed, involving two distinct rounds of collecting situational information, respectively described below under Study 1 and Study 2. During both rounds of collecting situational information subjects were asked to generate situation specifications, given certain traits. The format used for the situational specification was: 'When [event] then [behaviour]'. This instruction yielded behaviour-in-situation specifications of traits.

This trait-specification instruction provides the actual format through which the situations are defined. This empirical definition of situations is left unguided by explicit theory. This is how it should be, because taxonomic work and theoretical frames of reference are at odds with each other. Sneath and Sokal (1973) have made clear that, for example, taxonomic work in biology has suffered from theoretical predispositions: 'the theoretical framework ... has served as a "straitjacket" for taxonomic concepts and ideas' (p. 17; De Raad, 2000).

In the two studies described below, different approaches were used to develop a taxonomy of situations incorporating traits. Study 1 comprised two phases. In the first phase, the set of situations obtained in the first round was combined with a set of trait descriptive adjectives. Subjects had to indicate the likeliness of occurrence of trait-related behaviours in those situations (for details, see Ten Berge and De Raad, 2001). This produced a structure that had no direct reference to the behaviours of the subjects themselves (*internal* structure; see Wiggins, 1973, pp. 336–337). In the second phase of Study 1, the same set of situations was used in a kind of coping task (for details, see Ten Berge and De Raad, 2002). Assuming that people differing in personality relate differently to situations, subjects were asked to indicate how they deal with each of the situations. This procedure resulted in an *external* structure of situations, which is based on the subject's own dealings with the situations (Wiggins, 1973). In Study 2, the set of situations obtained in the second round was combined with a set of trait adjectives. For each combination of trait and situation, subjects had to indicate the extent to which the combination of the corresponding behaviour and the situation applied to them (for details, see Ten Berge, 2001). The latter procedure also yielded an external structure of situations. The three different procedures yielded somewhat different taxonomic results.

STUDY 1

Situation taxonomy

In this study, a set of situations was obtained by asking subjects (mostly first-year students of psychology) to generate for each of a certain number of traits up to five behaviour-in-situation specifications that they considered expressive of those traits (see Ten Berge and De Raad, 2001). For example, for the trait 'foolish' one might come up with 'he drank four vodka-martinis (behaviour), when he had to drive home from a party (the situation)'. A total of 290 trait terms were used, representing the Big Five trait system. A total of 150 subjects participated in this study, together providing a total set of 2234 specifications. The descriptions were stripped of their behaviour part so that further reduction would not be contaminated by behaviour-trait relationships. The remaining set of situation specifications was largely reduced on the basis of duplication and near-synonymity, resulting in a set of 242 situation descriptions (for details, see Ten Berge and De Raad, 2001). For a first subsequent study with this material, it was necessary to arrive at a smaller set, which was achieved by focusing only on the situations that were most frequently reported. To these were added some of the situation concepts from Van Heck's (1989) taxonomy. The final set consisted of a list of 132 distinct situation specifications. Representative examples are given in Table 8.1.

The consequence of applying an empirical definition of situations is that

Table 8.1 Examples of situation specifications (Study 1)

• Being reprimanded	• Having lost something
• Having a setback	• Wanting to convince someone
• Having to choose	• Being in a strange place
• Having a vacation	• Getting an assignment
• Being confronted with death	• Making a proposition
• Being at a social gathering	• Having high expectations
• Throwing a party	• Being challenged
• Running late	• Getting blamed for something

the set of situations which is generated contains specifications that may vary in different respects. They run, for example, from situations internal to the person, such as 'being ill' and 'being sad', to situations that are more external to the person, such as 'being teased' and 'getting an assignment'. On the continuum between these two opposites, there are situations like 'being in love', 'needing help', 'having to choose' and 'having a discussion'. These varying specifications are all considered elements of the set of situations according to the trait-specification model.

Combination of trait-related behaviours and situations: internal structure

The 132 situations were subsequently combined with triads of trait-adjectives. The triads were selected from the facets of the so-called AB5C model of traits (De Raad, Hendriks and Hofstee, 1992). Only those facets were used that combine two positive or two negative factor poles, because they contain the most trait adjectives. The trait adjectives of a triad were selected to represent the different meanings of a facet. Subjects ($N = 43$) were given the combinations of trait triads and situations. For each combination of trait triad and situation, subjects were asked to indicate the extent to which they expected a person with those traits to show behaviour that demonstrates the possession of the traits in the given situation. This yielded a matrix of scores, collapsed across subjects, for combinations of traits and adjectives, that was subjected to Principal Components Analysis. The eigenvalue pattern suggested a five-factor solution that was Varimax rotated. Alpha reliabilities for the five rotated components varied between 0.88 and 0.95. The results are represented in Table 8.2, through the five highest loading situational descriptions (Situations column) and the five highest scoring trait triads (Traits column). The illustrative items are grouped under labels of situation factors.

The first principal component in Table 8.2 is called *Situations of Adversity*. It consists of situational specifications in which someone has to deal with a problem, a negative experience, or a setback. The second component, *Situations of Amusement*, contains situations in which someone has a lucky break, hears good news, or is having a celebration. The third component, *Situations of Positioning*, refers to discussion, convincing and giving orders. The fourth component, *Situations of Conduct*, is bipolar, referring to situations where people have a positive, caring and soliciting attitude towards others on the positive pole, and showing lack of social behaviour and respect on the negative pole. The fifth component, *Situations of Daily Routine*, refers to going to bed, having dinner, being at school, and so forth.

Table 8.2 Varimax rotated principal components of situations (Study 1)

Situations		Traits	
Situations of adversity			
Being hospitalized	0.88	Insecure/unbalanced/nervous	2.42
Having a setback	0.87	Unstable/labile/inconstant	1.99
Being sad	0.86	Touchy/irritable/jealous	1.97
Making a mistake	0.84	Negative/surly/distrustful	1.87
Seeing something unpleasant	0.84	Dejected/depressed/gloomy	1.75
Situations of amusement			
Going out drinking	0.91	Lively/enthusiastic/extraverted	2.58
Being at a party	0.89	Exuberant/spontaneous/open	2.49
Throwing a party	0.86	Cheerful/joyful/merry	2.00
Making a joke	0.84	Optimistic/brisk/vital	1.83
Running into an acquaintance	0.83	Sympathetic/good-hearted/gentle	1.61
Situations of positioning			
Participating in a discussion	0.90	Accurate/consistent/persevering	2.15
Offering resistance	0.84	Decided/firm/energetic	2.03
Suing someone	0.83	Critical/versatile/inventive	1.60
Wanting to convince someone	0.83	Overbearing/bossy/captious	1.58
Wanting something different	0.83	Diffident/patient/sedate	−1.69
Situations of conduct			
Making obscene gestures	−0.86	Careful/virtuous/cautious	1.85
Being aggressive	−0.81	Meticulous/exact/conscientious	1.74
Gambling	−0.75	Slack/indifferent/antisocial	−1.79
Apologizing	0.82	Swaggering/conceited/boasting	−1.60
Taking care of someone	0.68	Egocentric/selfish/intolerant	−1.51
Situations of daily routine			
Going to bed	0.77	Patient/composed/quiet	2.50
Coming home	0.74	Commonsensical/imperturbable/cold	2.12
Having dinner	0.71	Negative/surly/suspicious	1.64
Being lost in thought	0.69	Balanced/stable/calm	1.58
Having to get up	0.68	Uncommunicative/introverted/stiff	1.40

Note
The numbers for situations are factor loadings; the numbers for traits are factor scores.

Relations between traits and situations

The five components can be viewed as a first sketch of a situation taxonomy developed from a trait perspective. Interestingly, through the factor scores, the triads of traits can be used to give meaning to this situation taxonomy (Traits column of Table 8.2). The trait triads that scored highest on the *Situations of Adversity* component were predominantly from the Emotional Stability factor. Traits that contributed to the meaning of *Situations of Amusement* were predominantly from the Extraversion factor. *Situations of*

Conduct were especially linked to the Big Five factors Agreeableness and Conscientiousness. *Situations of Daily Routine* were linked to Extraversion and Emotional Stability. Finally, *Situations of Positioning* were related to traits from each Big Five factor. From the Big Five trait perspective, the data, which for purposes of economy are not fully presented in Table 8.2, indicate that Extraversion was related to all situation types except *Situations of Conduct*. Agreeableness was related to all situations except *Situations of Amusement* and *Situations of Daily Routine*. Conscientiousness is related to all situations except *Situations of Adversity*. Emotional Stability is related to all situations except *Situations of Amusement*, and Intellect is related to all situations except *Situations of Adversity*.

In conclusion, it can be confirmed that there is a differential picture in which situations of a certain type, for example, *Adversity* and *Amusement*, seem to be especially suited for the expression of certain traits, for example, Emotional Stability and Extraversion. Other types of situations, for example, *Situations of Conduct*, seem to be suited for the expression of different kinds of traits such as Friendliness and Conscientiousness. This picture is also sustained from the perspective of traits: each type of Big Five trait seems to be more easily expressed in its own set of three or four of the five distinguished types of situations.

Dealing with situations: external structure

In the second phase of Study 1, an external structure was obtained. For this, the larger number of situations that resulted from the reduction procedure, the set of 237 situations, was given to 177 subjects (53 of them had to rate themselves, and these 53 subjects were each rated by one to three significant others). In case of the self-ratings, the subjects had to indicate the extent to which they were able to deal with the situations. In case of the other ratings, the subjects had to indicate the extent to which they thought their target person was able to deal with the situations. A classification of situations based on how people deal with those situations assumes that their traits or dispositions are (largely) accountable for it. People with a high score on a certain trait may, for example, have a preference for those situations that allow the expressions of that trait. In addition to the dealing-with-the-situation ratings, subjects had to fill out a Big Five personality questionnaire, the Five Factor Personality Inventory (FFPI, Hendriks, Hofstee and De Raad, 1999). The first four factors of the FFPI do have the traditional names Extraversion, Agreeableness, Conscientiousness and Emotional Stability. The fifth factor, called Autonomy with items such as 'can easily link facts together' versus 'follows the crowd', covers features of intellect and creativity.

For each ratee ($N = 53$), mean scores across self and other ratings were calculated for both the FFPI and the situations. The FFPI scale scores were computed and the responses to the situations were subjected to Principal Components Analysis.

The Principal Components Analysis of the situation ratings yielded a structure with 12 dimensions that were sufficiently reliable according to the criteria formulated by Hofstee, Ten Berge and Hendriks (1998). The eigenvalue pattern did not show a clear change. For this reason we compared several Varimax rotated solutions containing one to six components. The four-component solution turned out to produce the most interpretable results. In the five- and six-component solutions, three factors remained the same and the fourth split up both in the five- and in the six-component solution. The rotated four-component solution is represented in Table 8.3.

The four components in Table 8.3 are each represented by the eight highest loading items. The first factor, *Pleasure*, explains 27 per cent of the variance. The second factor, *Individual Adversity*, explains 24 per cent of the variance. The third factor describes situations of *Interpersonal Conflict* and explains 18 per cent of the variance. Finally, the fourth factor is called *Social Demand* and explains 26 per cent of the variance.

The meanings of these external structure factors of situations come close to the meanings of the first four of the internal structure factors. *Pleasure* may be seen as a replication of the earlier *Situations of Amusement*. *Individual Adversity* is similar to *Situations of Adversity*. *Interpersonal Conflict* comes closest to the earlier *Situations of Conduct*. *Social Demand* is related to *Situations of Positioning*.

Big Five traits and situation factors

Table 8.4 provides the direct correlations between the FFPI scales and the situation components. The correlations in Table 8.4 suggest that extraverts seem to be able to deal better with *Social Demand* situations than introverts. In addition, they seem to deal relatively well with *Interpersonal Conflict* situations and less well with *Situations of Adversity* than introverts.

Individual differences on Extraversion play a role in different types of situations. Like extraverts, disagreeable people deal relatively well with *Social Demand* situations. Differences in Conscientiousness do not seem to play a role in any of the four types of situations. Emotional Stability is related to three situation components, and finally Autonomy is related to *Pleasure* situations and, to a lesser extent, *Social Demand* situations.

To look further into this differential picture, for each of the Big Five factors as assessed through the FFPI, it is indicated in Table 8.5 from which situation factors the ten highest correlating situations originate.

The number of situations that distinguish people who are well able to handle the situation from those who are less well able differs clearly across the Big Five factors. For Agreeableness and Conscientiousness in Table 8.5 no such distinctions can be made. The table does not suggest any situations that

Table 8.3 Varimax rotated principal components of situation ratings (Study 1)

Situations	Pleasure	Individual adversity	Interpersonal conflict	Social demand
Getting his/her pay check	**0.82**	−0.03	0.06	−0.01
Hearing the good news	**0.80**	−0.08	0.19	0.25
It is a national holiday	**0.77**	0.11	0.13	0.01
Seeing something pleasant	**0.74**	−0.11	0.13	0.12
Having passed a test	**0.71**	−0.04	0.21	0.15
Walking along the street	**0.70**	0.19	0.18	0.34
Sitting on a terrace with a cappuccino	**0.69**	0.04	0.20	0.07
Having worked out his or her plan	**0.69**	−0.01	0.03	0.17
Being ill	−0.08	**0.72**	−0.18	−0.07
Having a slight accident	0.25	**0.68**	0.16	0.10
Having failed an exam	0.01	**0.66**	0.20	−0.02
Being forced into a corner	−0.13	**0.65**	0.08	0.24
Being angry	−0.02	**0.60**	0.24	0.08
Being the victim of a crime	0.06	**0.60**	−0.05	0.18
Not feeling very well	0.07	**0.60**	−0.23	0.10
Not being able to sleep	0.02	**0.60**	−0.04	0.20
Being teased	0.11	0.14	**0.69**	0.14
Someone is trying to pull his or her leg	0.28	0.29	**0.68**	0.24
Noticing that nobody is listening to him	−0.09	0.02	**0.64**	0.39
Telling someone to do something	0.28	−0.05	**0.63**	0.20
Wanting to beat down the price	0.18	−0.02	**0.62**	0.23
Being insulted	0.06	0.24	**0.62**	0.24
Being in the same circumstances as before	0.31	−0.05	**0.61**	0.22
Someone has a crush on him, but it is not mutual	0.22	0.03	**0.59**	0.11
Being in an unfamiliar environment	0.12	0.04	0.25	**0.79**
Being in charge	−0.03	0.08	0.01	**0.74**
Applying for a job	0.05	0.11	0.04	**0.73**
Having an important occasion	0.34	0.14	0.17	**0.71**
Being fond of someone	0.25	0.14	0.13	**0.70**
Having to speak in public	−0.02	0.06	−0.08	**0.70**
Being at a party	0.32	0.00	0.13	**0.69**
Having a discussion	0.23	0.05	0.15	**0.68**

Table 8.4 Correlations between FFPI scales and situation components (Study 1)

	Pleasure	Individual adversity	Interpersonal conflict	Social demand
Extraversion	0.20	−0.29	0.28	0.61
Agreeableness	0.19	0.21	−0.02	−0.42
Conscientiousness	−0.01	−0.17	0.15	0.14
Emotional Stability	0.01	0.42	0.36	0.45
Autonomy	0.42	0.16	0.13	0.29

Table 8.5 FFPI factors and factor origin of highest correlating ten situations (Study 1)

	Pleasure	Individual adversity	Interpersonal conflict	Social demand	Total
Extraversion	2	–	1	13	16
Agreeableness	–	–	–	–	0
Conscientiousness	–	–	–	–	0
Emotional Stability	1	15	6	13	35
Autonomy	2	3	1	3	9

Note
Listed are all correlations ≥ 0.47.

are handled better by agreeable and conscientious people than by disagreeable and unconscientious people. This may possibly be so because most people are sufficiently agreeable and conscientious to handle most situations well. For the other three Big Five factors the information is different. Apparently, there are quite a few situations that are handled better by the extravert, emotionally stable and autonomous person than by the introvert, unstable and non-autonomous person.

Combining the observations that may be made from Tables 8.4 and 8.5, the conclusion is that Extraversion, Emotional Stability and Autonomy are less situation specific than Agreeableness and Conscientiousness. From the situation point of view, one might conclude that the different types of situations differ in the number of Big Five dimensions for which they can distinguish between persons. *Pleasure* situations, for example, only distinguish autonomous from the unautonomous persons, and *Social Demand* situations can distinguish people on four of the Big Five factors, Conscientiousness excluded.

The distinction that emerged with respect to a differential role for Agreeableness and Conscientiousness on the one hand, Extraversion, Emotional Stability on the other, and to a lesser extent also Autonomy, is of particular interest since it corresponds with the distinction between character and temperament, respectively. Treatment information seems to say less about how a person deals with a situation than character information. In other words, temperament traits are less situation specific than character traits.

STUDY 2

Situation taxonomy

In this second study a fresh set of situations was collected, using a larger and more heterogeneous sample of subjects than in Study 1, in order to arrive at a more representative set of situations. In this case, 228 subjects (56 males and 172 females) participated, in age ranging from 15 to 82 with a mean of 34 years. Their educational level ranged from primary school to university, with 92 per cent having a higher education (details of methods and procedures are described in Ten Berge, 2001).

In addition to aiming at a more representative set of situations, the Big Five system was also more fully represented by systematically using trait terms from the various segments of the so-called AB5C model of traits (De Raad, Hendriks and Hofstee, 1992). All subjects were asked to think of one or more persons for each of three personality traits: for example, a friend, a colleague or a television celebrity possessing that trait, and to describe a maximum of five situations in which that person had shown behaviourally to possess that trait. The subjects were encouraged to describe the situations according to a 'behaviour-in-situation' format. For instructive purposes the subjects were given some examples for the trait *reckless*: 'when my brother had been drinking, he went behind the wheel', and 'when my friend crossed the street, she did not look out for traffic'. The total number of situations thus generated by the subjects was 3354, with at least ten situations having been generated per trait. These behaviour-in-situation descriptions were then stripped of their behaviour part.

The set of situations was reduced in two steps. During the first step the initial set was reduced to 454 situations on the basis of mere duplication and near-synonymity. The second step involved a more elaborate procedure in which two people categorized and subcategorized the situations. The sub-categories were inspected for vagueness, specificity and similarity. Too vague and too specific situations were removed, and situations close in meaning were represented by only one situation. This second step led to a final set of 142 situation descriptions.

Structuring the catalogue of situations

We provided subjects ($N = 65$) with combinations of traits and situations. The subjects ranged in age from 16 to 79, with a mean of 27 years. The subjects had to rate themselves on each of the trait-situation items. For this the 142 situations were used, and in addition 71 trait adjectives were used stemming from the best filled facets of the AB5C system of traits. This yielded a total of 10,082 combinations of traits and situations. These com-binations were put into a sentence form for which reason the trait adjectives were used adverbially: as in *when I said goodbye* (situation), *I behaved self-assuredly* (trait). For each sentence the subject had to indicate the extent to which the corresponding trait-in-situation would apply to them.

The trait-by-situation ratings were factor analysed, yielding an external structure of situations. Different rotated solutions of Principal Components Analysis were compared, rotating up to seven situation components. The six-component solution turned out to be the most interpretable one. Table 8.6

Table 8.6 Varimax rotated six-component solution of situations (Study 2)

Situations of amusement and prosperity		Situations of adversity	
Throwing a party	0.23	Having lost something	0.23
Being in love	0.23	Having lost	0.22
Doing something nice with friends	0.23	Having made a mistake	0.22
Having passed some test	0.23	Losing control over the situation	0.20
Being at a party	0.22	Not being able to reach someone	0.20
Having my birthday	0.22	Having to change my plans	0.20
Visiting friends	0.20	Doing something I am not allowed to do	0.19
Meeting my high school sweetheart	0.20	Being ill	0.19
Having a drink on a terrace with friends	0.20	Having to wait in a long line	0.18
Having visiting friends	0.19	Arriving at an appointment for nothing	0.17

Situations of interpersonal conflict		Situations of positioning	
Someone is bothering me	0.27	Being on the board of management	0.25
Being treated unfairly	0.27	Organizing an event	0.24
Someone is unreasonable	0.26	Being trained on the job	0.23
Having an argument	0.23	Being in a meeting	0.23
Someone does something behind my back	0.22	Having a job interview	0.21
Someone is jumping the queue	0.22	Having to give a presentation	0.21
Thinking someone is nagging	0.21	Teaching	0.21
Someone does not stick to agreement	0.21	Participating in a discussion	0.20
Someone is making a lot of noise	0.19	Having to make a decision	0.20
Someone is very insistent	0.18	Looking for a job	0.19

Situations of stress and emotion		Situations of involvement	
Partner commits adultery	0.42	A beloved person has deceased	0.33
Relationship is over	0.34	Hurting someone	0.25
Not being happy in relationship	0.30	Noticing someone in distress	0.24
Having a baby	0.21	Having to vacate my parental home	0.21
A beloved person has deceased	0.17	There are some shocking images on TV	0.19
Being in love	0.16	An accident is happening	0.18
Being fired	0.16	Someone else has problems	0.18
Having an argument	0.14	My house has been burgled	0.17
Going to bed	−0.14	Hearing bad news	0.16
Shopping for groceries	−0.15	Thinking I have a strong case	−0.18

contains the ten highest loading situations for every situation component. The loadings in Table 8.6 are quite low. This is due to the fact that the PCA was performed on a preprocessed data set in order to make it fit for a three-mode PCA (see Ten Berge, 2001). Nevertheless, the loadings can be used for interpretation purposes.

The first component, *Situations of Amusement and Prosperity*, contains situations such as *throwing a party* and *being in love*. This component is similar to the earlier *Situations of Amusement* (Table 8.2) and *Pleasure* (Table 8.3). The second component is called *Situations of Interpersonal Conflict*, containing situations in which two or more persons have a conflict of interests, such as *someone is bothering me* and *being treated unfairly*. This second component is similar to the earlier *Situations of Conduct* (Table 8.2) and *Interpersonal Conflict* (Table 8.3). The third component consists of *Situations of Stress and Emotion*, with, for example, *partner commits adultery* and *being fired*. This component has aspects in common with the earlier *Situations of Positioning* (Table 8.2) and with *Social Demand* (Table 8.3). The fourth component, *Situations of Adversity*, for example, *having lost something* and *making a mistake*, seems to be a replication of the earlier *Situations of Adversity* (Table 8.2) and *Individual Adversity* (Table 8.3).

The fifth component is called *Situations of Positioning*, referring to situations where people have to take a stand or have to give a work-related performance. It consists of situations such as *having a job interview* and *being in a meeting*. This component is similar to the earlier *Situations of Positioning* as represented in Table 8.2. Finally, the sixth component is called *Situations of Involvement*, and consists of situations in which a bond between two or more persons is expressed, or in which persons share grief or adversity. This component was not identified in the earlier two analyses.

COMPARING THE THREE SITUATION STRUCTURES

The three situational structures obtained and discussed in the preceding sections all resulted from applying PCA to the data. However, the ways the ratings were obtained clearly differed. In Table 8.7 the different results are summarized in order to facilitate choices to be made with respect to the most adequate situational structure thus far.

The horizontal position of the various situation components in Table 8.7 is made on the basis of face validity. Four types of situations are easily identified under the different perspectives of data collection: *Situations of Adversity, Pleasure and Prosperity, Positioning or Social Demand*, and *Conduct or Conflict* (see also Ten Berge and De Raad, 2001). The *Situations of Adversity* and *Pleasure and Prosperity* show similarity to Magnusson's (1971) Negative situations and Positive situations, respectively. *Positioning or Social Demand*

Table 8.7 Comparison of three situation structures

Method of data collection		
Is combination of trait x situation possible?	Are you able to handle the situation?	Does combination of trait x situation apply to you?
Situation components		
Adversity	**Individual adversity**	**Adversity**
Being hospitalized	Being ill	Having lost something
Having a setback	Having a slight accident	Having lost
Being sad	Having failed exam	Having made a mistake
Amusement	**Pleasure**	**Amusement/ prosperity**
Going out drinking	Getting his/her pay check	Throwing a party
Being at a party	Hearing the good news	Being in love
Throwing a party	It is a national holiday	Doing something nice with friends
Positioning	**Social demand**	**Positioning**
Participating in a discussion	In unfamiliar environment	On board of management
Offering resistance	Being in charge	Organizing an event
Suing someone	Applying for a job	Being trained on the job
		Stress and emotion
		Partner commits adultery
		Relationship is over
		Unhappy in relationship
Social conduct	**Interpersonal conflict**	**Interpersonal conflict**
Making obscene gestures	Being teased	Someone is bothering me
Being aggressive	S.o. is trying to pull leg	Being treated unfairly
Gambling	Nobody is listening to you	Someone is unreasonable
		Involvement
		Beloved person has deceased
		Hurting someone
		Noticing someone in distress
Daily routine		
Going to bed		
Coming home		
Having dinner		

and *Conduct or Conflict* show similarity to Van Heck's (1989) Joint working cluster and Interpersonal conflict cluster, respectively. The *Stress and Emotion* component seems to reflect elements of both *Positioning/Demand* and *Conduct/Conflict*. The *Involvement* component seems to have elements in common with *Situations of Adversity* and *Conflict*. The *Daily Routine* component only occurred in the first analysis.

DISCUSSION

Books on situations (e.g. Magnusson, 1981) and reviews of situation taxonomies (e.g. Ten Berge and De Raad, 1999) show a great variety of situation concepts defined from rather divergent perspectives. Examples are locations with a typical function (e.g. bus stop), gatherings with a clear goal structure (e.g. psychology classes), and interpersonal relations with varying organizing themes (e.g. intimacy or power). In this chapter, the discussion of situations and empirical studies reported were explicitly made from a trait-psychological perspective. The choice of such a perspective necessarily excludes certain types of situations, but the types of situations that are included matter to personality.

In the search for situations that matter to personality, three different procedures were followed in collecting data regarding situations, with the result that relatively comparable situation components could be identified among the different clusterings. All three situation structures were obtained with ratings that included situation descriptions which were generated given trait descriptors that, in turn, were considered representative of the various Big Five trait facets. Thus, the three situation structures may be considered as being relevant for further specification of trait-descriptive information. We can now suggest some four to six types of situations relevant under the perspective of individual differences, of which four are suggested to have stability across methods. This 'situational four' include: *Situations of Adversity*, characterized, for example, by having a setback, losing control and not sleeping well; *Situations of Pleasure and Prosperity*, characterized, for example, by throwing a party, hearing good news and passing an exam; *Situations of Positioning and Demand*, with examples such as being in a discussion, organizing an event or suing someone; finally, *Situations of Conduct and Conflict*, with examples such as making obscene gestures, being teased and being in doubt.

As with the Big Five personality factors, the Situational Four are to be seen as capturing a whole spectrum of situation concepts. The four dimensions emphasize recurrent meaning in those concepts, their commonality, at the cost of nuance. In discussions over the Big Five trait structure, critique has been expressed because certain trait concepts that had been judged as relevant, for example, sensation seeking, did not define one of the Big Five factors. Similarly, one might wonder why certain important situations or types of situations, for example, romantic encounters or physical danger, do have co-defined the kernel meanings of the Situational Four. If that were the case, one should conclude that the procedures followed apparently did not generate such situations; and assuming that the proper procedures were followed those types of situations should not be considered as mattering to personality. For practical reasons not all situations generated in these studies were listed in this chapter, only their factor-defining representatives. In the case of the examples above one would have to answer the question whether such situations might be captured by the Situational Four. Situations of *Pleasure and Prosperity* could well capture 'romantic encounters'. A related item 'Being in love' is given in Table 8.6. Situations of *Adversity* might capture 'physical danger', as for example indicated by the related item 'Having a slight accident' in Table 8.3.

The Situational Four have come about following psycholexical principles in which a sufficient number of subjects was asked to generate situation descriptions so that the result is to be considered as representative of the full lexicon of situations. The investigation confirms that systematic situational information is implied in trait concepts and that a few hundred subjects is enough to specify myriad situational references, constituting a full set of situation clusters.

Whereas in the preceding studies the commonalities among the situation structures were emphasized, the different methods of data collection yielded differences in results as well. Is it possible to draw conclusions about the 'best' structure or the more appropriate approach to arrive at a structure? Of the three approaches followed, the second and third should possibly be given more significance than the first because of their more direct connection to behaviour. The second and third situation structures are both so-called external structures, which have a more direct relevance to behaviour. The first taxonomy was built on internal data. Of the second and the third, the second is easiest to perform and follows the same methodology that is almost standard for the way trait factors are produced, namely by asking subjects to express how they are associated with certain qualities or objects of interest. In the case of traits, subjects are usually asked to indicate the extent to which traits apply to them or to others. In the case of situations, the degree of association comes about following a kind of 'typical coping' procedure, as in, for example, 'express the extent to which you usually deal with this situation'. The relative advantage of the more elaborate third procedure is that it may produce more refined and differential information regarding joint relations between trait concepts and situation concepts. This more specific type of information may be the reason why this third procedure yielded six situation components instead of four or five. On the other hand, the relative specificity of the third structure may also result from the fact that a more representative sample of subjects generated the situational data.

Given these emerging contours of situational factors that cover the domain of situations relevant from an individual difference viewpoint, there are several future directions for this enterprise. An obvious step is to perform the situational specification procedure as sketched in this chapter in other languages.

This should involve the generation of situations given a representative set of Big Five traits and preferably the situation rating procedure under the 'coping' instruction. In an ongoing study of the Dutch project on situations, the 'coping' procedure is being performed again on situational data generated by the representative sample of subjects, as described in Study 2.

An intriguing result that emerged from Study 1 is that regarding the differences between the emotionality or temperament factors Emotional Stability and Extraversion, on the one hand, and the factors Conscientiousness and Agreeableness on the other. Traits from Emotional Stability and Extraversion are expressed in more types of situations than traits from Conscientiousness and Agreeableness. The meaning of Extraversion and Emotional Stability is apparently less specified by situational context than the meaning of Agreeableness and Conscientiousness. For example, being punctual almost always takes place in an appointment situation. But being nervous is considered emotionally unstable in one situation (when doing shopping), but perfectly natural in another (when getting married). The distinction runs parallel to the classical distinction between character factors (Conscientiousness and Agreeableness) and temperament factors (Extraversion, Stability, Autonomy). Possibly the reactive nature of temperament is more intrinsically linked to a differentiating pattern of situational conditions.

The preceding difference between temperament and character factors is puzzling too. In the 'Trait Perspective on Situations' section I referred to temperament researchers who have suggested that temperament, because of its emphasis on form and style, would not be as situation specific as non-temperamental traits. The finding here at first sight confirms this: namely that temperamental traits are less specific than character traits. The outcome is simple, but the complication is that specificity may refer to situations, but not to behaviour. So, it is possible that character traits apply to a large variety of behaviours, and to a relatively small or specific set of situations. This possibility requires further study.

A last remark concerns the exploitation of these situational findings in the development of personality assessment instruments. Personality assessment instruments vary significantly in situational specifications. Some instruments have systematically and explicitly left out situational information. The majority of instruments are rather systematic where traits or behaviours are concerned, but ad hoc and unsystematic where situations are concerned. That is scientifically sloppy and rather uncommendable. These studies on situations do not necessarily lead to more specific instruments, but primarily to a more systematic representation of situational information.

REFERENCES

Alker, H. A. (1972) 'Is personality situationally specific or intrapsychically consistent?', *Journal of Personality* 40: 1–16.

Alston, W. P. (1975) 'Traits, consistency and conceptual alternatives for personality theory', *Journal for the Theory of Social Behaviour* 5: 17–48.

Argyle, M., Furnham, A. and Graham, J. A. (1981) *Social Situations*. Cambridge: Cambridge University Press.

Barker, R. G. (1968) *Ecological Psychology: Concepts and Methods for Studying the Environment of Human Behavior*. Stanford, CA: Stanford University Press.

Caprara, G. V. and Cervone, D. (2000) *Personality: Determinants, Dynamics, and Potentials*. Cambridge: Cambridge University Press.

De Raad, B. (1995) 'The psycholexical approach to the structure of interpersonal traits', *European Journal of Personality* 9: 89–102.

De Raad, B. (1996) 'Personality traits in learning and education', *European Journal of Personality* 10: 185–200.

De Raad, B. (2000) *The Big Five Personality Factors: The Psycholexical Approach to Personality*. Seattle, WA: Hogrefe and Huber.

De Raad, B., Hendriks, A. A.J. and Hofstee, W. K. B. (1992) 'Towards a refined structure of personality traits', *European Journal of Personality* 2: 81–96.

De Raad, B. and Perugini, M. (2002) *Big Five Assessment*. Goettingen: Hogrefe and Huber.

Endler, N. S. (1993) 'Personality: An interactional perspective', in J. Hettema and I. J. Deary (eds) *Foundations of Personality*, pp. 251–268. Dordrecht: Kluwer.

Endler, N. S. and Edwards, J. (1978) 'Person by treatment interactions in personality research', in L. A. Pervin and M. Lewis (eds) *Perspectives in Interactional Psychology*, pp, 141–169. New York: Plenum Press.

Endler, N. S. and Magnusson, D. (1976) *Interactional Psychology and Personality*. New York: Wiley.

Forgas, J. P. and Van Heck, G. L. (1992) 'The psychology of situations', in G. V. Caprara and G. L. Van Heck (eds) *Modern Personality Psychology: Critical Reviews and New Directions*, pp. 418–455. New York: Harvester Wheatsheaf.

Hendriks, A. A. J., Hofstee, W. K. B. and De Raad, B. (1999) *FFPI: The Five-Factor Personality Inventory*. Lisse: Swets Test Publishers.

Hofstee, W. K. B., Ten Berge, J. M. F. and Hendriks, A. A. J. (1989) 'How to score questionnaires?', *Personality and Individual Differences* 25: 879–909.

Hogan, R. and Roberts, B. W. (2000) 'A socioanalytic perspective on person-environment interaction', in W. B. Walsh, K. H. Craik and R. H. Price (eds) *Person–Environment Psychology: New Directions and Perspectives*, pp. 1–23. Mahwah, NJ: Lawrence Erlbaum Associates Inc.

Johnson, J. A. (1999) 'Persons in situations: Distinguishing new wine from old wine in new bottles', *European Journal of Personality* 13: 443–453.

Krause, M. S. (1970) 'Use of social situations for research purposes', *American Psychologist* 25: 748–753.

Larsen, R. J. (1992) 'Neuroticism and selective encoding and recall of symptoms: Evidence from a combined concurrent-retrospective study', *Journal of Personality and Social Psychology* 62: 480–488.

McCrae, R. R. and Costa, P. T. Jr. (1989) 'The structure of interpersonal traits: Wiggins' circumplex and the five-factor model', *Journal of Personality and Social Psychology* 56: 586–595.

Magnusson, D. (1971) 'An analysis of situational dimensions', *Perceptual and Motor Skills* 32: 851–867.

Magnusson, D. (ed.) (1981) *Toward a Psychology of Situations: An Interactional Perspective*. Hillsdale, NJ: Lawrence Erlbaum Associates Inc.

Magnusson, D. and Endler, N. S. (eds) (1977) *Personality at the Crossroads: Current Issues in Interactional Psychology*. Hillsdale, NJ: Lawrence Erlbaum Associates Inc.

Mannetti, L. and De Grada, E. (1991) 'Interpersonal verbs: Implicit causality of action verbs and contextual factors', *European Journal of Social Psychology* 21: 429–443.

Mischel, W. (1968) *Personality and Assessment* New York: Wiley.

Mischel, W. (1973) 'Towards a cognitive social-learning reconceptualization of personality', *Psychological Review* 80: 252–283.

Moos, R. H. (1973) 'Conceptualizations of human environments', *American Psychologist* 28: 652–665.

Murray, H. A. (1938) *Explorations in Personality*. New York: Oxford University Press.

Peabody, D. and Goldberg, L. R. (1989) 'Some determinants of factor structures from personality-trait descriptors', *Journal of Personality and Social Psychology* 57: 552–567.

Salgado, J. F. (1997) 'The five factor model of personality and job performance in the European Community', *Journal of Applied Psychology* 82: 30–43.

Saucier, G. and Goldberg, L. R. (1996) 'The language of pesonality: lexical perspectives on the five-factor model', in J. S. Wiggins (ed.) *The Five-Factor Model of Personality: Theoretical Perspectives*, pp. 21–50. New York: Guilford Press.

Schroeder, M. L., Wormworth, J. A. and Livesley, W. J. (1992) 'Dimensions of personality disorder and their relationships to the Big Five dimensions of personality', *Psychological Assessment* 4: 47–53.

Semin, G. R. and Fiedler, K. (1988) 'The cognitive functions of linguistic categories in describing persons: Social cognition and language', *Journal of Personality and Social Psychology* 54: 558–568.

Sneath, P. H. A. and Sokal, R. R. (1973) *Numerical Taxonomy: The Principles and Practice of Numerical Classification*. San Francisco: Freeman.

Strelau, J. (1987) 'The concept of temperament in personality research', *European Journal of Personality* 1: 107–117.

Ten Berge, M. A. (2001) 'Freebooters and prosperity: The structure of situations from a trait psychological perspective', doctoral dissertation, University of Groningen.

Ten Berge, M. A. and De Raad, B. (1999) 'Taxonomies of situations from a trait psychological perspective: a review', *European Journal of Personality* 13: 337–360.

Ten Berge, M. A. and De Raad, B. (2001) 'The construction of a joint taxonomy of traits and situations', *European Journal of Personality* 15: 253–276.

Ten Berge, M. A. and De Raad, B. (2002) 'The structure of situations from a personality perspective', *European Journal of Personality* 16: 81–102.

Trapnell, P. D. and Wiggins, J. S. (1990) 'Extension of the interpersonal adjective scales to include the Big Five dimensions of personality', *Journal of Personality and Social Psychology* 59: 781–790.

Van de Sande, J. P. (1996) 'Denken over situaties' [Thinking of situations], doctoral dissertation, University of Groningen, Groningen, The Netherlands.

Van Heck, G. L. (1984) 'The construction of a general taxonomy of situations', in H. Bonarius, G. Van Heck and N. Smid (eds) *Personality Psychology in Europe: Theoretical and Empirical Developments*, pp. 149–164. Lisse: Swets and Zeitlinger.

Van Heck, G. L. (1989) 'Situation concepts: Definitions and classification', in P. J. Hettema (ed.) *Personality and Environment: Assessment of Human Adaptation*, pp. 53–70. Chichester: Wiley.

Wiggins, J. S. (1973) *Personality and Prediction: Principles of Personality Assessment*. Reading, MA: Addison-Wesley.

Wolfe, R. N. and Johnson, S. D. (1995) 'Personality as a predictor of college performance', *Educational and Psychological Measurement* 55: 177–185.

Index